Praise for *The Soul of a Chef*

"One comes away awed by what great cooking demands of the practitioner, and reinvigorated too." —*The Washington Times*

"[*The Soul of a Chef*] has all the makings of a summer potboiler: suspense, intrigue, drama, pathos, and even a little humor."
—*Detroit Free Press*

"I'm sure [Ruhlman's] a pretty good cook himself, but I would urge him not to give up his day job, because he's a terrific writer." —*Newsday*

"Each section of the book is fascinating in itself, especially the introductory section on the Certified Master Chef exam, an ordeal of almost hellish intensity." —*Library Journal*

PENGUIN BOOKS

THE SOUL OF A CHEF

Michael Ruhlman has written for *The New York Times,* the *Los Angeles Times, Gourmet,* and *Food Arts Magazine* and is the recipient of a James Beard award for magazine writing. He is the author of *Boys Themselves, The Making of a Chef,* and *Wooden Boats* (Viking). He lives in Cleveland Heights, Ohio, with his wife and children.

THE SOUL
OF A CHEF

THE JOURNEY

TOWARD PERFECTION

MICHAEL RUHLMAN

PENGUIN BOOKS

PENGUIN BOOKS

Published by the Penguin Group

Penguin Group (USA) Inc., 375 Hudson Street, New York, New York 10014, U.S.A.

Penguin Group (Canada), 90 Eglinton Avenue East, Suite 700, Toronto,
Ontario, Canada M4P 2Y3 (a division of Pearson Penguin Canada Inc.)

Penguin Books Ltd, 80 Strand, London WC2R 0RL, England

Penguin Ireland, 25 St Stephen's Green, Dublin 2, Ireland (a division of Penguin Books Ltd)

Penguin Group (Australia), 250 Camberwell Road, Camberwell,
Victoria 3124, Australia (a division of Pearson Australia Group Pty Ltd)

Penguin Books India Pvt Ltd, 11 Community Centre, Panchsheel Park, New Delhi – 110 017, India

Penguin Group (NZ), cnr Airborne and Rosedale Roads,
Albany, Auckland 1310, New Zealand (a division of Pearson New Zealand Ltd)

Penguin Books (South Africa) (Pty) Ltd, 24 Sturdee Avenue,
Rosebank, Johannesburg 2196, South Africa

Penguin Books Ltd, Registered Offices: 80 Strand, London WC2R 0RL, England

First published in the United States of America by Viking Penguin,
a member of Penguin Putnam Inc., 2000
Published in Penguin Books 2001

12 13 14 15 16 17 18 19 20

THE LIBRARY OF CONGRESS HAS CATALOGED
THE HARDCOVER EDITION AS FOLLOWS:

Ruhlman, Michael, 1963–
The soul of a chef: the journey toward perfection /
Michael Ruhlman.
p.   cm.
Includes index.
ISBN 0-670-89155-X (hc.)
ISBN 0 14 10.0189 5 (pbk.)
1. Cooks—United States—Biography.   II. Title.
TX649.A1 R84   2000   99–053638
641.5'092'2—dc21

Printed in the United States of America
Set in Adobe Garamond
Designed by Betty Lew

For my mother,

Carole,

a beautiful soul

A work that aspires, however humbly, to the condition of art should carry its justification in every line. And art itself may be defined as a single-minded attempt to render the highest kind of justice to the visible universe, by bringing to light the truth, manifold and one, underlying its every aspect. It is an attempt to find in its forms, in its colors, in its light, in its shadows, in the aspects of matter and in the facts of life, what of each is fundamental, what is enduring and essential—their one illuminating and convincing quality—the very truth of their existence. . . . [I]t is, before all, to make you see.

Joseph Conrad
"The Condition of Art"

What interests me is how the quality of cooking in this country can be followed from a period of simplicity and function to one of goodness and bounty, then to an age of elaboration and excess, back again to functional (and for the most part, mediocre) eating. Finally, we hope, we are now in another epoch of gastronomic excellence.

James Beard
James Beard's American Cookery

Everything is relative but there is a standard which must not be deviated from, especially with reference to the basic culinary preparations.

A. Escoffier
Escoffier: The Complete Guide to the Art of Modern Cookery

CONTENTS

Part One

CERTIFIED MASTER CHEF EXAM

(OR THE OBJECTIVE TRUTH OF GREAT COOKING)

CHAPTER ONE

*C*hef Dieter Doppelfeld leads the way to kitchen station four, followed by two men in lab coats with clipboards. Brian Polcyn stands before these men attentive but at ease in a paper toque and chef's whites. He has set his stainless steel table with cutting board, slicing knife, bain-marie insert filled with hot water, and latex gloves.

Ron DeSantis glances at his clipboard and says, "Chef, would you please tell us what you have prepared?"

"Duck terrine," Polcyn answers. "Straight forcemeat with seared duck and shiitake mushrooms."

"And the sauce?"

"Orange-ginger."

Polcyn then begins the presentation, first submerging the terrine mold for several seconds in water simmering on the stove—just enough to warm and loosen it—then upending the terrine mold on his cutting board and lifting it off the terrine itself. Dieter Doppelfeld, who has run this test for the past nine years, Ron DeSantis, and the third master chef judge, Fritz Sonnenschmidt, an authority on terrines, watch silently. Polcyn's movements are unnatural and stiff, almost robotic; clearly he doesn't stand this straight while moving from stovetop to workstation at his restaurant or breathe so audibly. It's harder to drive a car perfectly when there's a cop on your tail.

Having successfully separated the terrine from its mold and pulled on the gloves, Polcyn removes the slicing knife from the bain of hot water, dries the blade. He places his left hand on the terrine, rests the knife on its center in preparation for the first cut, and for a moment holds still.

Polcyn measures five feet ten inches between his laced black shoes and his toque, which conceals abundant, wavy black hair. He is the thirty-seven-year-old chef-owner of Five Lakes Grill, a popular restaurant in the hamlet of Milford, Michigan, forty-five miles northwest of Detroit. He has been cooking professionally since high school and run the kitchens of some of Michigan's finest restaurants. He is a food consultant for Northwest Airlines along with such luminary chefs as Waldy Malouf, Nancy Silverton, and Todd English. He has twice been a guest chef at the James Beard House in New York City. He has appeared three times in the prestigious Bocuse d'Or competition. He once prepared a private meal for twelve for which the host, at a charity auction, had paid twenty-four thousand dollars. But never before in his twenty-two-year cooking career has he been as nervous as he is at this moment, his knife blade paused above this duck terrine, which he has seasoned with a Madeira reduction, inlaid with mushrooms and whole duck breast, and roasted to an internal temperature of 145 degrees.

Polcyn inhales sharply, strokes once through the terrine, once back, and he cannot believe his eyes. The knife has veered right. Polcyn stares at his hands as if they were not his own. The error ensures that the second slice will be slightly thinner at one end as well.

But the interior garnish of the seared duck breast is pink and glistening; he has cooked the terrine perfectly. He places the slices on a white plate, spoons his smooth bright orange-ginger sauce onto the plate, and sets it on the cloth-covered rolling cart for the judges to taste. Each judge samples the terrine and the sauce. Fritz Sonnenschmidt, a man who is very nearly a perfect sphere, asks, "Were you to do this again, what would you do differently?"

"I might have added some pistachios for color," Polcyn says. But other than that, he thinks it's pretty good.

Sonnenschmidt nods and looks to his left, beyond DeSantis, and says, "Chef Doppelfeld?"

"I thought it was very pleasant to eat," Chef Doppelfeld says. "Nice color, nice flavor."

There are some discreet clicks of pencil tips on clipboards. Before leaving, Ron DeSantis, a certified master chef like the others, a Culinary Institute of America instructor, and a former head chef of the United States Marine Corps based in Okinawa, says, "The major thing is your knife skills." He looks Polcyn dead in the eye and says, "You really need to have good knife skills."

"Yes, Chef," Polcyn says. He swallows at the insult and cannot hold his tongue. "Actually Chef, I do have the knife skills. It's just that sometimes they don't come out."

DeSantis leans into Polcyn's face and with quiet menace says, *"During these ten days they have to come out."*

"Yes, Chef."

The day before the Certified Master Chef examination began I arrived at the office of Tom Peer, food and beverage director at the Culinary Institute of America, the nation's most prominent cooking school. Peer was for years the executive chef at the Duquesne Club in Pittsburgh, and he was now the certification chairman for the American Culinary Federation, a trade organization representing tens of thousands of chefs. Peer oversaw the master chef certification program.

Peer had asked Dieter Doppelfeld to join us; Doppelfeld was an instructor at the CIA and the man who had managed the daily operations of the cooking test for the past nine years. He wore thick glasses and spoke with a mellifluous German accent. Doppelfeld wore chef's whites; Peer dressed corporate.

The Certified Master Chef examination meant different things to everybody who knew about it, the first clue to me that the test had some kind of genuine power. To Tom Peer it was a simple accreditation. "If you want an electrician to wire your house, would you rather have an electrician who was certified or one who wasn't?" he asked. Same thing with a chef; this test meant to certify that a chef had a specific range of skills and knowledge. But for others the test carried a mystique that had less to do with skills than a confirmation of some innate talent. For still others it was a like a mountain scaled, a solo ocean crossing. "There are two dates you never forget," Ron DeSantis told me. "Your birthday and the day you earn your CMC." This from a married man with two children.

Depending where in the industry chefs work, the CMC title can result in a higher salary, and in some circles it is a title of respect. But a large and vocal segment of the industry denigrates the test. There are clearly two camps, the public and well-known chefs who own popular restaurants and the competition-style chefs who teach in schools and compete in food shows. The prominent chef-owners of successful restaurants and celebrity chefs dismiss the CMC test as being out of touch with reality, a waste of time and money, and absolutely without meaning. Some well-known chefs like the idea of the test. David Burke, chef of New York City's Park Avenue Cafe, told me, "I think the test is great. It's got a lot to do with theory and technique that a lot of restaurant chefs never get to learn." But most popular chefs, upon hearing it mentioned, turn their heads as if they'd smelled something nasty.

On its surface the Certified Master Chef exam was plainly a cooking test, the only one of its kind anywhere, one that lasted ten full days and scarcely gave the chefs time to sleep. The chefs had to be great cooks in good physical condition, but they also had to be knowledgeable on subjects ranging from sanitation to restaurant management to tableside service. The goal of this test was to establish an industry-wide standard of excellence in the profession. The main work of the next ten days, though, the reason I was excited to be here, was cooking. I would be observing a long, hard, slightly bizarre cooking test. Ten days of all kinds of cooking styles, methods, and techniques ranging from American cuisine to classical French, charcuterie preparations such as foie gras pâtés and duck terrines, and baking and patisserie—by design all the kinds of cooking that, when perfected, make someone a master chef.

This cooking would be undertaken by six men and one woman who wanted to be called certified master chefs, or CMCs. I expected they'd be pretty damn good cooks, and a little off-center. Who other than the slightly demented would take this test? Each of these chefs had to travel hundreds of miles to the Hudson Valley and spend ten days away from their families and jobs to work really hard in someone else's kitchen. Most of them worked really hard all the time anyway, cooking day and night in their own hot kitchens. But here they would work harder, cooking and taking written and oral tests for days, days that would last twelve to sixteen hours, each under strict observation and mind-bending stress. For this they would pay a "tuition" of twenty-six hundred dollars to the American Culinary Federation. This did not include room and board, books, or equipment. Most of the chefs put themselves up in the Super 8 or the Golden Manor, two motels not known for luxury just down the road on Route 9. Some of these chefs had spent years studying for this test and spent money and time to travel to kitchens in other states to practice. With travel, room and board, and miscellaneous expenses, the cost of the test would be between four and five thousand dollars.

To review: ten days of grueling work, away from home and family, living in a motel, and spending thousands of dollars to take a test that an important part of your industry openly denigrates. This is simply not something that normal people *do*. But seven chefs were committed to taking it this year.

The likely result: failure. Failure is not just possible for these chefs; it is probable. Approximately 170 chefs have taken the test since it was first given in 1981. Only 53 have passed it. According to these odds, 2 of the 7 chefs here this year will be standing when the Day Ten mystery basket has been cooked, plated, served, and judged.

So not only did I expect to see close up some fascinating cooking that ranged from classical to modern, truly dramatic sauté and sauce work under pressure, but I figured I'd also be watching unusual souls in a struggle against likely defeat.

"I figured out where you're going to be from," Tom Peer said to me, leaning forward on his desk. "You're going to be from the National Council of Accreditation." When I said I'd never heard of this group, he chuckled and said, "That's because I just made it up."

I would wear a lab coat each day in the kitchen, and Chef Doppelfeld would loan me a clipboard. What my title was and what exactly I was doing for the National Council of Accreditation, I'd have to figure out for myself, Peer said.

In truth, I was a writer and freelance journalist who had asked to observe this odd one-of-a-kind cooking test. No outsider had ever been admitted to it or been permitted the kind of access I'd been promised. (No one had asked before, as far as I knew.) The people who ran the test worried that if I simply roamed the kitchens as a journalist, asking the chefs intimate questions and then writing down their answers in my notebook, I might distract them. The test is hard enough as it is without their having to endure someone who is nosy by profession. Also, they didn't want any chefs fretting over the possibility that I might broadcast their failures all over the country.

That I would be undercover had its good and bad points. A common concern dogs any thoughtful journalist: Are you altering the story you're reporting by your very presence as a journalist? This question would be moot since no one would know I was a journalist. My reason for being here, my lie, was to examine the test itself, not the chefs, for the "NCA," so no one would even notice or care that I was taking notes continually. I would have free rein in the kitchens; I could stick my face in their simmering sauces, open the oven doors where rabbit bones were crackling in oil, stand beside the chefs, and learn how to butcher Dover sole, and no one would think twice.

The drawback was that I would have to lie daily, and I was a bad liar. I tended to shake and stammer while lying, certain my sham disguise would be discovered and blow the whole deal.

A small price to pay, however, for what promised to be a thrilling assignment for someone who loves to cook. In Tom Peer's office I asked him and Doppelfeld how it was that so few people could actually pass this test.

Chef Doppelfeld, seated beside me in Peer's office, said, "Failure is usually that of basic cooking principles." All judges would stress to the chefs, and to me, that this test was all about the basics. Did the chefs braise properly? Did they season their food properly? When they were called in to the evaluation room, did they know that their artichoke

hearts could have cooked a little longer? There are several mystery basket situations throughout the test; the chefs are given trays of food they
have not seen before and have four and a half hours to devise and then
cook a four-course menu for ten. Did they use the food intelligently
and imaginatively? Was the meal properly cooked, well balanced, visually appealing, and delicious? You start with great meat, fruits, vegetables, and you do what it is your job to do: cook. How difficult is that?

Chef Doppelfeld's eyes enlarged behind his glasses, and he said, "I
am *not* going to put a *sea turtle* in your basket."

Yet less than a third of the chefs passed this test? Doppelfeld nodded
and confided that you could pretty much tell who had a chance and
who didn't by Day Five or Six.

"Is it possible that nobody will pass?" I asked.

Doppelfeld nodded, then said with genuine dismay, "If nobody passes,
I'll *weep*."

This grueling cooking test, simply the idea of it, had completely capti-
vated me, and it would become for me the beginning of a two-year immersion in the work of the American chef and professional cooking.
But for a long while I couldn't get to the core of my fascination with the
CMC exam. I asked Peer and Doppelfeld why they thought this test
was important. Doppelfeld explained that this profession, the profession of chef in America, was relatively young. For most of its history the
United States imported great chefs; we did not train our own because
we didn't have anyone to do the training; the country didn't even have a
cuisine it could call its own or any kind of tradition to speak of, beyond
the home ec–style teachings of Fannie Farmer, perhaps, or the world-
wide impact of McDonald's-style fast food. Yet in the past fifty years,
most noticeably in the past two decades, the culinary scene had exploded. Cooks had become chefs, and chefs had become celebrities.
Food magazines proliferated. National and local radio shows devoted to
food filled the air on weekends. An entire television network was created to broadcast food and cooking shows twenty-four hours a day.
Restaurants were becoming as famous as Broadway shows. And the work

itself—once the labor of the lower classes—had become fashionable. Parents, once proud to say that their child had entered law school, now boasted that their child was in culinary school. An industry that was still young, huge and growing ($336 billion in overall food service sales in 1998, $376 billion expected in 2000) needed recognized standards of uncompromised excellence, standards that were acknowledged by everyone. The Certified Master Chef exam aimed to create exactly that.

Had it been successful? Only in part, it seems. Some in the industry valued the credential. If a chef worked in a country club, a culinary school, research and development, or as a corporate or institutional chef—and many, many thousands did—the title might mean a salary increase of ten thousand dollars or more. But some in the industry criticized the test for rewarding culinary competition-style chefs, chefs who do not cook to feed but who cook to compete. To support their claim that the CMC test is irrelevant, celebrity chef-owners needed only ask what Charlie Trotter, voicing the view of most restaurant chefs, asked: "There are some great certified master chefs, but how many of them run successful restaurants?" (About 7 percent.)

Others noted that the test was not available to enough chefs to make it valuable. How many chefs would be willing to spend ten days of their life this way? How many would be willing and also be able to afford it? What if they were from a country outside the West? Some of the best chefs in the country, arguably, were neither American nor French but brought to America the cuisines of their homelands: India, China, and other non-Western countries. How did this test serve them? So perhaps the sheer low numbers of those to whom the test was available rendered the test irrelevant or scarcely relevant.

Yet for all the good arguments to dismiss this test, my fascination remained. While the reasons at the time were not immediately clear, the facts were these.

In February 1996 I entered Skill Development I at the Culinary Institute of America, a writer in student attire, in order to learn what the most prominent cooking school in the world said one had to know in order to be a professional chef and to write a true story about learning to cook professionally. One year later, having begun that first day by mincing an onion and having finished nine months later by working grill station at the school's final restaurant, I shipped off the manuscript. Then I sat in my room bereft. This couldn't be the end. I was still empty, and ravenous. Indeed I'd just started. I'd come to the Culinary looking for the knowledge to cook, but when I left, I found I didn't have that knowledge. I thought I did. But I didn't.

What I did have, though, were tools to learn the rest. I had some basic information about how food behaves under specific circumstances and, more important to me, information about how the human personality behaves under those same circumstances. This after all was why cooking mattered. It had less to do with filling your stomach or pleasing your mouth than with connecting yourself to something more powerful and extraordinary than sensual gratifications.

Don't ask me what! At the time I didn't know. But I knew it was out there. I hadn't moved my wife and daughter five hundred miles to a cow town for a year to learn how to make a superlative brown veal stock. I'd thought this was so, but after writing about the learning, I realized, again, that I needed to know how to make a superlative brown veal stock in order to learn the rest. What was the rest? I didn't know! But I meant to find out what it was and why cooking was so obsessively important. That was why I hustled to finagle a magazine assignment to get back to the CIA to watch this extraordinary cooking test. There was something here.

All America, it seemed to me, was busting at the seams to learn more about cooking, announcing its own passions and beliefs with fire and brimstone volume, dead passionate to eat at great restaurants, devouring celebrity chef cookbooks, filling supermarkets, from their own need, with products once unheard of there—Asian pears, taro roots, fresh morel mushrooms; would it be long before one could find fresh foie gras nestled between the Perdue chickens and Long Island ducks at the local Stop 'n' Shop? All of it, I understood, America's ecstatic clutching and cooking and feeding, was an attempt to fill its soul, each passionate cook's attempt to connect himself to a world that was receding through the computer screen of his home office, receding in the rearview mirror of his Jeep Cherokee sealed tight as a space shuttle from the atmosphere outside. America was cooking and eating, yet I knew this cooking and eating were merely the scratching of ghost itches on amputated limbs.

It was for me, anyway. And so I learned to make that basic brown stock. Once I knew how to make it, I not only realized how much more there was to know about food and cooking, but also sensed the fundamental importance of studying the work of professional cooking, to know the people who had been at this work all their adult lives. Somewhere in them was the answer to why cooking well was so fundamentally important.

Three months after finishing my narrative of learning to cook, I had returned to the Culinary to witness a test that claimed both to measure and to evaluate the basics, from which all truly great cooking originates, and to acknowledge or deny absolutely one's abilities as a chef. A range of cooking was performed over a short period by a variety of chefs; a search for the soul of a chef and the importance of great cooking might begin here. It became the beginning of a journey that led me to the kitchens and work of three outstanding but very different chefs, each of whom was distinctly American and, moreover, helped define what the American chef was, helped define the profession in this country, the work and the food.

The reason why the CMC test gripped me and proved the perfect place to begin my search for the soul of a chef at last became clear: It attempted to define the *truth* of great cooking.

I came to understand that all the varying impressions and thoughts about this test—from chefs who dismissed it out of hand as irrelevant, to those who revered it, to those who feared it or despised it—were only impressions, perceptions. Each described a reflection thrown off by a different facet of what I suspected might be a diamond. The very fact that the test existed was a claim that something solid and valuable and unchanging happened here.

But the idea that a few people could evaluate a chef's food, its creativity, its originality, and measure it objectively, evaluate it, compare and contrast its various attributes in order to render a final unarguable verdict about how good or bad this food was, and this chef was, was both intriguing and ludicrous. Imagine, say, a Certified Master Poet examination in which poets from around the country—not the celebrity poets and commercially successful poets such as Maya Angelou and Rita Dove, but rather the academics tucked away in towers teaching college English, the poets struggling with their work in virtual anonymity, publishing only in small regional journals—converged at one school and, under great stress and unusual conditions, were told to write poetry, in various styles and with unusual constraints of time and method, that would be evaluated by their peers. Their peers, master poets (but not the likes of Robert Pinsky or Richard Wilbur) would read this work, discuss it behind closed doors, critique it before the master poet candidates, and then, with absolute authority, render the verdict: "You are now a certified master poet" or "You are not." Those deemed unworthy would return to their obscure toil diminished in the eyes of their family, their colleagues, forced to admit they do not do master poet work, that they are and always will be mediocre poets.

Of course this is not ultimately what the CMC test does. Poetry is an art form. Cooking is a craft. (Oh, I know how the foodie blowhards—and even a lot of chefs—love to talk about food as art! But I'm sorry, noodles spun into towers and designs on plates with different-colored sauces do not equal art, so don't talk to me about food as art or chefs as *artistes*.) As with any craft, there were artful levels and shared standards of excellence. The test's very existence implied that great cooking, cooking at so-called master chef level, was not art, was only craft, the result of physical skills that were consistently measurable and comparable from one chef to the next. The Certified Master Chef exam aimed to set an objective standard of great cooking that existed regardless of this or that person's own taste and preferences, something that you could not do with an art such as poetry. Here one sought an objective standard of cooking that was true for all chefs no matter who they were, where they cooked, or how or why or whom they pleased or offended. This was cooking as Platonic form. Culinary essentialism. An objective standard. A truth.

This I wanted to see.

Peer and Doppelfeld had reiterated to me that this test measured "knowledge acquired over a period of time." But there was something more to their claims, something a little presumptuous, but maybe true. Fritz Sonnenschmidt claimed that he was a master chef as soon as he finished his apprenticeship in Germany; it was only a matter of learning the requisite skills and acquiring the knowledge. CIA president Ferdinand Metz, who had conceived and created the test, noted that only one person who had ever retaken the test after failing had passed, hinting that the Master Chef exam measures something innate. The way these master chefs spoke about the test suggested that there was a good deal more here than basic cooking principles. The unspoken claim by all of them was that you are either master chef material or you are not. You either have it or you don't, and if you don't, no amount of study and training can change that. When chefs earned their CMC, they were merely fulfilling what had been in them to accomplish all along. The Certified Master Chef exam measured and confirmed an inner greatness.

CHAPTER TWO

$\mathcal{L}$ecture Hall 2 is a classroom in the continuing education section of the Culinary Institute of America. A center aisle is created by four classroom tables on either side of the room. The lighting is fluorescent, and the room feels cool, sterile, and institutional. The first two chefs have arrived and are seated on opposite sides of the room, both dressed in their whites. Lynn Kennedy-Tilyou, chef de cuisine at a French restaurant in Memphis called La Tourelle, will be the second woman ever to take this test. William Guthrie, a third-generation cook, chef at the Hotel St. Germain in Dallas, has what appears to be a microphone attached to the collar of his chef's jacket; he's wired. William is forty-three years old and has been in the business since he was thirteen; he has, he tells Lynn, a thousand cookbooks. When there is a quiet moment in the room, William mutters, "This moment is like waiting to go into the dentist's office." Eric Kopelow, corporate executive chef for United Airlines, based near Chicago, arrives wearing corduroys and a brown button-down shirt. Mark Linden, executive chef of the Anchorage Hilton, has flown from Alaska with an enormous footlocker filled with clothes and gear. Each of these chefs speaks to one another easily, as if relieved not to be alone anymore, eager to share their anxiety.

Brian Polcyn enters, wearing a brown leather jacket. He takes the seat closest to the door and doesn't look at the others until they introduce themselves. He cordially responds but faces straight ahead and offers nothing that isn't asked for.

Finally, Neil Becker and Steve Jilleba stride in, exactly at five-thirty. Both look sporty, Steve in a blazer and Italian loafers, Neil in jacket and tie. Steve, executive chef at Sunset Ridge Country Club in Northfield, Illinois, is a giant beside Neil, a chef-instructor at the New York Restaurant School. They are talking and laughing as easily as if they owned the room and had little doubt as to the outcome of the test.

These are the seven chefs scheduled to take this year's Certified Master Chef exam.

Chef Doppelfeld hustles in several minutes late along with Tom Peer. Doppelfeld holds his arms stiffly at his sides and has a small stride that has the effect of making him seem always in a hurry. His face is a broad, open oval, his straight, thick brown hair is neatly trimmed, and his teeth are large. He is fussy and friendly at once and enunciates his words carefully.

"Good afternoon," he begins. "Welcome to za Culinary Institute of America. We have an exciting ten days ahead of us, ten days of comradeship, ten days of workmanship, ten days of *good cooking*. We have a positive attitude at the Culinary Institute of America, an attitude of success, and we are here to reinforce that idea." He smiles warmly at his guests and shakes his head rapidly. "We are not here to mess around with you and put nasty things in your basket."

Tom Peer steps in after Dieter has made general introductions. Peer's hair is pure gray, his eyes are ice blue, and he is nothing but friendly, almost too friendly. This is going to be fun, his demeanor seems to say. "Hi," he begins. "We're really excited to have you here. Some words of wisdom, some words of advice." He pauses. "We, the ACF, are going to ask you to cook. We're going to give you food and herbs. You're going to braise; you're going to panfry; you're going to sauté. Don't make it more difficult than it is. I'm sure you're going to do fine. Dieter will bend over backward to support you. We're here to help you do everything we can to make you successful."

Lynn believes this. She knows that the ACF wants as many CMCs as possible; the more there are, the more credibility the test will have. But she also knows that it isn't giving the titles away. She's pumped up and terrified at the same time.

Dieter first makes sure that everyone has comfortable lodging and reliable transportation before launching into an opening lecture on how the test works, beginning with the grading. The test comprises five major categories and ten minor categories. Each section of the test totals 100 points; 65 is the lowest passing grade, and the final average must be 75 or higher to earn the CMC title. Major and minor categories are weighted differently in determining the final grade. Asian cooking, a minor section, doesn't count as much as American cooking, a major; tableside service is worth a fraction of classical cooking. If you fail two majors, you will be asked to leave; if you fail a major and two minors or three minors, you will be asked to leave. Doppelfeld grows grave when he mentions Day Ten. "Fifty percent of your grade is Day Ten," he explains. "It's the hardest day of your life. You cook twice. You begin cooking at seven, you finish at eleven, and then at eleven-thirty you begin to cook again."

This of course is not barbecue-and-slaw cooking; this is complex and difficult cooking: four-course meals for ten, four portions served on plates, and a buffet platter for six, after nine strenuous days of cooking and little sleep. The first cooking test, nutritional cuisine, will not begin for another day and a half. For the first cooking test chefs will be given five hours to cook their menu, a half hour longer than most of the cooking tests that will follow. Then service begins, and the chefs have what will be a twenty-minute window to plate—that is, create four plates, three of which will be served to the judges as at a restaurant, one to be kept on display for reference, along with a buffet platter for six, for each course. "And believe me, twenty minutes goes very quickly," Doppelfeld says. "If you're not ready, if you're late, you go to the end of the line, and you are in big, big trouble. It's got to be on the money, push it out, get it out." Doppelfeld makes a fist, holds it at his sternum, and makes pushing motions back and forth, cooks' sign language for working hard, beyond hard. "There will be runners there to take the food away. Just push it out."

Doppelfeld then moves into Cooking 101, just to make sure everyone's on the same page. "Car-a-mel-i-za-tion is a *big thing*. Vegetables need to be caramelized, so don't cut your vegetables this big. . . . If your

menu doesn't call for consommé, don't *make* one, so you don't have to
worry do I have the right ratio of egg white to tomato. . . . Some people
think that root vegetables do not need to be cooked. If you feel that
way, convince Richard Czack!" Czack is a CMC, an administrator at
the Culinary, and will be a judge of classical cuisine; he's a stickler for
properly cooked veg—veg, that is, that doesn't go crunch when you bite
it. "Fork tender means: If I stick a fork in it, I feel no resistance. Osso
bucco should not be like chewing a hockey puck. . . . We are looking
for good, solid cooking techniques. A sauté is a sauté; a braise is a
braise; a broil is a broil. *To sauté* means to jump. Sauté is the finest thing
we eat. But not if it's cooked two hours in advance. Freshness is very
important. . . . I am not *interested* in curlicues. This is not for *Gourmet*.
I want straight cooking. . . . Put the concepts together so they work. If
it's American cuisine, don't give me *Dover sole*. . . . In classical cuisine, if
Guide Culinaire says do it with twelve truffles, that is what you should
do. Remember that sole Véronique requires you to *peel* the grapes. This
is the most important thing to do. That is what Mr. E decided to do. I
can't argue with him. He's dead. . . . Charcuterie, if you bring your
forcemeat up to seventy degrees, don't be surprised if it has little holes
in it. . . . Nutritional cooking, make it look good, make it taste good.
Little bit of acid, a little bit of herbs, a little bit of infusions, they all
give you flavors."

Doppelfeld refers to the test as "our little project while we are here
together" and reminds the chefs to concentrate on each day's work separately, worry about tomorrow tomorrow.

"Are notes allowed in the kitchen?" William asks.

"Notes are always welcome," says Doppelfeld.

"Are cookbooks?"

This seems a bad sign to Doppelfeld, and he says, "I do not think a
cookbook is practical."

Mark Linden asks, "Are we responsible for our apprentice?"

"Because you are in a managerial position, you are responsible."

"For the mystery basket, if something's not working out the way you
expected it to, can you rewrite your menu?" asks another.

"No," Peer responds. "Could you do that at your hotel or restaurant? No. If it's not acceptable there, it's not here."

When there are no more questions, Chef Doppelfeld takes seven sealed envelopes and says, "OK, let's draw for charcuterie. Can we do ladies first?"

Lynn smiles, offers a facial curtsy, and takes the first envelope. She opens and reads assignment seven: "Terrine, 2 lobsters, 1 pound each of scallops and shrimp, 4 Dover soles, and 12 mussels." Lynn is a big girl, with straight dark blond hair, a round, open face, and a sweet Tennessee accent. She is almost childlike in her excitement. "I make lobster terrines all the time," she says quietly. Eric Kopelow, the United Airlines chef, is pleased to have drawn an assignment that reads:

> Galantine
> 3 each ducks
> Duck foie gras "B" grade

Eric loves to work with duck, he says. Brian Polcyn has drawn duck too, but his assignment reads "Terrine," and he must use some kind of mushroom along with the three ducks, not foie gras. William Guthrie will be given two rabbits and green peppercorns for a terrine, Steve Jilleba and Neil Becker both have drawn chicken and foie gras galantines, and Mark Linden has drawn the same assignment as Lynn except that he gets salmon instead of sole.

A sense of beginning and excitement and heightened nerves has arrived as the seven chefs carry their assignments into the continuing education dining room for a meal prepared by the Culinary Institute's American Regional class. But the table is quiet as the food begins to arrive. Lynn sends back her soup and then sends back her salad, untouched. Eric says, "I feel like I could puke." There are some mumblings about classical procedure. Neil tells everyone how humbled he is to be here.

Lynn says, "This is going to be the hardest ten days of my life," a prediction that will soon prove incorrect.

CHAPTER THREE

*F*riday begins before 7:00 A.M. with Dieter's "housekeeping chores" and instructions for the next assignments and classes. Brian Polcyn, who had eaten silently but well the night before, returned to the Golden Manor to study, was in bed after eleven, slept well but woke feeling achy. He's hoping it's not the beginnings of a cold. Mark Linden, far from his Alaska home, jarred awake all night long and doesn't reckon he got more than two hours' sleep.

Today's work begins with a lecture on sanitation and oral presentations on related subjects (toxins and bacteria, how restaurant design can aid sanitation, how to handle leftovers). This will be followed by lunch and another three hours of lecture on nutritional cuisine, a visit to the CIA storeroom, with the rest of the evening being spent in the computer lab working out the nutritional analysis of their recipes for the cooking practical tomorrow.

Their mission is not simple. They must create a delicious four-course meal that contains no more than 800 calories, 15 to 20 percent of which must be protein, 25 to 30 percent must be fat, and 50 to 55 percent must be carbohydrate. Each meal must have less than 150 milligrams of cholesterol, and they are allotted 900 milligrams of salt. They are given two proteins—40 ounces of meat and 24 ounces of fish—but these again are not known in advance and are once again drawn by lot. Lynn is happy when she draws chicken and grouper—two healthful items—but she is typically upbeat and would likely have reacted the same if she'd been given foie gras or sweetbreads. Brian draws the assignment that reads "mussels and pork loin." He shakes his head, then shrugs and says, "It's gotta work." William is complaining to no one in particular that he drew duck and shrimp, two high-fat, high-cholesterol items. The rest of the ingredients they choose themselves following a trip to the CIA storeroom.

Lynn beams at all the beautiful produce and changes her menu to include some of the butter greens she sees and some blood oranges. "I love shopping," she says. She writes a list of items she may want to use. So does Polcyn. Perfect morels have arrived from Washington, and Polcyn says, "Everyone's gonna have morels on their menu tomorrow." But he's not pleased with the rest of the produce. "I cook kind of seasonal," he says. As it's early in spring, the full bounty of the Hudson Valley is not yet available. Everyone is searching the vast storeroom of the CIA and writing a list, except for William, who spends the entire time searching for jasmine rice. He does not seem to have gotten a break from his nerves. During nutrition lecture he continually asked how much you could go over or under the allotted requirements. When he asked if egg substitutes were available, the nutrition instructor, Catherine Powers, said, "If you want to use egg substitutes, I suggest you go out and buy them. I don't believe in substitutes. They don't taste good. We're looking for healthy cooking without substitutes."

While the CMC test has changed little since it was first given, the changes it has seen result from changes in our culture and our increasing knowledge about food and cooking. In the early eighties the nutritional cooking section was a minor category that tested chefs on special dietetic needs, cooking for diabetics, for instance. But as the country's nutritional focus shifted, so did the CMC exam to reflect better what we know about nutrition, mainly that nutrition and healthy cooking techniques are important to American consumers and can actually result in good, satisfying food if you know what you're doing. The focus today concerns how to boost flavor without boosting fat.

After a tour and examination of the CIA storeroom the chefs return to the computer lab, where nutritional analysis programs tabulate the protein, salt, cholesterol, carbohydrate, and fat content of the recipes they write. Nobody likes all this sitting. These people are cooks, and a day without some kind of cooking, the beginning of a major cooking test, makes them edgy. One of the nutritional judges, James Hanyzeski, observes, "They're still in the white-knuckle phase." Then to the group he says, "Don't be nervous. I don't think you're going to have fun, but pay attention to the details and cook the way you want to cook. Be happy with what you're putting out; follow your style."

All of them seem to think that they'll be OK once they can get into a kitchen and start cooking.

The chefs return to the Culinary Institute of America the following morning at around six-thirty and meet their first assistants, CIA students of varying abilities, who will aid them in their prep work. Brian Polcyn says hello to Ezra Elkon and leads him to a table in the corner of the dining room to discuss the morning's plan of action.

Brian has drawn position three, behind Mark and William, and he and Ezra charge the kitchen at exactly seven-forty. The room has just begun to feel busy. The first thing Brian does is tape the prep list (assistant's duties highlighted in yellow) and plating diagrams to the wall. "It's gonna be a little hairy," he tells Ezra, "but it's gonna be good. If you have any questions, don't hesitate to ask. I'm feeling better today because I get to cook. Otherwise I'm depressed." He squats at the oven and says, "Every day this is important. I want you to check the temperature of the oven. We don't want any surprises."

Continuing Education Kitchen I is a big fine space, a double teaching kitchen where as many as eight chefs and their assistants can work at the same time. The room is divided into four quadrants, and each quadrant has a double range with eight burners, two ovens, a steam kettle, two prep tables, and two lowboy refrigerators. At either end of the kitchen is a wall of tall, deep refrigerators where parstock, such as vegetables and stocks, are available. The kitchen quadrants are bisected by a large aisle used for dry storage cages, a grill, huge steam kettles, a cage for pots and pans, more stainless steel tables for additional prep space. Running the length of the kitchen on either side are windows. One set, long observation windows, is for looking in; students and instructors curious about the test can stand in the hall and watch the cooking. The back of the kitchen looks out onto a large quad that fills with culinary students between classes. Today is bright and clear, ornamental cherry trees in the quad are in bloom, and the kitchen is filled with natural light.

Dieter scurries past Brian's station, halts when he sees the prep list and several elaborately sketched plating diagrams taped to the wall, "Oh, my *God*," he says, "it's like the Olympics," then scurries off. Culinary Olympics happen once every four years in Frankfurt, Germany, and are presumably not unlike an international CMC exam.

"We're gonna organize our station by course," Brian explains. He pokes his nose into the bag of mussels and winces. "These don't smell too good." He looks through them, finds one that has opened and discards it. He lowers a bag of green beans onto a scale and says, "We've been shorted on our green beans. I need a quick count on these."

Mark Linden, the Alaska chef, who sports a spare mustache and whose light brown hair is heading toward gray, has his assistant mincing shallots and small-dicing yellow peppers as he poaches pears that eventually will be grilled. Grilling is a great technique of healthy cooking because it introduces flavor without calories, a smart move here.

William Guthrie remains on unsteady ground. Before his seven-twenty start time, he had called out to Chef Hanyzeski, a judge today, and ran to him with the words, "Chef, the world is coming in on me." He is struggling with his menu, which begins with shrimp cocktail (served in a hollowed-out onion) and is followed by salad, a duck stir-fry, and a baked fruit dessert. He has located the jasmine rice, but he cooks it in too much water (Carolina white rice requires a two-to-one water-to-rice ratio, how William cooked his jasmine rice, which requires less water), and he must recook it following Dieter's suggestion.

Dieter will help this way, though it is a bad sign when one of the chefs aiming for a CMC title can't cook rice properly. Nevertheless, he's eager to assist, even prod the chefs in the right direction if they veer. Lynn, for instance, has overordered the Bibb lettuce that so excited her the day before, but she does not realize it; she's focused on butchering her grouper. Dieter, however, does realize it and says, "Chef, will you be needing all this lettuce?" Lynn, distracted, simply says yes, and Dieter bobs off with a shrug, saying, "Well, she didn't get the *hint.*" As he instructed the chefs at the beginning, "Utilization is very important. If you order twelve pounds of mushrooms, I don't have a problem with that. But I expect to see you *use* twelve pounds of mushrooms."

Neil Becker, the culinary instructor from New York, has gotten a happy surprise. The proteins he drew were salmon and turkey breast, and he'd expected he'd find on his tray forty ounces of boned turkey breast. Instead he finds a turkey with its legs and wings removed. Now, in addition to the breast meat itself, he has the skin, which will keep the meat moist and self-basted as its roasts, and he can also use the bones. He's smart enough to pounce on this good fortune, immediately boning the breast, chopping up the bones so he can get the most flavor out of them in the short time he has; he gets them roasting so that he can add them to his chicken stock to fortify that flavor for his eventual sauce.

"Si," Neil calls to his assistant, "where are those wood chips?" Neil will also use smoke as a flavoring element for the turkey. These are perfect moves.

By nine o'clock the kitchen has begun to rock. Fourteen chefs and assistants are in constant motion. Dieter is scurrying zigzag paths throughout, removing scraps and garbage from workstations (everything is evaluated), attending to people's needs (Eric can't figure out, for instance, how to put together the juicer that he'd requested for his red pepper *nage*), and muttering critiques to himself along the way: "Those bones are too big; he's not going to get a good sauce out of that," and, carrying two lamb tenderloins away from station seven, "He gave me the best part of the lamb back; he tells me he can't *use* it!" Dieter has two assistants, both CIA graduates. Tuan ("Butch") Rafael, a cook in Arizona, and Joe Scully, executive chef of the Druid Hills Golf Club, who has volunteered ten days of his life to manage the chef assistants because he hopes to take this test eventually and will get an inside view of it by working. One CIA instructor is wandering the kitchen as an observer, and two others, Ron DeSantis and James Hanyzeski, both

CMCs, are serving as proctors. Hanyzeski, now thirty-four years old, was at the time he took the test, the youngest to pass the exam at age twenty-seven. These men, who wear suits beneath their lab coats, will observe cooking technique, station organization (called mise en place), sanitation (do they change their cutting boards after butchering poultry, for instance? Do they keep their meat and fish on the bottom of their lowboys to avoid drippy cross-contamination?), and how well they work with their assistants.

Hearing of excessive waste coming out of station two, DeSantis heads to the hall and looks into a blue recyclable bin where food scraps are discarded. He dips into one and spears a romaine core with his pencil. He stands upright and rotates the lettuce core before his eyes by spinning the pencil in his fingers. He returns to the kitchen and looks into a pot at station three, where Brian Polcyn is simmering artichoke hearts. Polcyn, who is off to the side, notices DeSantis and stops working. He watches DeSantis, at first, it seems, worried that he's done something wrong. Then, realizing he hasn't, he grows annoyed and conveys a clear get-the-fuck-outta-my-pot anger. He clutches some bay leaves and shakes some peppercorns out of a bottle and tosses them into the pot, and DeSantis wanders off.

Polcyn has created a strong menu. Steamed mussels with artichokes, saffron rice, and fennel with a tomato coulis will be followed by a salad course, farm greens with asparagus and red peppers in a potato vinaigrette. His main course will feature sautéed pork tenderloin with a morel mushroom sauce, wild rice, and green beans, and he intends to make an angel food cake with raspberry puree for dessert.

Regularly throughout the morning Brian asks Ezra to take a break from cleaning and halving the morels, or cutting the beans or dicing the potatoes, to sweep the floor. The proctors will be watching for such things; he wants his station clean at all times. Brian stands at the stove and holds a saucepan to Ezra. "This is the juice that came out of the mussels, a little wine, some stock from the vegetable scraps. I'm gonna cook off the fennel in this. See how I'm building flavors. I've only got so much stock. If I run out of stock, I have to use water, and water doesn't have a whole lot of flavor."

Hanyzeski makes the rounds checking salt and oil. Chefs must measure out their salt ahead of time. He approaches Polcyn's station and asks to see the recipe analysis. "You have no additional salt?" he asks.

Brian says, "I have about a sixteenth of a teaspoon."

Reading the analysis, Hanyzeski says, "You've got five hundred thirty-five milligrams of salt."

Brian computes quickly: "So that leaves me with three hundred sixty-five milligrams."

"That's about a teaspoon and a half. Do you want me to measure that out for you?"

"Thank you," Brian says, and returns to cooking. He tastes the fennel, which has cooked in the mussel juice and wine stock. "Needs a little salt," he says, raising his eyebrows. To Ezra he says, "You see, the braising liquid for the fennel now becomes the base of our tomato sauce."

Behind him, Lynn Kennedy-Tilyou in position six is furiously at work on a menu of grilled grouper with green tomato mango chutney and red beet coulis, hot pepper chicken with sweet potato puree, black bean sauce, fennel and wild mushrooms, and chocolate spice cake with strawberry relish. When she grinds her toasted spices for the chicken entrée, she and her assistant start coughing their heads off and everyone in the kitchen turns to see what's going on at station six.

The first cooking practical is running smoothly now, and as service for the first chef approaches, the tension and energy in the kitchen grow palpably intense. The air is alive with cooking noises, sizzling oil, the clank of pans landing on burners, but no voices. Everyone is working fast. Dieter begins to marshal the runners, student recruits. Plates go into ovens to heat, and soon Mark Linden's window opens, and his first course, grilled scallops with a gazpacho sauce already plated and set out on the prep table, is out to the judges that instant. DeSantis, clipboard and pencil in hand, calls off time intervals. He touches a gooseneck and a plate to feel for heat and scratches a note on his clipboard. Mark and Cheryl, his assistant, work furiously to complete the plating—in all, forty items—within twenty minutes, and when the last course disappears with two minutes to spare, Mark is so relieved that he embraces Cheryl with gratitude.

Polcyn has been keeping an eye on William's station as he finishes his morel sauce. William's one of those intangibles he wants to avoid. Polcyn holds the saucepan to Ezra, who grabs a tasting spoon and tries it. "See how that—you tasted it before—see how that salt brought it up?" Ezra smiles and nods. "OK," Brian continues, "first course is hot, second is cold, so at about quarter after, we'll plate the second course, and as soon as the first goes out, we'll put the second course right up here." He slaps the stainless steel table, then turns to the stovetop and negotiates some extra burner space from Lynn. "No problem," she says. She's hustling too, with her window opening in an hour, but she does not catch an early error. When she turned on her oven, she set it to 350 degrees, not all the way up to 550, as she would have in her restaurant back in Memphis. Polcyn uses the borrowed burner to sear his pork tenderloin.

William is attempting to get his shrimp cocktails out, but everything is taking longer than he expected, and he is yelling at his assistant. DeSantis, who stands behind William taking notes, is quiet except to call out times. "Ten minutes, Chef," he says. Then: "One minute, Chef." William yanks his dessert—sliced star fruit, kiwi, papaya, and banana in parchment paper—out of the oven and tosses each onto a plate, and off the desserts go. He has scarcely made it.

Polcyn's window is already open, and he calls to DeSantis, "Chef, where are my runners?" Only then does he begin to plate his first course. Each chef has attempted to send the first course out the moment the window opens, so when Polcyn doesn't send his out, hasn't even begun to *plate* it, it seems to be a clear mental mistake, an error in judgment.

DeSantis calls out, "Chef, you have fifteen minutes."

Polcyn takes an extra moment to add more tomato coulis to one of the first-course plates. "These are very hot," he says to the runners, who are now lined up and waiting. He has yet to send out a plate. "Make sure the mussels are evenly distributed," he says to Ezra, who is putting the mussels on the platter. After seven minutes the first course vanishes, and up come the salads. Polcyn tosses the greens in his vinaigrette and plates them by hand atop the asparagus. DeSantis helps sponge the plate rims and set them on trays for the runners. "Chef," Polcyn says to DeSantis, placing the seared pork tenderloin on a cutting board, "this is ten portions." And he begins to slice. When the meat is plated, he places a perfectly roasted walnut half on top of the wild rice. Out go the entrées, and then the desserts, and Polcyn takes a breath. He has made his window with thirty seconds to spare.

He was never worried, he says, and feels good about the food he sent out. When asked why he waited so long, dangerously so, it seemed, to send out the first course, he becomes angry.

"I'll tell you why I did it," he says. He is still pumped on the adrenaline of service, and he points in the direction of station two. "Because that guy was late. And I wanted to put as much distance between my food and his. At my restaurant I want to make it as pleasant for my customers as possible. Those judges are my customers." To send his food out simultaneously with William's was simply not how he believed his food should be served.

Steve Jilleba has sent out his first course already, and Steve will be followed by Neil and, after Neil, Lynn, like clockwork. But Lynn's service, because of her oven temperatures, becomes a quick nightmare. Nothing is cooking as it should, and she sends out her grouper undercooked and then the chicken, raw in the center. This has her so rattled that she creates a platter for eight instead of six and does not have time to fix it. It's a disaster. As she works, assistants are carrying in large sheet trays filled with lobster and sole and salmon and pork and duck and rabbit and turkey, checking off all items on the requisition list. Charcuterie prep will begin immediately after lunch.

When each chef finishes cooking, he breaks down his station, cleans it, and packs up his tools. Polcyn carries his in a big red Craftsman toolbox. Neil Becker has all kinds of fancy equipment like digital-read thermometer with probe and wires, a couple of small silver thermoses in which he can hold his sauces piping hot, and a single nonstick pan, which he brought specifically for this day of the exam and which he used to sear his turkey. "That's the only thing nonstick pans are good for," he explains. "Otherwise, they're useless because you can't develop any fond."

When the stations are cleaned and the equipment is packed, the chefs can head to the dining room across the hall for a meal, though no one wants to eat. Neil will head to the quad to have a smoke. Soon they will be called, in order, to Lecture Hall 2, which has been changed from a classroom to a judgment hall. The tables are no longer in rows but instead run the length of either wall and are covered with white cloths. At the head of the room sits another long table covered in cloth where three judges sit, taste the food, discuss it, and mark the grade sheets.

They evaluate it in six categories, granting a set amount of points for each one: serving method and presentation (0–10), preparation (0–10), nutritional balance (0–10), menu and ingredients composition (0–5), creativity (0–5), and flavor, taste, texture, doneness (0–25), resulting in a score of a possible 65 points for each course. This is divided by the number of courses and added to the kitchen proctor's score of up to 35 points for a total score out of 100 points.

On the tables against the wall sit their platters and one plate for each course; this serves as a kind of visual reference if the judges need to refer back to one or another of the courses.

In the center of the room rests a single chair, and here each chef sits, listening to the critique. The chairs are all the same—generic plastic and steel classroom chairs—but the chair in the center seems several inches lower than those of the judges.

The chefs wait quietly at the back of the dining room to be called in. Mark Linden returns, having passed with a strong score in the low eighties, and William Guthrie takes his place. The judging lasts between five and ten minutes. When William sits back down in the dining room, he slumps in his chair and tells the others that he did not pass. He seems to be surprised but more in a kind of numb shock. When the others ask him why, he explains that the judges—Tom Peer, Hanyzeski, and Catherine Powers, the nutritional instructor but not a chef, master or otherwise—didn't like his stir-fry with rice. They expected a more complex entrée. Likewise with the plain baked fruit. He doesn't go into the painful details.

Brian returns and sends big Steve into the chamber. Brian sits heavily, looking beat and discouraged. For a moment a collective gaze hangs on Brian: Has he failed?

He says, "No, I passed." But clearly he doesn't like the score, 76. He explains the critique: His mussels should have been featured, not simply mixed into the dish; the judges thought his pork was a little undercooked, but the biggest thing they criticized was the seeds in his raspberry puree served with the cake. Why did he leave the seeds in? He tries to answer it himself, slumped in the chair. "I guess I was thinking that I needed every bit of flavor and moisture I could get." Then he shakes his head and says, "What was I thinking?"

Lynn too has failed. She is not surprised, but she has been dealt a shock. She arrived today confident and ready. Maybe too confident. She studied more than a year to be here and practiced mystery basket situations. This failure, the first step out of the starting block, rattles her.

No one eats; there is scarcely time. Lynn has taken her blows in the judging room: Not only was her chicken raw (a real no-no), but the coating of dried ground hot peppers was too spicy to eat comfortably, and generally her entire menu, the very conception of it, was a hodgepodge, they said, confused. Now, with scarcely a break, she must head back into the kitchen and make that seafood terrine.

She is tired and can't think clearly. She heads to station five with her equipment, followed by her new assistant, Lon, who has been in class all morning. She has approximately three and a half hours to make and cook her terrine. She will serve it tomorrow morning. Nothing more today will be judged, but she has no concentration. She gets to her station and can't begin, can't focus. Lon, however, has enough training and sense to understand what is happening. First he encourages her, tells her it will be OK, says leave it behind you. It is all she can do to apologize to him. He asks her what he can do, and she shakes her head. This is not a rigidly timed preparation, but there are time constraints—four hours to prepare and cook their items and accompanying sauces—and she is losing time in her shock. Almost absentmindedly she finds her equipment list and prep list, written the night before, and this saves her. Lon takes the lists from her and begins to assemble her equipment at her station: cutting boards, sanitizing fluid, ice baths, Robot Coupe, hotel pans, pots. "I'm sorry, Lon," she says, "I need to get my head together." By the time Lynn has got her thoughts in order and her spirit not fully alive but at least vertical, Lon has gathered the equipment and has already made some headway in the prep list by peeling shrimp.

Lynn begins by boning four Dover sole. She can do this in her sleep, and the sheer mechanics of it lead her mind back to the kitchen. When she has finished boning the sole, she starts a stock by sweating the bones with some onions. She will reduce this stock till it has a clean, rich flavor and use it to fortify the scallop and shrimp mousseline that will form the bulk of the terrine; she will inlay this terrine with large chunks of lobster and mussels and flavor it further with cream and wine and fresh basil. Her kitchen senses have reengaged, and she's cooking again.

CHAPTER FOUR

A master chef hopeful who is not comfortable with forcemeat should be advised to keep that four or five thou and stay home, don't take this test, steer clear. CMC candidates must love forcemeat. They must have a deep and enduring passion for it, a thrill of grinding and pureeing meat and wrapping it in other animal products or molds and cooking it all very gently; they must be expert in sauce work, and possess clever and wily palates in combination with a powerful but judicious sense of seasoning, for all these things come into play with forcemeat.

Forcemeat, to speak broadly, is anything ground and then cooked, but it usually refers to meats that have been ground and seasoned for pâté, terrine, or sausage. The word *forcemeat* has only a coincidental relationship to the word *force* because forcemeats are in fact forced into sausage casings, or inside other meats or skins or inside molds; the word actually derives from the French verb "to stuff," *farcir.* Forcemeat was originally a meat used for stuffing. In many American restaurants today the word *farce* is used to designate stuffing, whether for a quail or a ravioli. Chinese dumplings use what can be called forcemeat. A farce of bread, egg, and herbs is made all across America on the last Thursday of November and cooked inside a turkey. Oscar Meyer bologna and salami are forcemeat preparations. Beef forcemeat, fried and served in a bun, is an American classic; the sauce is typically ketchup, and the dish often has cheese melted on top.

But here at the Master Chef exam, the forcemeat was refined, classical, a garde-manger technique that would be used not only during the next two days for the charcuterie and buffet sections of the test but would also play a formidable and fascinating role in classical cuisine and mystery basket tests. While it is classical and elegant, with aristocratic overtones, utilitarianism is what it's founded on: avoiding waste.

Lynn made seafood terrines at her restaurant, so her draw was not only a contemporary assignment but one she was already comfortable with. Her forcemeat would be made by pureeing raw shrimp and scallops with egg and cream, to be flavored with wine, a concentrated fish stock, and basil.

Likewise, Brian's duck terrine is a contemporary classic. He serves a pâté-of-the-day at his restaurant as one of his menu's starters and makes duck terrines all the time. His forcemeat today, prepared on the heels of his low-fat, low-salt nutritional menu, would be a mixture of duck, pork butt, and pork fat, first ground and then pureed. Floating in the center of this forcemeat would be a whole duck breast, called an interior garnish, which he has seared in a sauté pan. He would deglaze this pan with Madeira, reduce it, and add it to the forcemeat as an intense seasoning. Brian loves forcemeat preparations, but that doesn't make this assignment any easier. When asked if he is "just making a terrine," he replies with annoyance, "When you're making it for Sonnenschmidt, who is the authority in the country, it's not *just* a terrine."

Neil and Steve, who are working as a kind of team through this test, studying together, taking breaks together, helping each other with their various menus, have both drawn galantines. While the galantine is not a lot different from a terrine—the grinding, seasoning, and garnishing are the same—it is a more complicated and old-fashioned poultry and game bird preparation. You see it at food competitions but not on a lot of menus today for pretty much the same reason: It's a pain in the neck to make. Still, there's something exquisite and intriguing about the galantine, partly because it's difficult and partly because the idea of it is an elegant use of the entire bird.

Galantine—there is a long-standing debate on the origins of the name itself, mainly whether it derives from the word for gelatin or from *galine,* old French for chicken—indicates that the forcemeat is rolled inside the skin of the bird to form a perfect cylinder and, typically, poached in the appropriate stock and served cold. A variation of the galantine is the ballotine, which is a galantine served hot.

If you're the sort who loves to mess around for hours in a kitchen, the galantine is something you'll want to try. Here's how it works. Start with a whole chicken and remove its skin in one piece; this can be tricky, especially at the drumsticks and wings, but if you start by making the initial incision down the back of the chicken, it's really not all that difficult. Next, scrape off all the fat and trim it so you have one unbroken rectangle of skin; this is your cooking vessel. Bone out the meat completely. Wrap up your chicken forcemeat (the dark meat from the chicken ground with equal parts pork butt and fatback) and interior garnish (the seared breast meat from the bird as well as anything else lying around, truffles, foie gras, something tasty) in the skin you've prepared to make a tight cylinder, using plastic wrap to get it very tight. Next, remove the plastic wrap, tie this cylinder up in cheesecloth, and poach it in the 170-degree chicken stock that you've made from the chicken bones. When the interior temperature of your galantine hits 160 degrees, remove it from the heat and let it cool in that same stock. When it's cold, it's ready to unwrap, slice into perfect disks, rest upon a good sauce—Cumberland, perhaps, or mustard sauce, depending on the interior garnish—and finish with some fresh-picked thyme leaves or perhaps a fried sage leaf. It should be delicious and juicy and fun to eat.

All these fancy kitchen shenanigans are of particular value today simply because restaurants rarely serve them, so the only way we can know about them is to make them in our own kitchens. But among the most interesting elements of forcemeat in general is the fact that it is an emulsion. We typically think of an emulsion as being a heavy liquid created by blending a fluid fat such as clarified butter or olive oil with egg yolk: hollandaise sauce, mayonnaise. We certainly don't think of it as something you can bounce. But in fact forcemeat is an emulsion of fat, protein, and water. The grinding and pureeing of the meat and fat disperse the fat throughout the meat so that you have one uniform force. Fat makes it juicy and delicious. There is a reason no one used forcemeats in the nutritional cooking section of this exam. Without the fat, you'd have very dry, dull forcemeat.

The emulsion, then, is what makes the forcemeat preparation elegant not only in taste but also in concept. Because fat becomes soft at warm temperatures, and because emulsions are by nature unstable physical systems, the forcemeat emulsion can break. This is why Dieter warned people not to allow their uncooked forcemeat to reach room temperature or they might find little holes in their terrine slices. What happens when a forcemeat breaks is the same thing that happens when your béarnaise sauce breaks: The fat separates out. In terms of the terrine or galantine, what you would see is your pâté shrinking inside its mold, which is filling with grease, or your stock filling up with fat. And what you will serve to your guests is what amounts to shrunken and desiccated sausage.

The main way that you avoid this breakage is to keep your forcemeat below forty degrees until you cook it. This would be easy if you worked in a refrigerator, but most chefs work in hot kitchens, and adding to the ambient heat is the fact that the very act of turning meat into a farce, grinding and pureeing it, heats it. This means that you had better know to keep your grinding tubes and blades and dies and your food processing blade and bowls frozen until you're ready for them, and always keep this forcemeat in bowls that are resting on a bed of ice.

Though you can be a successful restaurant chef and have not a clue about galantines, a lot of food knowledge and technique are involved in a single preparation, and this is why they are prominently featured in the CMC exam.

As the chefs convene around Dieter and Chef Sonnenschmidt for the charcuterie introduction, Brian looks exhausted but says, "I'll get a second wind as soon as I get in the kitchen."

Dieter begins the discussion by saying to the group loudly and emphatically (and, it seems, with a private joy of his own), "It's OK to use salt! It's OK to use *fat*!" This is an important reminder because they have been so intensely focused on avoiding salt and fat for the past two days they need to refocus on classical technique, which adores fat. To cook nutritional hard and fast all morning and then move into charcuterie is jarring.

Chef Sonnenschmidt, seated, gives a brief lecture on charcuterie and this section of the exam, a minor subject. The judges, he explains, want only to see "the fundamentals of charcuterie." The basics in this case mean a proper ratio of fat and meat to ensure a good emulsion and attention to appearance (when you look at it, you should want to eat it; it should all but scream out its deliciousness), and then it must actually taste good. One terrine or galantine, one sauce, proper method, follow directions, demonstrate good thinking by using all that is offered to its best advantage, and don't get fancy. Piece of cake.

Into the kitchen they go for four and a half more hours of work, Lynn slow and dazed, her assistant saying, "It'll be OK, it'll be OK."

In the kitchen distinctions among the chefs appear, their personalities emerging through a stiff shroud of anxiety and nervous energy. Brian remains hip, confident, serious; he knows this material cold, has been a cook all his life, and loves to work in the kitchen. He's just doing what he does at his restaurant. Steve Jilleba, a country club chef, is huge and towers over the stoves in his backless kitchen clogs and white socks, but he has almost no visible emotions. The suggestion of a smile threatens once in a while, but mainly he is as dour as his brown, droopy mustache, so much so that he seems placid, not nervous about this at all. When I bring this to his attention, he makes his face twitch like a lunatic; yes, he's as nervous as the rest of them.

Both he and Neil, who is short and compact, Steve's physical opposite, work like technicians. Neil, a born and bred New Yorker with a dark complexion and thick black hair and mustache trimmed short, teaches galantines to his students. He also enters food competitions, so this garde-manger work is familiar to him. And yet, when he's finished rolling his galantine, he still has a good half pound of forcemeat, which leaves him no choice but to roll this into a basic roulade and admit that he misjudged the quantity. "I feel like I'm making stupid mistakes," he says, securing his galantine within cheesecloth. "I've made a thousand of these."

Steve is preparing the exact same thing—a chicken galantine with an interior garnish of chicken breast and foie gras—and he creates a compact little bundle, perfect as a pipe, about two inches in diameter and about nine inches long, wrapped in the clean, unbroken skin of the chicken. Dieter has been walking the kitchen, admiring Steve's craftsmanship throughout the slow hours of the afternoon. But then he sees Steve do something that turns him around: At the end of the day, after his galantine has been cooked, Steve wraps it tightly in plastic wrap. The proper method is to cool the galantine in cheesecloth in the cooking liquid because as it cools, it absorbs some of the flavor and moisture of the stock. After perfect steps throughout, Steve has sealed off this extra flavor, apparently in the interest of keeping the shape perfectly round. This is what makes Dieter mad. Taste is paramount. "This is *not* a *food* show," he whispers with real anger.

Eric Kopelow, thirty-eight years old, is responsible as head chef of a major airline for fifteen thousand meals every day dispersed on hundreds of planes during thousands of flights throughout the world. He travels more than he stays at home with his family, logging about half a million miles in the air each year, visiting every international city United Airlines flies to twice a year and all major domestic cities, eating at restaurants and planning menus that can be made in bulk, can stand up to the unusual circumstances of high altitudes and severely limited cooking facilities, and are not overly complicated. Catering companies outside his control prepare the food that he and his staff design in the corporate kitchen outside Chicago.

None of this work, though, requires him to make a single duck galantine as he has been asked to do today, an unfortunate fact. Eric seems to have only a vague understanding of the galantine method and at best a fuzzy expectation of what his finished work should look like. He removes the skin from the duck, but he leaves large chunks of breast meat still attached, apparently to serve as interior garnish. Duck skin has on it about a half inch of fat that, when rendered, is great to cook with but is no fun to eat. It's hard to scrape off this fat, and it helps if the skin is partially frozen, but you've got to get rid of that fat some-how. Eric does not. He moves from this error to another when he grinds good foie gras for his forcemeat. This was why Sonnenschmidt had expressly instructed the chefs to demonstrate good thinking by using what you have well. You don't grind up your most expensive item so that it gets lost; you feature it. When Eric goes to roll his duck galan-tine, what with all the fat, attached breast meat, and too much force-meat, he finds that it is a bad approximation of a football. But he keeps barreling forward. When it is rolled and tied, the galantine is so big that it won't fit in a pot but must be poached in a roasting pan. It is not a happy afternoon for Eric.

Sonnenschmidt likewise wanders the kitchen, observing. Sonnen-schmidt, the author of *The Professional Chef's Art of Garde Manger*, is considered an expert on classical garde-manger technique and a knowl-edgeable culinary historian. Officially, he is culinary dean at the CIA and, unofficially, a kind of godfather and benevolent spirit on campus. He hails from the former West Germany and is often seen arriving and departing beneath his green felt homburg, of which he is profoundly proud. He is so round that he actually teeters back and forth sideways as he walks.

As he wanders the kitchen, he rarely speaks and does not offer ad-vice or help to the chefs as Dieter does. When he sees that Neil has misjudged the amount of forcemeat, he whispers to me, "Making too much forcemeat is not necessarily bad. But you must know how to make use of it." When asked how one would make use of plain cooked forcemeat, he answers, "You serve it with a cold salad," and tod-dles off.

He stays to only midway through this charcuterie preparation, but before departing, he nods to me to observe the giant Steve, who stoops to put the finishing touches on his perfect galantine; he works like a craftsman of miniature wooden boats, each detail perfected to scale. Sonnenschmidt then teeters to station four so that I may observe Eric's galantine, an abomination in progress.

Sonnenschmidt then leads me into the hall and says, "Does a cook need to know this? No. Does a chef? Maybe. Does a master chef? Yes."

He makes some jokes with Dieter and DeSantis, who are passing through, and with hearty laughter he departs.

Because the tone of the kitchen all afternoon does not include a service, the chefs are a little slow and must suddenly hustle to get their products cooked when Dieter asks them to start cleaning up and clearing out. Lynn just gets her terrine in before Dieter tells them to leave. The terrines will finish cooking during his buffet lecture.

Once they all have reconvened in the dining room at tables near Dieter, and after this long, long day in the kitchen, Dieter says, "Good job today. Keep your strength. It's not going to get any easier."

He runs down tomorrow's schedule: serving their terrines and galantines in the morning—judges want to see unwrapping and cutting—and then, after a quick coffee break, buffet preparation from 10:00 A.M. to 9:00 P.M., eleven hours, including an hour break for dinner, during which they must leave the kitchen. It is a major subject demonstrating a range of garde-manger techniques on a single platter: two main items, two garnishes, and a salad, presented with architectural exactitude. Again Dieter concludes with his usual advice: "Remember that it should *taste* good. I want good color and flavor combinations. This is a real exercise in harmonious tastes. I want to see good cutting, strong lines, appealing presentation, a good game plan for the buffet. This is not a food show. It's a *practical*. This is a *working* food platter."

They once again draw lots. Lynn is wiped out and discouraged. She was here, hopeful and ready, at 7:00 A.M., and now, more than twelve hours later, she is very nearly a different person. She will return to more study and preparation in her motel room to fashion a game plan for the preparation and execution of buffet platter. She opens her envelope and discovers that for her platter she will be working with duck products. She has lost her confidence. "Neil," she says, "can I call you? I don't know what I'm going to do with the foie gras."

"Absolutely," he says with genuine encouragement. "Call me."

It's 8:00 P.M. when they head into the cool spring air, the end of Day Two.

CHAPTER FIVE

*N*eil Becker arrives the following day at 6:30 A.M. in bright clean whites. He is first to present, and there is an elaborate station set up in order to serve his galantine. At 7:00 Dieter Doppelfeld, in CIA chef's whites, and Fritz Sonnenschmidt and Ron DeSantis, wearing lab coats, appear at Neil's station, DeSantis complaining about how cold it is. He likes a hot kitchen.

Neil has been ready for ten minutes and is standing bolt upright, hands clasped behind his arched back, toque riding high.

An assistant rolls a wooden cart set with tablecloth and silverware to Neil's station. All say good morning. Then Sonnenschmidt says, "Chef, first will you tell us what you have prepared?" There are a lot of Germanic accents aloft on the breeze at the CIA, and here in a quiet kitchen, issuing from Sonnenschmidt, it can be vaguely intimidating, given the martial undercurrents associated with it in this regimental setting. But Neil is a New York City boy, and New Yorkers have their own bellicose instincts; he is ready.

"Chicken galantine with foie gras, chicken breast, smoked tongue and pistachios."

"And your sauce?"

"Orange-cranberry."

Then Neil sets to work. He takes two steps to the stove and dips his gloved hand into the gelatinous chicken stock to lift the galantine, which is bandaged head to foot, as it were, in cheesecloth. He wipes the cylinder clean and brings it to the cutting board, where he removes the cheesecloth. He then transfers it to a clean cutting board and pulls on a fresh pair of latex gloves for the all-important cuts. This is not strenuous activity, but every now and then he exhales quickly and abruptly. He removes his slicing knife from a bain-marie of hot water and dries it with paper toweling he has ready. He grips the galantine firmly with his left hand and rests the blade in the center fast against the base knuckle of his index finger. He inhales, then slowly pushes the blade through the galantine and slowly draws it back and through to the cutting board. It is a perfect cut. For the first time he sees the interior of his galantine; until that moment he does not know how it will look and if he has been successful in preparing it. It is beautiful. The foie gras is large and pink, the pistachios and tongue provide bright dots of green and red, and the breast meat is pale as a moon in this small disk.

He repeats these perfect cuts to create two identical slices. He places each on a separate plate, which he has ready at his station. He spoons the orange-cranberry sauce and sets them on the rolling cart for the judges.

Dieter, with knife and fork, lifts one slice off the plate and holds it horizontally at eye level, checking the smoothness and the evenness of the cut. He likes that the foie gras is prominently displayed. The judges taste. Their slow nods suggest the galantine has a good flavor, but they say nothing as they mark their score sheets—pencil tips on clipboards click-click-click in the quiet kitchen.

Sonnenschmidt says, "Now. If you were to do it again, is there anything you would do differently?"

Neil appears troubled by this question. "I would have made it a little thinner and longer. Tightened it a little more to get rid of a few more air bubbles." Clearly he's stretching. He doesn't want to presume that it's perfect, not in front of Sonnenschmidt, but it's pretty damn good. Then, remembering a genuine, measurable error, he says, "I would have made less forcemeat." Sonnenschmidt asks to see the leftover roulade. Neil ducks into his lowboy and hands Sonnenschmidt the excess force, sighs, and shrugs.

"And what would you do with this?" Sonnenschmidt asks.

Neil pauses for a moment to think, then says, "I might serve it with a cold salad."

The judges thank him and depart. When the scores are tabulated, his will be a 92.

Eric, at station three, peers over a low wall separating the range at his station from station two, where Mark Linden is about to upend his seafood terrine before the three judges. Eric appears serene, almost blank. After a moment, though, it's clear that it's not serenity but rather a kind of braced stillness, the kind you see in someone who's seasick, the moment he understands capitulation is inevitable, after which he lurches for the ship's rail. He looks that bad, and one cannot help feeling both pity and wonder: *Why on earth do you want to be here?*

He says he hasn't slept more than three hours, tossing and turning from worry. Finally, when he woke at three forty-five, he could no longer sleep and lay awake till dawn, thinking about his galantine, floating in a roasting pan of greasy stock. He says only that he is "not comfortable" with it.

When the judges have finished with Mark, at station two (a decent seafood terrine, though a fraction overcooked at one end), they appear before Eric.

The scene—judges, the set station, solitary chef—and dialogue are all but identical to what I saw at Neil's station except for the galantine, an albatross on a cutting board. Eric pushes his knife through it four times for three slices, serves each on a plate, sauces them, and places them before the judges. As he's slicing, Dieter peers at the stock in the roasting pan which has a yellowish oil slick on top; both duck fat and foie gras fat have leaked out of the galantine. Dieter tastes the poaching liquid and makes a horrid face.

When the judges have tasted, they mark their score sheets but begin talking immediately, DeSantis first, saying the taste of orange is overpowering. "That's the first thing that hits your mouth," he says. "And it stays there. Way too much orange."

Sonnenschmidt says, "The sauce is too pale in flavor"—Eric had described it as a Dijon-peppercorn sauce—"you don't taste the pepper."

Sonnenschmidt then asks what Eric would have done differently. Eric knows now that he should have scraped off the fat, and he would have used less forcemeat so that it wasn't so enormous, but he more or less mumbles this because he's simply so upset and discouraged by it all. Even this is a kind of failure. Dieter wants to hear a complete description of the many errors. He must like Eric a good deal because for the first time Dieter appears to be very angry, as if Eric had disappointed him personally.

He begins by holding his hand to the uneaten portions, saying, "Three different slices, three different sizes," and from there moves into a litany of errors: The interior garnish is an uneven dice, it's far too fatty, his poaching liquid is filled with fat, and why did he grind up perfectly good foie gras? Dieter stands beside Eric at his cutting board, and Eric stares down at his galantine, which lies there ruined, like a bad car accident. "I'm not talking about nutritionally sound," Dieter says. "I'm talking about craftsmanship. This is *very* poorly done."

Dieter leaves. It's especially rough treatment because Dieter typically affects the benevolent old uncle lending a hand, encouraging even in failure. Not this time.

Eric dumps his galantine in the garbage. "I knew it," he says, then: "What can you do?" He drops his cutting board into the sink at his station and runs hot water over it. On to ten hours of buffet preparation.

Steve Jilleba is a stark counterpoint to Eric. His galantine is so perfect that after he's finished slicing, Dieter picks up one half of the cylinder and puts his nose to it, beaming. He rushes to me with the galantine. The foie gras is pink and glistening. He holds it to my nose, and I smell a powerful blast of foie gras. Dieter gives me one solid nod. This, his face seems to say, is what a galantine is all about!

William has been assigned the rabbit terrine, and there at his station is a white terrine mold, inside of which is a shrunken terrine with a top layer of pure fatback, into which he has laid a row of thinly sliced button mushrooms. Just a glance at the station, a glance at the chef, though, gives one the impression that something is badly wrong here.

It's not that William won't look you in the eye; it's that when he does, he inspires extraordinary unease. He has a narrow face, and straight dark hair falls across his forehead. He has shaved but not very well, and the stubble is pronounced against his pale skin. He wears a neckerchief, as all the chefs do, but not a T-shirt beneath it, so there's a gap of more pale flesh and straggly chest hairs between neckerchief and chef's coat.

This physical impression of something being not quite right extends to his station. Again, it's not simply that it's sloppy and incomplete; there's something wrong about it in an almost otherworldly way. The first clue is that instead of a long slicing knife waiting happily in a bain of hot water, there is a serrated bread knife with a white plastic handle lying flat on his cutting board. His terrine mold sits on a sheet pan stuck in spilled aspic that's solid as rubber. And the terrine itself: shrunken and with aspic filling in the gaps, and the button mushrooms obviously meant to be garnish, as if William didn't realize this would be the eventual bottom of the terrine, not the top.

The scene only gets worse.

After Sonnenschmidt says, "Chef, will you tell us what you have prepared?" William answers but then, looking at the rolling wood cart, asks the judges if they have any plates. Sonnenschmidt says, "You should have plates at your station." Dieter has Butch, an assistant, rustle up some plates for William.

William turns out his terrine and begins his cutting. He has placed a scale at his station. With the serrated knife he saws off a slab of the rabbit terrine and, oh so carefully, places it on the scale. He then examines the weight of the slice before setting it on a plate. DeSantis, blank-faced, looks at Sonnenschmidt, who looks back at DeSantis. This is past being humorous; this is bad. Butch, behind the judges observing, whispers, "It's like being at a gory movie; it's so gruesome you don't want to look, but you can't help yourself." After William has placed on plates three large slabs of varying thickness, the judges taste. No one speaks. Sonnenschmidt, as always, asks, "If you were to do this again, is there anything you would do differently?"

"You mean under better circumstances?" William asks.

"No, under the *same* circumstances," Sonnenschmidt says sharply.

William fidgets and says he would have seasoned it more and added veal demiglace to the forcemeat.

Dieter doesn't want to touch this and remains silent the entire time.

DeSantis asks him why he got so much shrinkage. William said he wanted shrinkage. "You *wanted* this to shrink?" DeSantis asks.

"Yes."

"I don't understand that," DeSantis says.

William tries to explain that he wanted the entire terrine to be coated in aspic.

Sonnenschmidt says, "For a terrine, you would want aspic only on the bottom."

DeSantis asks, "What's the purpose of the fatback?"

"To hold the mushrooms in place," William says.

Fatback is to emulsify into the ground meat, not to be a separate element that you eat, and not to hold mushrooms that wind up on the bottom of your terrine, so when DeSantis hears this, he's had enough. "You've got some *real* problems here," he begins. Mercilessly and without regret he runs through every mistake he's seen. It quickly grows too gruesome for Butch, and he departs.

Brian Polcyn, at station six, is ready and waiting at his station when the judges arrive. He has made a duck terrine with interior garnish of seared duck breast and shiitake mushrooms, to be served with an orange-ginger sauce. Perhaps still tasting blood from the Guthrie devastation, DeSantis will lay into Brian on his uneven slicing and furthermore doesn't want to hear any backsass excuses. Polcyn nevertheless scores solidly in the mid-eighties.

The final contestant is Lynn, who is no less discouraged now than when she left last night. Returning to her hotel room, she broke down, weeping, but the emotional flood exhausted her utterly, and she fell into a hard black sleep. Though well rested, she nevertheless has been thinking all morning that if she fails this section, she will take herself out of the test voluntarily and return to Memphis. She has a serious concern about her terrine. Because of time constraints, she had to pull it when it measured two degrees lower than she wanted it to be.

Lynn is only the second woman to take the test—the first was Lyde Buchtenkirch-Biscardi, a CIA instructor who passed strongly and currently teaches charcuterie—so Dieter and the others are secretly pulling for her. Also, she's a bright presence in the kitchen, and it's hard not to be hopeful for her.

After she announces to the judges what she has prepared—seafood terrine with whole grain mustard sauce—she takes her terrine to the pan of water boiling on the stove. A dip of between five and ten seconds should be sufficient to loosen the terrine, but Lynn holds the terrine in for longer. Her back is to the judges so she does not notice their expressions, which begin as raised eyebrows and escalate to wide-eyed, open-mouthed stares as Lynn continues, astonishingly, to leave it in the hot water. Dieter, who watched her make the terrine, knows the sole could actually overcook and disintegrate if she leaves it in and any gelatin she'd added to the mousseline forcemeat, which holds the entire terrine together, could melt. It may already be too late.

Sonnenschmidt and DeSantis keep turning to each other to see how the other is reacting, and their alarmed, incredulous smiles eventually turn to plain worry. DeSantis actually covers his face with his hand. Forty-five seconds pass, and Dieter can't take it anymore. He hurries away, whispering harshly, "Why doesn't she take it *out?*" He can't watch. Still, Lynn stands at the stove staring at her terrine in the simmering water, occasionally checking the edges, tugging at the plastic wrap that lines the mold.

At last she removes the terrine and brings it to the cutting board. Dieter returns with a sigh, but worried the whole thing will just spill out onto the cutting board when she removes the mold. She upends the terrine and carefully lifts it up. The terrine holds, and Dieter exhales.

Lynn rewraps the terrine, gently, in plastic to keep it secure as she slices—another dangerous move considering how warm it must now be. (This is the last thing Lynn is worried about; there's not a drop of gelatin in it to melt, and if anything, the terrine is undercooked.) She slices and serves two separate plates.

It's a gorgeous terrine. The slim outer rim is pure white Dover sole with a fine line of deep green seaweed inside that; the scallop and shrimp mousseline is bright and pale and flecked with basil; packed in this are huge chunks of lobster, and mussels, and whole scallops.

Dieter lifts one of the plates and holds it up at an angle. He knows from the sheen of the lobster and the way the mousseline glistens that Lynn has cooked it perfectly. If it tastes good, if it only tastes OK, Lynn will surmount this hurdle.

DeSantis is bent over the plates at a right angle, staring. He tastes. He nods. Sonnenschmidt tastes and nods. Lynn is cleaning up her station; she can't bear to watch or listen. DeSantis takes another bite and, chewing with eyebrows raised, says, "That's a *good* terrine." Sonnenschmidt concurs. DeSantis takes a third bite and says with genuine surprise, "That's the best seafood terrine I've had in my *life*."

The judges eat every bit of what she has served. Then Sonnenschmidt, a leading authority on terrines, asks whether Dieter would mind if he wrapped up one-half of this terrine to take home. Dieter nods happily, proud for Lynn. When the judging is done, Sonnenschmidt tucks the firmly wrapped half terrine under his arm, says, "That's why I work for free," and laughs as he toddles out of the building.

Lynn is elated. As she's cleaning up, she says to Lon, her assistant, "I've got my *Terminator* glasses on."

Her score: 98. Reportedly the highest anyone has scored in that category ever.

CHAPTER SIX

$\mathcal{B}$uffet is a major category and perhaps the one most unfamiliar to those who are not professional chefs. We've all been to one kind of buffet or another: a variety of foods, spread down a long table, perhaps on a piece of furniture actually called a buffet. It's a meal you receive standing up, often having waited in a line. Sometimes you serve yourself; sometimes servers portion the dishes for you. At nice Sunday brunch buffets there's often a chef cooking to order and you can have a fresh hot omelet instead of the soggy hash browns steaming in a hotel pan. Buffet-style restaurants originated and flourished in France at big railway stations before high-speed trains and club cars arrived; such restaurants could serve food immediately to a guest about to take a long journey. Within American restaurants the salad bar is a kind of buffet, and some restaurants offer buffet every day. In kitchen parlance, buffet can mean serving a large group the same menu. But classically, buffet simply designates cold food served from platters.

The person responsible for working with cold food, or the station preparing cold food in restaurants, is called garde-manger. Often leftovers or unused meats, fish, and vegetables from various parts of the kitchen are funneled to garde-manger station. Sometimes the garde-manger is meant to hunt scraps on his or her own and must be a deft scavenger. The term itself actually means to keep what is to be eaten. Part of what that means is not throwing out leftovers. Using leftovers requires a range of skills. Leftovers are the raison d'être of the pâté, terrine, and galantine. The two uncooked ducks not sold last night that will otherwise go bad can, with some pork butt and whatever garnish might be lying around, be turned into a duck terrine or galantine serving twenty people. Leftover vegetables can make vivid and extraordinary terrines. So knowing how to turn leftovers into forcemeats and mousses and mousselines is an invaluable skill for the garde-manger.

Another body of skills the garde-manger needs is methods of preservation. True garde-mangers are the great preservers. Salt has been a preserver of fish for thousands of years, doing the same for cod as it does for pork. Sugar too preserves; put sugar on berries that are about to go bad, let them sit overnight, and then cook them into a delicious sauce or simply make—what else?—preserves. Pack lemons in sugar, and soon you will have what are called preserved lemons. Sugar pulls water out of protein too, and mixed with salt, it makes a great meat cure. If you find you have an extra side of salmon on your hands that will go bad if you simply leave it in the fridge, cover it in salt and sugar for a few days and your salmon will be cured. Trim the tail off that salmon first, make a salmon mousse, and you have used two different methods of preservation. Let the cured salmon sit unwrapped in the fridge till it feels a little sticky, and then smoke it (a third preservation method on the same item) because that smoked flavor makes the salmon especially delicious.

Meats can be smoked too, as can forcemeats such as hard sausages. Soaking meats in a brine is a preservative, a way, for example, of keeping beef edible for a long time. Soak and ferment some cabbage in brine, and serve the resulting sauerkraut with your corned beef or smoked sausage. (Freezing of course is a relatively recent method of preservation in most parts of the world, but not one typically valued as a garde-manger skill.)

The confit is another method of preservation. Duck legs, poached in their own fat, then stored submerged in this fat, will keep for weeks and weeks and may be the very best way of all to cook and eat duck.

So methods of preservation are among a garde-manger's chief techniques, but for a contemporary buffet, more skills than that are needed. Buffets can include salads and canapés and roasted meats served cold. These options too will come into play in the Certified Master Chef exam, and they must be combined with a chef's sense of design and composition, because the chef's buffet platters must be beautiful to look at; they should be so enticing that you can hardly keep your hands off the food. It is an important section of the test because it requires so many different skills all at once. In fact, if one section of the test best measures the true overall talent of a chef, this may be it because of the variety of skills needed and because as a rule cold food is harder to make delicious than hot food. You need some real muscle employed with elegance and balance to make cold food taste great and look so good you want to devour it. The platter must have a variety of cooking methods on it, contrasting textures, flavors, colors, and it must all make good culinary sense.

This is why Master Chef candidates need ten hours of prep time and, the following day, two hours in the afternoon to assemble their four plates and a platter for six—twelve intense hours to create and serve a cold meal for ten people.

Brian sits down with Eric in the dining room during a buffet prep meal break. Brian is feeling pretty good. He drew a pork platter for the buffet—"a good muscle," he says of pork—and his game plan is mapped out: spice-rubbed and smoke-roasted pork loin, straight pork terrine, a grilled vegetable terrine, bean salad, and sweet potato tart. All his items are simply stuff he's worked with and developed over the course of his career as the chef of restaurants in the Detroit area, though the conditions here are a little different. At his restaurant no one menaces him about his knife cuts. Also, the fatigue even after Day Two is something to contend with. "You get back to your room at nine," Brian says. "You're dead fuckin' tired, and you've got to put this elaborate buffet together." But he has been so thorough that he has made a kind of spreadsheet to ensure perfect variety of methods, flavors, and textures:

Item	Flavor	Color	Texture	Height	Method
Pork Loin	Smoky/Spicy	Natural	Solid	Low	Roast
Terrine	Light	Bl/Gr/Wh	Smooth	Low/High	Bake
Grilled Veg	Fresh/Clean	Colorful	Firm	Low	Grill
Tart	Sweet/Rich	Orange	Soft	Medium	Braise
Salad	Acid	Green	Crisp	Medium	Poach
Sauce	Sharp	Yellow	Creamy	N/A	N/A

Brian met Eric here at the Culinary, where they took a practice class for this exam. Brian's worried about Eric. He's noticed that Eric has not been eating very much over the past couple of days. Eric has a thick brown mustache and large, gentle blue eyes, eyes that are distant now. The galantine episode was rough on Eric. Brian looks at the large white dinner plate in front of Eric. On it are a plain piece of bread, a piece of cheese, and a piece of ham, untouched. That and a cup of black coffee.

"You should eat something, man," Brian says.

Eric doesn't respond. Brian can see that Eric is in a bad place right now. It's as if they've jumped out of an airplane, Brian thinks, and Eric has just realized he doesn't have a parachute.

"Eric," he says, "come on, focus on the day to day. Focus on one thing at a time. You've got a list. Just do one item at a time, and it will all come together."

Eric looks at Brian, then looks away. "What am I *doing* here?" he says.

This hits Brian like a slug of lead. He knows at that moment Eric is going down, and realizing also that Eric could drag him down too, he withdraws emotionally from Eric, pulls his own ripcord, lets Eric plummet.

Back in the kitchen at station two, Brian rocks through his items with rhythmical expertise. He doesn't even have to think much; it's all planned, he's done it before, and it ain't brain surgery. He begins with his first main item, a pork loin. He sears it. Then he coats it with a dry rub of cumin, paprika, saffron, salt, and pepper, to give it a little color and high spice level; cold food needs heavy seasoning and boosted eye appeal.

Next he puts some hickory chips in a roasting pan and puts the roasting pan over a burner. He sets a rack over this, raised above the chips by balled aluminum foil, places the seared seasoned loin on the rack, and covers the pan with a lid. Soon the chips begin to smoke, and for the better part of an hour that pork loin roasts in the smoke. Brian has used three different methods of bringing flavor to this pork loin: searing, seasoning, and smoking. When the loin hits 150 degrees, he takes it off the rack. Next he will manipulate the shape for further eye appeal: After it rests for several minutes but while it is still hot, he wraps the pork loin in plastic and puts it in his cooler in a hotel pan under another hotel pan with weights. The weight will give it a uniformly oval shape that will set once it's cold.

He crosses this item off his list and continues with the next item. He is required to use a pork tenderloin somehow, and he has decided to feature it as the interior garnish of a pork terrine, straight forcemeat with chunks of black truffle and pistachios. (There are different categories of forcemeat, which is why Brian specifies his as "straight"; for a "gratin" forcemeat, some of the meat is browned before it is ground and pureed; a "country-style" forcemeat is coarsely ground, not pureed, and usually includes liver.) He roasts and cools the pork terrine with a weight on it.

He has decided on a lean vegetable for his salad, a simple green bean salad with sautéed shallots, strips of tomato, and bacon and tossed in a bacon vinaigrette. He cooks the beans and shocks them in ice water, lightly sautés the shallots, mixes the vinaigrette. Item by item he checks them off his list.

On his Japanese mandoline, he slices eggplant, carrots, zucchini, and yellow squash lengthwise and grills them; he also grills sliced red pepper and mushroom. When they are cool, he begins to assemble his grilled vegetable terrine. He lines a terrine mold with plastic wrap. He adds a small amount of gelatin to a second vinaigrette and coats each slice of vegetable with it as he layers them in—widthwise so that they hang over the edge of the mold—first the eggplant, then the carrot, the zucchini, squash, and down the center he layers the red pepper and mushroom. He folds the flaps over to seal it up and tightly finishes wrapping it in plastic. He loves this dish and sometimes serves it at his restaurant with a tomato coulis, often adding goat cheese as well. It's simple and always perfectly seasoned because each piece of veg is individually coated with vinaigrette and the gelatin in the vinaigrette holds the whole thing together when you slice it. It will be a healthful, tasty, and vibrant item on his platter

Finally, to introduce a starch to the plate, he decides on a sweet potato mousse tart, baking the tart shells blind, then filling them with roasted sweet potatoes that have been pureed with cream and a little gelatin and seasoned. He spreads these in the tart shells and then, when they have cooled and set, finishes them by pouring up to the rim of the tart a film of aspic that will give the tarts an appealing gloss. He likes the tart idea also because it will introduce a wedge shape to the platter, giving him now several different shapes: oval, small rectangle, large rectangle, and triangle and also the circle of the tart. It's a smart platter, and he's able to clean up and leave with time to spare.

The conclusion of Day Three, a Sunday, is gentle, with everyone finishing at a different time and without the frenetic activity and crescendo of a hot kitchen's service. Indeed this is the first of two days during which the chefs don't serve hot food under pressure. Even Eric leaves the kitchen feeling a little better. He has worked his way through each item of his seafood platter: poached salmon, a seafood terrine, lobster mousse. The mechanical work of the kitchen has for the moment brought him out of his tailspin.

CHAPTER SEVEN

*M*onday morning at seven, the chefs convene in the Escoffier Room, one of the CIA's four working restaurants, one devoted to classical French cuisine. Whereas mornings are typically spent discussing and being tested on nutrition, sanitation, cost control, and the like, this morning the chefs will demonstrate a passing familiarity with front of the house topics and tableside service. Patrick Culot, a front of the house instructor and former waiter, maître d', captain, and sous chef at various restaurants in New York and in his native Belgium, runs the class. The chefs today will bone, serve, and sauce a roast chicken or a Dover sole and prepare and serve either crepes Suzette or bananas Foster. Culot will demonstrate each, and then the chefs will try it themselves. People are tired, but the mood is light. Even Eric seems to be enjoying himself a little. He appears to have gotten a good night's sleep and feels confident about the day ahead.

The class begins, however, on an ominous note. At the stroke of seven, with all the chefs seated in the elegant dining room of the restaurant, many drinking coffee out of china cups and saucers, Culot takes attendance. He has the list beside him, and he hunches over it, checking off each name with a pencil. When he reads the name William and no one responds, he looks up and asks, "Where is William?"

Lynn says softly, "He's no longer here."

Exaggerating slightly his accent, Culot says, "Lost in zee battlefield," and draws a line through the name.

William called Lynn at her hotel room to let one of the chefs know that he was leaving, and this was appropriate, for she was the first person he spoke to upon arriving at orientation.

The day before, during buffet preparation, Brian had one of the few chances to see what his colleagues were doing. Buffet prep allowed for such breathing room. "The guy was doing funny things with cans," Brian said, recalling William's activities.

The proctor that day confirmed that bizarre preparations were happening at station four, where William worked. The cans were Pepsi and Sprite. He was wrapping skin around one and baking it. He was stuffing the other with meat and roasting that.

Joe Scully, the Atlanta chef who had come to assist Doppelfeld and organize the apprentices, was a tall, lean husband and father, thirty-eight years old with curly dark hair, studious round glasses, and an perpetual bounce in his step. He was a constant observer throughout the exam, and he said of William, "You know how men are from Mars, women are from Venus? This guy was from *Pluto*. It was as if he had no reference point."

At about seven o'clock that night Chef William took the stairs to Dieter's office on the second floor of the building to say that he thought he could finish in two hours, but he didn't think he was going to pass.

Dieter knew William was not CMC caliber, understood that they shared no standards, that it was a different language William was using here, and not one that meant anything to Dieter. "You do not take a perfectly good piece of meat and stuff something through it and cut it into little pieces," he said, referring to William's strip loin. "I suppose you can make quail confit, but a confit takes at least forty-eight hours." And of course there was the jasmine rice. Still, Dieter did not want to come to any hasty conclusions and said, "Let's go down and talk to the proctors and see where you stand." Dieter would find that even he couldn't finish in two hours with what William had begun.

Eccentric as William was, and in part because none of the other chefs really knows what anyone else is doing, the first casualty is nevertheless felt by everyone. As Scully remarks afterward, "When someone crashes and burns, everyone feels it."

When the tableside service class has finished, all sit for a lunch of the Dover sole and roast chicken they've been practicing on. The table is generally quiet; fatigue has set in. Neil says with a sigh, "Day Four," and Brian says, "Is it Day Four? God, it feels like Day Eight." There is some discussion about how odd the proctoring feels, and Brian in agreement says, "There is a proctor in my motel room."

After lunch Brian and I take our coffee cups to the dishwasher's station, and I ask him why he's taking this test. He sounds almost angry in response, and the intensity of his words surprises me. "I'm not doing this for the title. I'm not doing it to prove anything. The only thing you've got to prove anything to is yourself." He shakes his head. "I don't know. There are so many reasons why I'm taking this test. I'm doing it for the education. It's a great education. So it's a no-lose situation. I'm doing it for my staff, and I'm doing it so that I can attract the highest-level employee." Then he says, "I don't *like* doing this."

Nor, he adds, do his wife and five children. Brian's oldest child, Alana, is thirteen, and his youngest, Ben is two. His wife, Julia, works at the restaurant when she's not taking care of the kids. Five kids keep her pretty busy, so before leaving for New York, Brian made eight dinners for her that would be ready either to pop in the oven or to throw together in a hot pan. They included a carbonade de boeuf à la flamande, which is an old classic, pot roast with onions braised in beer (it's important to use brown beer, he notes), chicken cooked in rice, stuffed pasta shells, lasagna, and New England clam chowder. He left her a list of them and what order they were to be served, since some were frozen and some only refrigerated. ("Kids should have good clean flavors and wholesome food," he says. "Kids today, man, their idea of a good meal is McDonald's. My kids, they can't even read, but they pass a McDonald's sign and they start screaming for McDonald's." It's not easy pleasing all five kids of varying ages, but the meals he's chosen are ones that everyone agrees on. Just don't put anything green in there, not even chives, he says, because they'll spend the whole night picking out the green bits.)

Balance is the key, he says. He wants to be a good husband and father, a good businessman, a good cook, and a good chef; he wants to make enough money to support and raise his family well, he says.

But the CMC test, in fact, has little to do with these stated goals, so I wonder, really, why he's taking the test. I don't ask again. He's got to hurry back to the kitchen to begin his platter construction.

It's quiet and cool in the kitchen and feels almost like an architectural design class with diagrams of platters at the various stations and, in addition to knives and steels, rulers and string. Brian is slicing his terrine with the pork inlay and has his assistant, Charlie, stand a spatula flat on the board and flush against the terrine—"like a carpenter's square," he says—to see how close he's come to a perfectly vertical cut, thinking of DeSantis with each stroke. Brian shakes his head. He lays the slices on a sheet tray that he's covered with plastic wrap. Dieter walks by, tilts the tray, evidently notices the slightly different thicknesses. Dieter grimaces and walks off, and Brian says, "They could see it from St. Andrews Road," which is nearly a mile away. "Now is *not* the time to be practicing your knife skills," Brian says. "But I guess you're always honing your skills." He looks at the inlaid tenderloin, which is slightly off center. On a platter where everything is symmetrical and perfect, anything even slightly out of place seems magnified. "That's a mistake," he says. "They're going to get me on that. I put it in wrong. *Stupid* mistake."

He measures the placement of each terrine slice and pork slice with a ruler. He uses a string to create perfect curves as he lays each slice on the platter. He steps back every now and then to check the appearance from a distance. "See how it all flows down?" he says to Charlie, mimicking the elliptical patterns with his hands. "Nice and simple. Keep it simple."

Steve Jilleba, the big man from Illinois, has made a rabbit pâté en croute, which is absolute perfection to look at, a game hen terrine, and added rabbit glace to the forcemeat. He's also made a red pepper mousse and a vegetable salad. His face has yet to make an expression, but he did say earlier that he was coming down with a cold and this concerned him.

Neil drew turkey, again. He doesn't like turkey. "When we do *international*, I'll draw turkey," he says, shaking his head. He's making a smoked herbed turkey breast, and he's also stuffed the turkey wings with giblets, pine nuts, and currants, turned them into ingenious miniature galantines, but with the last joint intact. He's also making a maple-cured pork tenderloin, marinated green beans, barleycorn salad with pecans and mushrooms, and a cranberry sauce.

Dieter likes what he sees for the most part. Everyone seems to be moving through a solid game plan. "If they all pull through today," he says quietly, "they have a good chance of having a big class"—that is, a big crop of new CMCs this year.

The two hours fly, and soon platters and plates go out. The work is intense, given the necessity of perfect plating: each piece, sliced perfectly and placed perfectly. During most of the last hour these chefs are at permanent right angles over their platters.

When runners come to take Brian's platter away, he looks angry.

"You know what's going to happen?" he says. "They're going to rip me a new asshole. You know what they're going to get me on? *Slicing.*" Brian grits his teeth. "They're gonna say, 'You want to be a master chef and you can't even slice a *terrine*?'" The spector of DeSantis won't go away.

As is always the case, the chefs lean against the white walls of the hallway outside Lecture Hall 2, where, tonight, Ferdinand Metz, president of the CIA, a superstar for America in the culinary Olympics for many years, and the man who instigated the creation of this exam, will judge. He will be joined by Richard Czack and Dieter Doppelfeld.

Brian drew position two and thus has more than an hour to wait while the judges evaluate the four platters that followed his. He uses this time to write down his own criticisms: bad slicing, off-center inlay, and he thought the pork loin was slightly overdone. He knows Metz and Czack are the judges, and he wants to be prepared. But he also writes down arguments in his favor, noting the variety of methods, flavors, and textures employed on one harmonious platter. Brian considers it an intelligent platter especially since he put it all together after a long day, "dead fucking tired," two nights ago. But Metz and Czach are in there, so he doesn't know what to expect.

All are mainly quiet as they wait in the hall lined up on either side. Lynn looks particularly nervous: If she doesn't pass, she'll be asked to leave. Because of her failure the first day, she's on a day-to-day basis for these four days, all of which are major cooking tests; if she fails one, she's out.

Mark goes in and come out, Brian follows and comes out—no new asshole—Steve, Neil, all of them fairly strong passes.

Eric is silent. He and Lynn are the last to be called in to the judging. Eric enters quickly, and when he emerges from the judging room, Lynn enters immediately, unable to bear waiting an instant longer than she must.

They all remain in the hallway to draw their assignments for tomorrow's section of international cooking. When Eric says, "I don't believe it," everyone stops talking and turns to him.

He has failed buffet. He leans against the wall and looks at the ceiling. His eyes begin to tear up. "I don't believe it." Then he says, "I'm out."

"*What?*" Neil says. "You're not out."

"I'm not going through with it."

"Come on, man," Neil says. "Stick with us."

Still looking up, Eric just shakes his head.

"Come on, man, there's nothing but cooking ahead of us."

At last he looks Neil in the eye and says, "You don't understand. I felt good about that. I felt *good* about it."

Steve Jilleba says, "Shake it off."

It's futile, Eric is thinking, two failures in a row, and this last one for something that he thought would easily pass.

Neil continues a passionate argument for staying in. "If you drop out now, then you have to take the entire test over again. Don't drop out now. You'll be second-guessing yourself for the rest of your life."

Eric just shakes his head, looking lost.

Lynn emerges from the judging room with long strides and a big smile. "I get to come back," she says. She is so happy she wants to keep talking about it, but she glances at Eric and looks down. "I'm sorry, I'm just so . . ." She needs some kind of release, she needs to share this. Brian understands this and says, "Awww," opens his arms wide and Lynn receives his big brotherly embrace eagerly. It feels so good, she hugs Neil, who's standing right there and smiling with her.

CHAPTER EIGHT

Entering Lecture Hall 2 when the scenery has changed from class-room to judging chamber, and the bets, as it were, have been placed, is not a fun part of the day. What follows can be elating, and it can be bruising, even devastating, as it was for Eric. Each chef steps in to face three certified master chefs who have already come to a conclusion about the candidate's food. The atmosphere is not festive; it's like a Senate hearing, sometimes hostile. The judges render a verdict on the CMC candidate's work, and the experience can feel cold. Dieter Doppelfeld makes every effort to keep the judging as objective as possible. Dieter is one of the judges for buffet; one might argue that he should not be a judge because he knows who has created each platter, perhaps even watched mistakes in progress, and the possibilities of favoritism or the reverse may color his impressions. On the other hand, Metz and Czack are tasting and evaluating blind, and all discuss their impressions among themselves as they judge without regard to the name of the chef. At this level of evaluation the proof is in the pâté, not in the chef or the judge.

When Brian enters, he greets the judges and sits in the solitary chair about a yard in front of the three judges. The room is stark, the floor cool tile. Metz is in the center, leading the evaluation, and his first words to Brian are: "What happened to your thumb?" He has noticed that Brian's right thumb is bandaged, sliced on a mandoline during the nutritional cuisine practical. Brian explains this to Metz, who nods and advises him to take good care of it.

Only then does the critique begin, first with Brian's evaluation of his own platter, then the judges'. Brian finds the critique genuinely helpful. Metz, for instance, suggests that Brian's off-center pork tenderloin happened not because Brian put it in wrong, as he thought, but rather because he put too much weight on the terrine, causing the inlay to shift as it cooled. Brian realizes this and wonders, "Why did I put so much weight on it? That's what this test makes you do. I would never have done that at my restaurant." Richard Czack calls out for special mention the fact that he could see the grill marks not only on the outside layer of terrine slice but also on interior layers. This was how closely Czack examined each item—five of them on Polcyn's platter alone, some thirty throughout the late-afternoon judging. Brian will score an 85, having lost serious points for excessive waste at his station during prep, noted by the kitchen proctor.

I have a moment to speak with Metz as he leaves the judging hall. He is lean in an elegant suit, his light brown hair and mustache neatly trimmed as always, his face slender with high cheekbones and strong chin. I ask for his thoughts in general on the buffet performance. "They all clearly have a valid reason for being here," he says. "There is no one in left field." In general he is pleased, and he offers, by way of example, the pork platter, which was perhaps the best. "Simple, simple, simple," he says. "One line going this way, another this way. . . . His roast pork was *perfectly* cooked. That indicates a level of maturity."

I ask then about a particular seafood platter, wanting an explanation for why Eric failed. Why did every platter pass, I wonder, but not this one? Metz does not refer to the chef, or even what the chef did, only to the food. The food was what it was.

"The aspic had no flavor," Metz begins. "You would have some acids and herbs in it. And you have a lot of expensive ingredients there. Aspic is simply to hold them; it shouldn't be like a rubber ball." He shakes his head. "He served one sauce for both main items. The salmon was a little dry." Also, he notes, the terrine was cut in giant slabs containing big, inelegant chunks of meat for garnish. "It didn't look good," he concludes. "When you look at it, you should want to eat it."

I ask Metz some general questions about the CMC test itself. He readily acknowledges that the number of certified master chefs is small and that it does not have a huge impact on the industry, but he hopes that it does in some ways "serve the industry" by setting a standard of excellence. How does he respond, I ask, to claims that the CMC exam is elitist and the related fact that if there were more CMCs (and therefore less elitist-seeming), the test itself might have more impact in the industry?

Metz answers that he does not care how many CMCs there are. Volume is not the point. Standards are the point. "If we do like they do in Europe and give it to Joe because Joe is a good guy . . ." He finishes this comment with a shrug. Indeed the test and the title would have little meaning if that were the case and would likely seem even more elitist. Maintaining the standard, not increasing the number, he believes, will make this test valuable.

My last question regards the notion of this test's measuring something innate, that if you aren't master chef caliber now, you never will be. Some people have it, and some don't. Is it possible that some chefs, no matter how devoted to their craft they may be, no matter how much they train, practice, and study for the Master Chef exam, will never pass it? Yes, he says, he believes this may be so. This test measures something innate.

Dieter Doppelfeld is in the judging room. "The cards fell about where they would fall," he says. Everyone, that is, has cooked to his or her abilities. I ask him, then, why does someone pass and someone fail.

The platters still sit out on the white tablecloths on tables running the length of either wall. He takes my elbow and pulls me to Brian's platter. "When you see this," he says to me, "you *smile.*"

And I do. The pork is pale pink and glistening with juice. The terrine is vibrant and inviting with multicolored layers of grilled vegetables, the beans are bright green, glistening with the vinaigrette, offset by the red strips of tomato and pale shallot, and the sweet potato tarts are bright orange and creamy-looking. Dieter picks up the uncut section of pork loin and holds it for me to smell; it's redolent of hickory smoke and spice. "This takes a lot of craftsmanship," Dieter says. He pulls me to Steve's platter on the other side of the room and says, "When you see this, you want to *eat* it." Steve's platter is beautiful, particularly with its showpiece rabbit pâté en croute. Dieter looks at me, looks at the platter, than back to me, to make sure I understand. I do, and nod.

Dieter directs me to Lynn's duck platter, with foie gras pâté, haricots verts, pears. To me it doesn't look bad and doesn't look good, but I don't have the immediate urge to taste anything as I did moments ago. Dieter regards the platter for a long moment, shrugs, and says, *"Interesting."*

Finally, he takes me to Eric's platter, and a look of genuine sadness comes over him. "When you see this . . ." He doesn't finish the sentence or need to. He tilts his head to regard the platter, removes the gooseneck sauce container, steps back, tilts his head the other way, then shrugs as if to say, "A little better, anyway." The thick slabs of terrine, chunks of seafood held together in aspic, do not call out to be eaten. Quenelles of lobster mousseline rest on top of dull tomato petals. Dieter lifts a quenelle and breaks it in two. It appears grainy. "The lobster doesn't taste like *anything*," Dieter says. "There is not one grain of salt on these damned tomatoes, and the onion relish doesn't taste like anything either!"

And so from Metz and now from Dieter, I had clear responses and had been shown evidence I did not doubt.

When the food has been cleared and a classroom atmosphere has been restored to the judging chamber, the chefs reenter to draw their assignments handed out by chef-instructor Anton Flory. Eric accepts one but does not open it. You can see the look of futility in his eyes: *You don't understand, I felt good about that, I felt* good *about it.*

I can see this. I can see clear distinctions in these chefs. Without my even tasting a morsel of the food, their personalities and abilities are now close to the surface. *They either have it or they don't:* Those are the words the chefs who passed continually used. "What is that 'it'?" Tom Peer asked me rhetorically. "I would love to know what 'it' is." Certainly "it" is not a single thing or element or trait or piece of knowledge but a combination of skills, knowledge, and will. Perhaps "it" is even more, a passion for the work of cooking and a love of food enhanced and refined over many years, acted out daily, something that is almost outside oneself, certainly beyond one's control. This is conjecture, of course, but what *is* visible are clear differences in the way these chefs work and what they produce. After just four days, long and fast as they were, I know something new.

That night, after transcribing the day's notes and trying to make sense of this test, I make a prediction based only on what I feel, having watched these chefs up close for four days. "It's clear to me today," I write. "Steve and Neil have it. Mark is borderline, has passed everything but don't know if he'll have the numbers. Lynn, if she makes it through, won't have the numbers. Eric will never be a CMC."

This is presumptuous, of course, but even more interesting than my blanket verdict on Eric, whose only measurable failure has been in the field of classical garde-manger, a specialized segment of the realm of culinary arts that has little to do with his own work as a chef, is my prediction so early in the test regarding Brian. "Brian," I write, "is borderline, but borderline for his—I don't know. Something. His independence maybe. But I think he'll do it with pure will and love and intelligence."

Why do I think independence is a liability?

Brian Polcyn began cooking at the age of fourteen and never looked back. Born in 1959 in Pontiac, Michigan, the youngest of five in a blue-collar family—his father worked in a spring factory that supplied the automotive industry; his mother raised the children—he first worked as a dishwasher in a family restaurant that served roast beef and instant mashed potatoes. In high school he spent part of each day in vocational training, then attended Schoolcraft College in nearby Livonia, graduating with an associate degree in culinary arts. He was formed, as were an unusual number of Michigan chefs, under Milos Cihelka, then chef of the Golden Mushroom. Cihelka was in the first class of certified master chef candidates and was apparently the reason Greater Detroit had the highest concentration of CMCs outside Hyde Park. Of the five chef instructors now teaching at Schoolcraft, all were certified master chefs or certified master pastry chefs, and several others worked in the area.

After five years under Cihelka, Polcyn landed a head chef job at The Lark, one of the state's premier restaurants. After disagreements with the owner, he left to open his own restaurant called Pike Street Grill in Pontiac, a run-down, crime-ridden city Brian referred to as Beirut. His restaurant became a trendy and chic spot to dine and helped resuscitate Pontiac by luring other businesses.

Brian opened Five Lakes Grill in Milford, where he and his family lived, in 1985. The 124-seat restaurant and bar—brick walls, hardwood floors—now averages between thirty-one and thirty-five dollars per check and serves about a thousand people a week. His mother works here along with his wife, Julia, handling the books. He met Julia where most important things seemed to happen to him: in the kitchen. Brian was sous chef at Travis Point Country Club in Ann Arbor; he recalls a love-at-first-sight scenario when Julia, an architecture student and waitress, first walked through the kitchen door. They had their five children over eleven years.

Not the least remarkable element of Brian Polcyn's story is the fact that he has been able to achieve what so many in the industry fail at: balance. Brian is a happy and good husband (according to the only person fit to judge) and, also according to Julia, a great dad, wrestling with toddler sons in bed in the morning, not missing his daughter's soccer games or staring down her potential suitors in their Milford living room. This, along with operating a successful restaurant: working the line himself, prepping and expediting, schmoozing the crowd. He soon received an offer from Schoolcraft College to teach as well, and because he was a chef (you never say no to more work), he accepted the offer.

But Brian was a cook at his core. That was what he did and who he was. So when he was asked to cook at a Super Bowl benefit in San

Diego, he brought in his own stocks, worked his own station, served eight hundred portions of pumpkin-truffle risotto with fried sweet potato filaments, "sweet potato hay" he called it, finishing each portion *à la minute* because risotto is best that way, all the while watching Emeril Lagasse ("He didn't even cook, man," said Brian) and his own friend Todd English move through the room trailed by TV cameras and, Brian recalled, "little girls in black batting their lashes." Drew Carey came back to Brian's table for a second helping of risotto, more gratifying to Brian than TV cameras. When Brian arrived at the Detroit airport the following day and hauled his trunk off the luggage conveyor, a woman read the name of the restaurant on the side and said, "Five Lakes Grill! That's one of our favorite restaurants. Are you Brian Polcyn?"

Two weeks earlier, on a wintry Saturday morning Brian left the restaurant sipping a large cappuccino in a paper cup, a big blue winter coat over his whites, and crossed the street to a jewelry store, looking for something for Julia's birthday. The salesman showing Brian some bracelets and earrings noticed his chef pants and asked where he was from.

"Five Lakes, across the street."

The man beamed, then pleaded, "Why can't you open for lunch?"

"We'd need to do a hundred covers a day to make it worth it."

"*We'll* all go," the man said.

Brian counted the employees and said, "That's five. Now all we need is ninety-five more." He thanked the man and returned to the restaurant to begin work. By the time Julia arrived with the kids ("Ben! Dylan!" he shouted at his two- and three-year-olds. "Out of the kitchen!"—too many sharp things lying around), he was boning venison for that night's menu—240 reservations on the books—braising red cabbage, and dicing butternut squash, leaving only to speak with Julia or take a call in his tight, book-lined office from a prospective sous chef, sensing his current sous chef was about to leave ("You can tell," Brian said. "It's like a marriage. When someone's fooling around, you can sense it").

Brian was about as representative a contemporary chef as I was likely to find. He was a good cook, well grounded in the fundamentals, ran a fine popular restaurant, and supported his wife and five children well. But once he entered the hermetic world of the Culinary Institute and the CMC exam, the elements surrounding his cooking—his family, the hip, homey restaurant with its familiar glovelike kitchen, perpetual praise from the people who ate at Five Lakes—all fell away to lay bare his cooking, ten do-or-die days of it.

CHAPTER NINE

*B*rian Polcyn stands in the doorway of the east dining room, and at exactly 3:20 P.M. Joe Scully says to him, "Ready." Brian bolts from the gate and with long, steady strides barrels into the kitchen. He sets his red Craftsman toolbox at station five and removes from the lowboy cooler two large sheet trays filled with a variety of meat, seafood, vegetables, fruits, and legumes. It is the first time he has seen the materials he must use to build a three-course meal for ten in the category American regional cuisine, due in exactly four and a half hours.

Four chefs, staggered at twenty-minute intervals, are already cooking, and the kitchen is alive with the noise and smells and heat of the work.

Brian's first and most immediate task is to concoct a menu given what he sees on his tray, and during the next twenty minutes Brian does no cooking. As his assistant sets the station, Brian works with a pencil and a legal pad, glancing at the products on the sheet pans beside him, then scribbling like a sketch artist on his pad. Brian calls to his assistant to have a look at what they will be preparing. "A nice light seafood ap," he says, more or less thinking aloud, as he often does. "I'm not happy with that salad, though. A little out of nutritional balance. I'm gonna add some potatoes." He's glad to see those four rabbits, as any good midwestern cook would.

Here are the materials Brian has to work with. On the first sheet pan:

4 rabbits
5 skate wings
1 pound scallops
2 lobsters
1 pound of bacon
pork fat
caul fat

And on the other:

tomatillos
bosc pears
chayote squash
almonds
dried cherries
red beans
Texmati rice
1 pineapple

Brian has a half hour to create his menu using as many of these in-gredients as possible. He also has available parstock, which includes items such as stocks, a variety of lettuces and vegetables, and assorted other items to supplement what he sees on the tray.

Each chef has received the exact same tray, the contents of which were determined by Dieter. Dieter likes these trays and wants to see some good thinking about using these products.

"Ten portions," he explains to me. "If there were another rabbit, maybe everyone would have a hind leg. But there are only four." He gives me a wily little grin. "But there are ten skate wings." This allows for an entire skate wing per person, something to center a course on. "There's a pound of scallops," Dieter continues. "What are you going to do with a pound of scallops?" Certainly you can't base a course around them, not given an ounce and a half per person. Dieter waits a moment, then says, "You make a forcemeat. And there are red beans on those trays. If you put beans on your menu, you better get them *cooking*."

Anton Flory, who was a member of the class of chefs taking the very first Master Chef exam in 1981, is today's kitchen proctor. Chef Flory is bone thin; a toque hides thinning black hair but not the long, straggly eyebrows above a prominent nose. When an enormous smile cuts a swath across his narrow aging face, it is the face of an undertaker. His Austrian baritone is resonant and rich. "Your menu, Chef?" he asks Brian at 3:50 P.M. Brian has finished and is already gathering the par-stock he needs. He hands Flory the menu:

Pan-fried skate with lobster sauce
Farm greens salad with asparagus, potato, and
roasted red peppers
Stuffed roasted rabbit with morels, natural juices,
braised leeks and carrots, and spaetzle

Then, at Flory's bidding, Brian places all the items he will not be needing on a sheet tray and sets it at the far end of the station. It is immediately taken away. Brian begins to bone his rabbits, saying, "Charlie, blanch me three tomatoes." He bones the first rabbit in a flash and then, throwing his head back, winces. "Shit, I gave back my caul fat. Charlie, go get Chef Scully for me." He needs the caul fat, a transparent stomach membrane, veined with fat that will melt in the oven, to wrap his stuffed rabbit in.

Charlie vanishes, and moments later Joe Scully appears. "What can I do for you, Chef?"

"Chef," Brian says, "I made an error. I suppose it's too late to get back my caul fat."

Scully says softly, "No, it's not too late, Chef."

Scully checks this with Dieter. It's an error on Brian's part, but not a substantial one, and there is leeway since Brian caught it in time.

Brian finishes boning all his rabbits, separating their parts in different pans: dark meat from the legs and thighs for the farce in one, loin in another, and bones, which he'll roast and use to make the sauce, in yet another. Dieter suggested making a forcemeat from the scallops to extend them through ten portions, but Brian and others make a forcemeat from the rabbit to extend four rabbits into ten portions, a classic garde-manger technique.

Among the four other chefs working at breakneck speed, there are similarities and differences in their chosen menus that seem to be indicative of their talents. Lynn has decided to use those scallops as an appetizer, in a dish of pan-seared scallops with pears and toasted almonds. Not an auspicious sign, given Dieter's reason for including so few scallops on the tray. For her second course she makes a skate chowder, another potential error in conception. Not only did she return seven skate wings, keeping just three to chop up, but she does not ask herself if it is wise, in a three-course meal, to serve two seafood courses, back to back. Her third course is braised and stuffed rabbit with artichokes and red beans, beans that she does not immediately get cooking.

Dieter says nothing, but already he is a little disappointed in Lynn's menu, which lacks complexity. Even so, she is already in the shit, moving a little too fast, her toque staining early with sweat. "I'm just trying to figure out how I'm gonna get this *done*," she says. This is sudden-death cooking for her, and she knows it.

Mark Linden, the Alaska chef, is likewise feeling the heat early. He began twenty minutes after Lynn in position two and straight off made some mental errors that may cause problems and already intensifies the anxiety, almost to the point of being unbearable for him. He has called his second course a consommé, for instance, which adds an unnecessary degree of difficulty to his menu: The judges here are sticklers for perfect clarity in consommés. His main course is a rabbit ragout, which, after he hands in his menu, just doesn't make good sense to him. The problem is that he doesn't like rabbit. He doesn't like working with rabbit, and he doesn't like eating it, and because of this, he has scarcely worked with rabbit in his twenty-year culinary career.

Not long after he turns in his menu he stops—plain stops. He's going to walk out. Can't do it. Won't happen.

Chef Flory, who, despite his grim visage, is as sweet and avuncular as Dieter, sees that Mark has panicked and stops at the station. "Let's just stop for a moment and take a look at where you are," he says gently to Mark. He examines the menu and concludes that all is not lost. In his rumbly Austrian baritone, haltingly deep for a man this skinny, he says, "Except for the consommé, everything is simple. Pan-seared skate. Rabbit ragout. Rice and beans." He shrugs. Mark knows how to do all this. The consommé was a blunder, but let's just put our head down and get to work, they agree. Flory has calmed Mark. Mark digs his heels in and begins to cook.

Neil Becker, in position three, has scarcely begun but shakes his head, saying, "I'm sweatin'." Sweat or not, he has created an intriguing, even ingenious menu:

> *Mixed seafood in a lobster broth with chayote squash and*
> *artichoke hearts*
> *Mixed greens with a pineapple vinaigrette and toasted almonds*
> *Pork-stuffed rabbit with cranberry chutney, red beans, and*
> *rice with sunchokes and green beans*

He has used a remarkable number of items from his tray, returning only the tomatillos and bosc pears. Polcyn, by comparison, has used nothing from his nonmeat tray. Neil's only error is not tasting those little dried red berries; they are cherries, not cranberries, but he's been drawing turkey almost every day so this is a mistake caused by perseveration.

Dieter stops to watch Steve working. He loves what he sees: "A lot of hot pans under control," as Dieter puts it. Steve maintains constant silent motion without seeming hurried. He has come down with a full-blown feverish cold, but once he gets his solid frame moving, it's just too much weight to slow, and he freight-trains through a thoughtful menu:

> *Sautéed scallop-and-lobster cake, sautéed skate wings with*
> *pineapple-chayote relish*
> *and marinated kidney beans*
> *Mesclun salad with poached pears and a dried-cherry*
> *vinaigrette*
> *Roast stuffed loin of rabbit with stewed artichoke hearts and*
> *sunchokes*

Steve is in position four, followed by Brian in position five, the last of the group. Yesterday, when the group showed up for the 7:00 A.M. class on food service management, Eric was not present. I asked Dieter. Dieter nodded and said, "He folded his tent." Eric wanted to be able to walk off this campus of his own accord, Dieter said, not because he was being forced out.

The candidates now numbered five, and after food service management and lunch they returned to the classroom for a lecture on international cuisine, given by Chef Flory, and then headed into the kitchen, one after the other at twenty-minute intervals, to cook their international menus in four and a half hours. The menus were all European, except for the South American menu, drawn by Lynn: black bean soup, matambra (marinated flank steak rolled around a stuffing of bread crumbs, hard-boiled eggs, yellow corn, and, separate and whole, carrot sticks and spinach leaves), along with deep-fried sweet potatoes, spaghetti squash, and snap peas.

Brian landed a Spanish menu of gazpacho, stuffed squid, saffron risotto, and grilled veg. Mark Linden made a German menu of liver dumpling soup, sauerbraten, kartoffelpuffer (potato pancakes), and braised red cabbage. Steve drew the Austrian menu of griessnockerl suppe (meat broth with farina dumplings), zwiebelrostbraten (strip loin, flattened, pounded, dusted with flour and sautéed, garnished with crisp fried onions dredged in paprika-spiked flour), bratkartoffel (home fries), cauliflower polonaise, and braised Swiss chard. Neil drew what was probably the trickiest menu of all, the Swiss menu, which, after a classical cheese soufflé, called for a rathsherren topf, a mixed grill: fillet of veal, calf's liver, filet mignon, veal sweetbreads, veal kidney, smoked slab bacon, all of which had to be grilled to order, except for the sweetbreads.

Everyone passed comfortably. They had drawn their menus and methods in advance, so there were no surprises. The judging, though, rattled Brian, who came out with a mediocre score. The judges told him his gazpacho lacked a depth of flavor because he did not roast the hard, bland Roma tomatoes he was given, and they also said the color was not so good because he pureed those tomatoes in a food processor, not with a food mill, making the soup pale by introducing too much air into the puree. "I can't believe it," he said after the judging. "They *hated* my *soup*."

After international they headed back to their motel rooms in the dark to rest up before a long day that began with a four-hour class on cost control followed by the American regional section of the exam, their first mystery basket situation.

During the long hours of cooking I have time to talk with the chefs who are working the exam, such as Chef Flory. We are near station two, where Mark is cooking like crazy to have his consommé, skate wings, and rabbit ragout ready on time. Flory watches and says, "Nerves."

Given this stress and the work involved, remembering Eric's sad, disbelieving eyes, and imagining all that was to come—the hardest part of this exam was still ahead of them, *days* away—I ask Flory, "Why do these people *do* it?"

"We always reach for what's beyond our grasp," he says. The undertaker's smile peels across his face; his baritone rumbles. "It is in our nature. Otherwise we'd be in a *sea of mediocrity* that's out there." He flicks bony fingers in the direction of the window.

Chef Flory issues a guttural laugh and departs.

At 5:30 P.M., with two hours and twenty minutes till his window opens, Brian drops his lobsters into a court bouillon (quick, or "short," stock)—a mixture of water, wine, herbs, and vegetables—and covers the pot with a hotel pan so that it returns to temperature as quickly as possible, while apprentice Charlie peels carrots and asparagus and chops herbs. In another pot Brian caramelizes mirepoix. His rabbit bones are roasting but not well. He has put too many in the pan he's chosen, so they're bunched up, steaming to gray and not really caramelizing.

When the lobsters are cooked, he removes them and separates the meat from the shell. He quickly chops the meat and then the shell. He turns to the stove and lifts the pot in which the lobsters have cooked and takes it to a chinois resting in a bain-marie to strain the liquid.

"Any flavor the lobster has distributed will be in here," he explains to Charlie. "The vegetables have no more flavor in them." Brian walks to the stovetop and stirs a pot, manically announcing his movements to his student apprentice; he's his own color commentator. "I'm sweating vegetables in here, no color. I'm gonna flame it with brandy. I'll add these lobster bones, chopped. Why did I chop them?"

Charlie shakes his head.

"Maximum flavor extraction. That's what the judges are looking for here, good cooking principles. There are caramelized vegetables back there." These will be for the rabbit sauce. He glances at a steel bowl on his station and says, "Also, a little trick with lobster and shrimp sauce, add a little tomato product. Brings up the color and the flavor. Brandy and tomato paste, good flavors."

At five-fifty he removes his rabbit bones from the oven, puts them in the pot with the caramelized vegetables, and sets the roasting pan on top of an open flame. He pours chicken stock into the hot pan. "What's this called?" he asks Charlie.

"Deglazing," Charlie says.

"Very good."

Once the bones are simmering gently, Brian grinds his forcemeat, rabbit leg and thigh meat, pork, and pork fat. He keeps this ground meat in a bowl resting in a larger bowl filled with ice. "Ideal temperature for an emulsion is thirty-four degrees," he says. He seasons the ground meat, then puts it in a Robot Coupe, purees it, adds a little flour, a little cream, and purees it some more to emulsify the cream into the meat mixture. Last he folds sautéed morel halves into this forcemeat and begins spreading the mixture onto the boned rabbit loin.

But he doesn't like the color, too uniformly brown. Dieter is at the station observing, and Brian asks, "Chef, is there any spinach?"

"No," Dieter says, "Zer ees some arugula."

"It's not part of parstock?"

"No."

"I'm safe," he says, but shakes his head. At his restaurant there is always spinach lying around. Brian doesn't stop moving—there's no time to waste, move, move, move, steady and smooth—and continues to wrap the forcemeat in the rabbit loin. He then secures the entire loin in a film of caul fat and grabs for the next one.

Joe Scully could be twenty-five years old by appearance: lean, runner's physique, youthful mien. He is in fact a husband and father of three, pushing forty; he intends to be in Brian's spot next year. For a country club chef, a CMC title will mean a salary boost of ten to twenty thousand dollars and push his income, which includes some business side dishes, into the six-figure range. He also wants the challenge of it. This test is exciting to him. So for his own preparation, he watches all the chefs carefully. At 6:14 P.M. he stands back from station one, observing Lynn. Lynn has a million pans going; her toque, the second one she's gone through, is tearing from sweat and has become partly unfastened in back. She is moving from prep table to stovetop, to prep table and back in a frantic dance toward her open window.

Scully sees that she's in serious weeds. "She's got sixteen minutes," Scully whispers, "and she's still cooking her *ass* off. I'm not even going over there. I'll wait till six twenty-five."

I follow Scully as he walks to the center aisle of this big double kitchen. He glances at Mark Linden, who looks pretty much exactly like Lynn. Scully says to me, "He started off on the wrong foot, and he just never recovered." You have to catch this off-on-the-wrong-footness immediately, Scully says, then know enough to recognize it for what it is and make the necessary adjustments; otherwise you're a goner. "It's a little like when you get into an argument with your wife," he explains. "There's that moment when it could go either way, one moment when you can say, 'Honey, I love you, and I'll do anything I can to make this better.' But once you pass that moment, there's not a lot you can do."

Scully hustles off to make sure everything will be set when Lynn's window opens.

It's six-twenty, and Brian begins to make his herbed spaetzle. "We've got an hour and a half, Charlie," he says.

"How are you doing?" Charlie asks.

"I'm feeling"—Brian pauses to think—"all right. Not great, not bad."

At six thirty-five, Brian strains his lobster sauce. Mark Linden begins to wipe down his station in preparation for service. And Lynn is completing the platter for her scallop dish, having already sent out the first-course plates to the judges. She's moving too fast—never a good sign. Her hat is about to slide off, and her jacket is partly out of her apron, an echo of her sloppy, too-fast movements and disarray. She takes four bowls out of the oven, using side towels, and sets them on her station. She ladles her seafood chowder into the first bowl, but it's so hot the soup starts boiling hard as it hits the bowl, sending up a shower of spatters that lands on the bowl's rim and burns there. She hesitates only a moment: No time, she's got to serve it. These are about as deep as weeds get, and there's nothing for her to do but push on through them to the end. She is at the center of a great commotion: Runners wait; Flory stands with clipboard in hand; a crowd has gathered at the observation window pressing to see. Lynn begins slicing her stuffed rabbit for her final course. Scully orchestrates the runners and says to Lynn as she begins to plate, "Let me know when these can go, Chef." As runners take trays into the hall, Scully, worried a returning runner will collide with a runner carrying food, calls into the hallway, "Don't let anyone bust 'em." CIA chef-instructors John Reilly and Rudy Smith, both potential CMC candidates, are among the crowd in the hallway watching the food as it zips past them on large trays.

Lynn's last plates go out. Then she puts the finishing touches on her platter. She stands upright, breathing hard. She takes one deep breath and wipes her brow with the back of her hand. To Scully, she says, "That can go"—then turning to Chef Flory—"and I'll start packing."

He tries to comfort her, but Lynn, whose face is bright crimson and glistening with sweat, shakes her head and says, "My beans aren't cooked." Flory tastes one and says nothing. Lynn is exhausted and discouraged, wiped out. She just didn't know what to do with that food when she pulled the sheet trays and saw what was on them, and she never recovered.

As she begins to clean up, I look to Chef Flory. "She has made too many errors," he says sadly, then heads to station two, where Mark has started to plate.

For an hour and twenty minutes more, chefs will be pushing to get their food out. The busyness intensifies, and so does the pressure. Strangely, though, big Steve wants to check on his pal Neil. Steve is so well organized and ready that he can leave his station and causally ask, "When are you going?" Neil doesn't even look at Steve to answer, just keeps moving, and Steve strolls back to his station.

At seven twenty-five Brian checks the internal temperature of his rabbits: They're at 120 degrees. He'll pull them when they hit 130. As service approaches, he calls off all the items he needs, from plates to goosenecks to sauces. He asks Charlie if the plates are clean; one bad plate that didn't get thoroughly washed can throw off your whole service. Charlie has set two sautoirs on the stove for Brian to sauté his spaetzle in; Brian holds them up, doesn't like the straight sides, and gets two sauté pans with sloping sides so that he can jump the spaetzle cleanly.

At seven-forty Brian begins to sauté his skate wings in a mixture of butter and oil. He turns one with his tongs and it's so delicate the meat pulls apart. He takes the pan off the heat and dips to his Craftsman toolbox for an offset spatula, then continues cooking.

"Time, Chef?" he calls to Scully.

"Your window is gonna open in one minute."

"One minute it is," he says. "I'm gonna be saucing this platter and also using a gooseneck."

"Your window is open, Chef."

Brian ladles lobster sauce onto the plates; it's a good nappé consistency—that is, it nicely coats the back of a spoon—bright peach-colored, and filled with chopped lobster. "Maybe a little heavy on the lobster," Brian says. "Bring me a tasting spoon, Charlie." He removes some of the lobster meat from the sauce. He places the skate wings on the sauce, garnishes with a little chive, and out they go. He puts together a small platter for six. "Should I sauce the platter?" he asks. It looks plain without sauce, so he sauces it, and out it goes. Immediately Brian pulls up plates with cold asparagus and roasted red pepper from his cooler. He tosses endive with dressing and plates it. Suddenly Brian halts—just a skip in his movements, really—and says, "I smell burning butter." He turns to the stove behind him, where the two sauté pans sit over flames. "Got a problem here, Charlie, got burnt butter." He dumps the butter, wipes the pans, and sets them off the heat.

"You've got sixteen minutes left in your window," Scully says.

Brian finishes tossing the mixed greens, plates them, says, "Asparagus at six o'clock," to the runners, and his second course is out.

At eight o'clock he sautés his spaetzle in fresh butter. He removes plates from the oven and sets them at his station. Charlie has cut the butcher's string from the four rabbit loins resting on the cutting board. Brian steels his knife, slices the rabbit, two strokes, forward and back, for each slice. He plates the spaetzle first, then the braised leeks.

"That's a nice touch, Chef," Scully says, liking the leeks.

Brian's carrots are bright orange and cut in long obliques. He rests the rabbit loin on the leeks, sauces each plate. He pauses to look at the plates, says, "A little herbs on her would be nice," and he looks for the herbs, which Charlie is in charge of. He looks around some more. "I used all my herb, *Charlie?*" Charlie bolts for more chives in the reach-in cooler and then has to go to the other side of the kitchen to find a cutting board.

"He's giving it his best shot, Chef," Scully says.

"That's all I can ask," says Brian.

Charlie returns, cuts chives like a bandit. As Brian's plated food sits, he puts together the platter. He glances at Charlie and says, "Keep going, Charlie, you got it."

The final touch, freshly chopped chives, is placed on each plate and the platter for six, and out they go. His service is done.

"Chef," Brian says to Flory, "would you like to see what I have left?" Brian shows him a half pound of unused forcemeat, a few spaetzle, a little extra sauce—in all, excellent utilization.

"Good job," says Flory. "But you sent back so much stuff."

"Yeah." Brian agrees, wincing. "I didn't really like *any* of that stuff.

Pineapple, ahn. Cherries, I could have used cherries, I suppose. I don't like sunchokes. I just didn't want to compromise my philosophy."

It does not seem to concern Brian, though, that this is not a test of his philosophy.

As always, the chefs lean against the wall on either side of the fluorescent white hallway, beat from this second consecutive day of hot cooking, Day Six. An extra body waits as well, dressed in street clothes: Lynn's husband, who has lived with her through each day of this test. He watched her cook, and as they waited, she told him all the mistakes she made. Lynn at position one is called in first. There is little talking.

After ten minutes the door opens, Lynn emerges, and to her husband she pulls a finger across her neck.

"My beans were raw; my artichokes were raw. Dieter got a raw scallop." She shakes her head and looks at the floor. "Oh, and two seafoods," she adds. "I thought shellfish and one that wasn't was OK."

Neil shakes his head and says, "No, always keep your fish together."

Lynn smiles to the group, ever hopeful. "It's almost a *relief*," she says.

Brian gives her a big hug of congratulations and support. Lynn and her husband say their good-byes. She gives them all business cards with the name of her restaurant and says "If you're ever in Memphis . . ."

After they've gone, and while waiting to be judged, Brian says, "If I fail *one* thing, I'm walking out. One thing."

Neil's dark eyes enlarge. *"Really?"*

"It feels good to tell myself that," he grumbles.

Neil soon finds that he has scored a stellar 93 today. Every day on every section he has scored in the high eighties and low nineties. The little guy from New York is burning this test to the ground.

Steve too has received a strong pass.

Brian is the last to enter the judging chamber. All wait to hear how he has done. When he emerges, he nods to the group with a small, tight smile and takes an immediate right, through the door and away into a cool, dark night, clutching the envelope containing tomorrow's cooking assignment, the most difficult yet. Tomorrow's items are so obscure, so deeply rooted in the history of a foreign country, that when he reads them, he won't even know what they are. He will have to look them up in the Book:

> *Consommé à l'Orge Perlé*
> *Filets de Sole à la d'Orléans*
> *Poulet Sauté à la Catalane*

CHAPTER TEN

*B*rian steps into his white Jeep Cherokee and turns left onto Route 9 for the five-minute drive to the Golden Manor motel. The Jeep has a serious dent, a whole quarter panel is caved in, but the car's still running strong, an apt metaphor for the chef at the wheel. Brian has scored a 75 in American regional, a blow to him. He was pleased with that food; he thought that food he sent out was pretty damned good. More than that, he *knows* it was good. So he's mad, but also a little afraid: *My God, what do I have to* do? He knows he's borderline. Six long days cooking as well as he possibly can, and he's *borderline.*

Brian cut a deep gash in his thumb the first day cooking and must live with this fact daily. Each morning he obsessively swathes his cut with ointment and wraps it tightly. He is concerned about this cut—was even before Metz cautioned him about it—knowing that if it becomes infected, it can hurt his cooking and knife work. He needs both hands to be healthy. Already he must wear a rubber finger cot over it, which is uncomfortable and gets in the way. He can't afford to let it get worse. One more thing to worry about.

The duration of this test has begun to chip away at Brian's psyche. Fatigue not only weakens his faculties and diminishes his spirit but lays open to infection crucial patches of his mind. He can't salve and wrap these. He bolts awake throughout the night, thinking he's overslept, the perpetual nightmare.

He jolts awake in the first days of the test, having dreamed that his Jeep, with all his kitchen tools, is stolen. By degrees it registers that he is sitting upright in absolute darkness, in a grim motel, 750 miles from his wife, Julia, and their five children. The Jeep is still there; it won't be stolen. He turns over in bed and tries to sleep more. He bolts awake again; his thumb is throbbing.

When he wakes at five-thirty—all these chefs, already awake from stress and hitting the switch before it even has a chance to sound, rarely need to turn their travel alarms off—Brian steps softly to the bathroom. He squints for a moment at the brightness, then regards his toiletries— razor, shaving cream, comb and brush, toothbrush and toothpaste, soap—evaluating it for its neatness, handling, storage, economy. To Brian's barely conscious brain it is simply the morning's mise en place, and he can hear over his shoulder the gentle, menacing clicks of the lab-coated proctor's pencil tip marking an evaluation of his bathroom shelves.

On the night of Day Six, having received a score of 75 for his work, Brian has at least two more hours of study and preparation ahead of him before he can sleep. He was in the continuing education building before 7:00 A.M. and didn't leave it till after 9:00, but he can't let up now. Classical cuisine—cooking as prescribed by Auguste Escoffier in the first years of this century, largely foreign to most contemporary chefs—is without doubt the most difficult cooking he will be asked to do here and thus requires more study.

But there is another layer to his mounting anxiety, a fact he has told none of his fellow chefs, one that he really doesn't like to admit himself. This is not the first time he's taken the CMC exam. Four years ago he arrived in Hyde Park for this very same test. He was thirty-three years old and cocksure of himself; he'd made a success of a high-end restaurant in a depleted city, Pontiac, Michigan, been widely written about in the state, and he'd trained under Milos Cihelka, himself a CMC. For the first six days of that test the young Brian Polcyn rode high, felt un-stoppable. He was exactly like Neil, in fact, crushing each section of the test day by day. Then he hit classical cuisine, and it was like running into a locomotive barreling full steam the opposite way. He failed badly, and with one engine gone, the tailspin began. After Brian failed Asian cuisine, it was Ron DeSantis, increasingly Brian's nemesis, who said these words: "Chef, we cannot allow you to continue."

But he was full of himself then, he says. Now he's got his mind right. However, those words, that voice, still ring in his head: *Chef, we cannot allow you to continue.*

Brian has created a small fortress of cookbooks in a motel room that is otherwise colorless (that nothing, pea green motel color), and among those books is *Escoffier: The Complete Guide to the Art of Modern Cookery.* He needs only this book, and in it he looks up his recipes, numbers 589, 1996, 3195, and reads.

His consommé should be simple. Escoffier calls for ordinary consommé—that is, consommé made from white beef stock, with a garnish of cooked barley. The tricky thing about the consommé is that it's got to be perfectly clear. And here at the CIA *perfectly* means "perfectly," date-on-a-dime-at-the-bottom-of-a-gallon clear. A spoon shouldn't blur beneath the surface; it should sparkle. Absolute crystal, that soup. This is not difficult to achieve if you were taught correctly when you first learned, but the tricky part is the garnish; that soup's got to *stay* clear. If you haven't properly prepared your garnish, the garnish will cloud the consommé on contact.

Not much studying required here, just sound cooking methods.

The next item, though, is a little more involved: Filets de Sole à la d'Orleans. Escoffier recommends coating the fillets with a whiting forcemeat into which you've mixed chopped truffles. You then roll them into paupiettes (see recipe 2000, page 231, for your basic paupiette method). Next, fill a small, round cooking dish (preferably a porcelain cocotte) two-thirds full "with a Salpicon of shelled prawns, mushrooms and truffles mixed together with a little cream." Not quite sure what a salpicon is or what Mr. Escoffier thinks it is? Turn back to page 51 for the method: a tiny dice, one-fifth of an inch, bound with a little liquid.

Place the paupiette, which has been shallow-poached, on top of your salpicon, and coat it with a tablespoon of Sauce Crevette. Can't remember how to make that crevette sauce? Page 20, number 110: Add some fish stock and cream to a fish velouté or a béchamel (see pages 8 and 9, numbers 20 and 25 for those); reduce; stir in some shrimp butter and red coloring butter for a nice shrimp-pink appearance. Once your paupiette is coated with sauce, place a slice of truffle on top and one nice prawn in the center of that, and your Filets de Sole à la d'Orleans is good to go.

On to the last course, the amazing poulet sauté. The poulet sauté describes a way of preparing a chicken so that each of the chicken's parts can be perfectly cooked, beautifully presented, and easy and delicious to eat. It is an efficient method in both its utilization and its cooking because the entire dish and its accompanying sauce are cooked in the same pan. The poulet sauté is truly one fine way, maybe the finest, to pan-roast and serve a chicken. It is also a great contemporary method because of its efficiency and because of its removal of all the fat.

For a proper poulet sauté preparation, begin with a medium-size chicken, and remove the legs. Separate the leg and thigh at the joint. Remove the bone from the thigh, the femur. If the thigh is fatty, and these days it usually is, scrape the fat out of the various layers of thigh muscle.

Next, neatly cut off the bottom of the drumstick to remove the cartilage; scrape the bone clean so that no tendons stick there; this will allow the meat to seize up around the top of the drumstick for a neat appearance and juicy, dense bites of dark meat.

Cut off the wing tips so that only one section of wing, sometimes called the drumette, remains attached to the carcass. Then take the breast and wing joint off the carcass in one piece. Remove the skin from the breast. Cut the bottom of the wing joint off, like the drumstick's, to remove the cartilage and allow the meat to ride up toward the breast, leaving a clean, dry bone for presentation.

Season the four pieces of chicken with salt and pepper, and they are ready to cook.

In a very hot pan, sauté the chicken to brown it on all sides; then pop it in the oven, and finish cooking, removing the breasts while they're still rare, returning them during the last minutes of cooking. When the legs and thighs are cooked, remove the pan from the oven, transfer the chicken to a dish, and keep it warm. Deglaze the pan, add your sauce components, and serve this over the chicken or reheat your chicken in the sauce.

The final beauty of this preparation is that once you've got your chicken properly butchered, it can be adapted to countless recipes. Escoffier includes just sixty-five poulet sauté recipes, but the variations are infinite.

For a simple poulet sauté, add minced shallots to the pan, then deglaze with vermouth, add a little chicken stock, and reduce. Delicious. Have a hankering for a Provençal roasted chicken? Do the same thing, only after it's cooked, add garlic, diced tomato, sliced calamata olives, and finish with a chiffonade of basil. Want Poulet Sauté avec Fine Herbes? Add fresh-chopped tarragon, chervil, parsley, and chives.

Brian Polcyn, in the dim light of his room at the Golden Manor, must plan for a Poulet Sauté à la Catalane, however, a recipe for ten using five chickens, rather more complicated than a quick deglaze-and-reduce method. For the Catalane, Brian must, when the chicken is cooked, deglaze his pan with white wine, then add some Sauce Espagnole (thickened brown veal stock, a contemporary version of which, called fond de veau lié, will be made personally by DeSantis and provided to all chefs who need a foundation brown sauce). Brian will then add quartered mushrooms that have been sautéed in butter, thirty glazed onions, thirty small chestnuts halved and cooked in bouillon, forty chipolata sausages halved, and a dollop of tomato fondue (page 49, recipe 315, meaning melted tomato, but tomato paste will do), reheat the chicken in the sauce, and serve.

He will choose a vegetable dish (haricots verts with butter) and one starch dish (Riz à la Turque, rice pilaf with saffron and tomato fondue) from an approved list to complete his all-Escoffier menu.

He then sets about writing his prep list. It is more elaborate than any he has written so far. Instead of simply creating a list of what needs to be prepped, he writes the time at which each item will be prepped,

blocking off each hour, and the final half hour, and last, he has written
down exactly what must be done during his twenty-minute service window. He is determined: Classical will not take him down this time.
When he has accounted for every minute of his four-and-a-half-hour
cooking practical, he at last allows himself to sleep.

CHAPTER ELEVEN

*F*our of the seven chefs remain on Day Seven. Each will cook a different menu. Brian has drawn position three and paces the East Wing dining room. Waiting to begin is, for everyone, one of the hardest parts of the day, especially today, classical, and especially for Brian, whose failure four years ago in this category hangs behind him like a cloud bank.

I ask him if he's nervous.

He looks a little angry and says, "Of course I'm nervous."

I ask what makes this section of the test so particularly difficult, and Brian answers, "All the building blocks. Each step has to be done perfectly for the good end result."

At two-forty Brian strides to station three and tapes his prep list to the tile wall, puts Charlie to work, and is up and running himself, first boning chicken and sole. By three o'clock Steve in position four has begun, and the energy in the kitchen is palpable but usual. It's quiet, a little spooky even. Not even during buffet setup, when no one was cooking anything, has the kitchen been so silent. Yet at the same time it's never been so busy. The air feels about two hundred pounds per square inch.

"It's the little details that add up, that they forget to do," Chef Flory, again the kitchen proctor, says of classical cuisine. "They forget to flatten the fish, which tenderizes it and prevents it from shrinking up and squeezing out the forcemeat." I notice that Steve has his assistant wiping clean his mushrooms. At Brian's station, oddly, mushrooms are soaking in a bowl of water.

Chef Flory sees me looking at the mushrooms, soaking up all that tasteless fluid, and nods, intoning in his Austrian bass, "Eet makes a leetle deeference een flavor een zee end."

But Flory likes classical cuisine partly because, he says, "There is no room for interpretation. You prepare it the way Mr. E. wrote in the book." The smile rips across his face. "Ninety years ago!" And he laughs.

Indeed, right there on page 231, Escoffier writes that before you spread the forcemeat on the sole, "lightly flatten them with a moistened cutlet bat or heavy knife so as to prevent shrinkage," as Flory noted. Everything is spelled out exactly.

I leave the kitchen to stop by Tom Peer's office to ask for a more complete evaluation of the American regional section of the exam, specifically more detailed information on Brian and why he got a 75 and where he stands.

"He's borderline at this point," Peer confirms, then goes on to last night's food, pretty much point by point off the top of his head. The carrots were overcooked. Brian's forcemeat was a little grainy. "There's one way to make forcemeat," Peer says. "You grind it, Robot Coupe, push it through a tamis." Brian didn't push his forcemeat through a tamis, a fine-mesh drum sieve. I ask him to clarify the word *grainy,* and he says, "When you rub your tongue against the roof of your mouth, it's not smooth."

Peer squints to remember, then runs down the list. The sauce for Brian's rabbit was light (in part, no doubt, because the bones didn't get nicely caramelized), not enough greens on his salad, the vinaigrette was too acidic, and there was too much of it. The lobster sauce tasted good, but he chopped up good lobster meat; he should have saved the claws and used big chunks of the meat from the tail. The biggest problem by far, though, what hurt him almost beyond repair, had nothing to do with the actual cooking but rather had to do with thinking, his *decision* to cook so few of his mystery basket items.

Neil, for instance, didn't just use his almonds, didn't just toast them and serve them; he candied his almonds as well. That was an extra step the judges liked. Peer notes that Neil used the pineapple to make the vinaigrette; that scored big. They want to see that you can work with chayote squash, with sunchokes, utilize a lot of different products well.

In the face of all Brian's errors, I ask, what on earth saved him?

"It tasted really good," Peer says.

When I return to the continuing education building, Joe Scully is leaving the kitchen. "How's it going?" I ask.

He shakes his head seriously and says, "It's a pressure cooker in there. Cooking from that *book* fucking *sucks*."

Even Scully looks mad.

Indeed the kitchen remains so quiet you can almost hear the steam rising off the consommés.

It's been a long day for Ron DeSantis when he enters the judging room at about 6:15 P.M. Today was Day One of his class, the St. Andrew's kitchen, the first restaurant CIA students cook in. It's an especially involved day because he's got to get up at 4:30 to ensure his kitchen is well prepped (an entire new staff arrives and must be ready to cook a menu they've never seen for a packed restaurant by 11:30); lecture begins at 7:00 A.M. and then, between 11 and 11:30, DeSantis cooks one of every single item on the menu—four pizzas, nine starters, eight entrées—very quickly, explaining as he cooks the details of each as well as the plating instructions to his student cooks. After this class he heads to Lecture Hall 2 to give the classical cuisine lecture to four Certified Master Chef candidates. "First," he says to Brian, Mark, Steve, and Neil, "congratulations for being here. It's not an easy task; it's not an easy decision." Then, enlivened by a strong cappuccino, he moves into his lecture. "Today will be an interesting day because it's a style of cooking we don't use a lot," he says, and quickly notes the misconceptions: "Classical cuisine is not rich and heavy; it's *light*. It's not rich and fatty; it's *nutritious*. It's not wasteful but cost-*effective*. . . . The beauty of the classics keeps revealing itself." The man loves this style of cooking, chose the recipes himself, and will lead the judging four hours later, taking the center seat at the head table, and laying his *Escoffier* before him.

Lyde Buchtenkirch-Biscardi joins him in the quiet, sterile room. Buchtenkirch's thick, wavy hair has gone gray, but her bulk proclaims a hearty youthfulness. The woman is built like a backhoe. In fact she *owns* a backhoe. Buchtenkirch is the only female CMC. When she took the test in 1990, her assistant, a young cook from Cleveland named Michael Symon, was struggling to lift a hot gigantic stockpot off the stove; Symon, a stocky former high school wrestler, was no slouch, but as he groaned at the weight of the pot, Buchtenkirch, who was in a hurry, swatted him aside and hefted the pot herself with a clean-and-jerk grunt and impressive speed. Buchtenkirch was the first woman to enter the Culinary Institute of America as a student in 1970. They tried to make her wear a skirt. She said, "I wear pants like the rest." Buchtenkirch is also renowned in the area for extraordinarily beautiful wedding cakes with fine, intricate sugar work. The woman can bake you a showpiece cake and dig you a swimming pool all in the same weekend.

Buchtenkirch takes a seat on DeSantis's left and asks about the dishes DeSantis has chosen.

"I tried to get live trout," he says, "but it was too difficult." He explains the logistical problems and expense of bringing in live fish and tells her he went with sole.

"Did you get fresh sole or frozen?" she asks.

"Frozen," Ron says.

Buchtenkirch shrugs and says, "Frozen performs pretty well."

Rumors had been in the air that live trout might make an appearance during this test. This would be for a tricky preparation called truites au bleu. It doesn't get more French classical than that. Escoffier writes, "For this preparation, it is absolutely essential to have trout which are alive."

He describes the dish further: "About 10 minutes before being re-quired remove the trout from the tank, stun them with a sharp blow on the head, empty and wash quickly. Immediately place in the boiling liq-uid whereupon the fish will quickly curl up and the flesh split open."

It's this unusual nose-to-tail curling action that makes this prepara-tion unique and is the reason the fish must be only recently deceased. Escoffier recommends serving these with a hollandaise sauce and melted butter. They can be served cold too with a vinaigrette.

It's regrettable that DeSantis was unsuccessful in his efforts to pro-cure live fish; the potential for comedy is rich. Imagine, in the frenetic rush toward service, the chefs catching ten trout each, stunning each one as the others flop around on the cutting board and onto the floor, then gutting them and cooking them. This would have been something to see.

Richard Czack is the final judge to arrive. He removes his suit jacket and hangs it on a hanger at the back of the room. Czack is trim and spry, and what remains of his hair is closely cropped and white. The man graduated from the Culinary Institute of America nearly forty years ago, in 1958, and has been an instructor and administrator at the school for decades. When he took the CMC test, it was rumored, he did not get up at five-thirty every morning. He got up earlier, so that he could get in some invigorating laps at a local pool before the work began. He sits on DeSantis's right. At exactly six-thirty the first con-sommés arrive, and Czack says, "Ron, why don't you tell us what we'll be tasting?"

For the next hour and a half the three certified master chefs, all CIA grads from different decades, taste food prepared as prescribed by Escoffier more than ninety years ago. At first it is not an entirely happy experience. Consommés have fat floating on top; fish is overcooked; forcemeat is skimpy or squeezed out; quenelles are tasteless. The judges remain ruthless as Brian's first course, regular consommé garnished with barley, arrives.

DeSantis peers into the cup, and says, "This has a lot of *particles* in it."

Buchtenkirch says, "It's *cloudy.*"

"It is *very* cloudy."

"I know what they're going to say," Czack says. "'It was absolutely clear till I put the barley in.'"

"Then we need to hear how they prepared it," says DeSantis. "Did you wash it, blanch it, then cook it, or did you just cook it?"

They're not impressed with the flavor either, and Czack concludes simply: "This is not a good showing."

Servers arrive bearing the second course, placing before each judge Filets de Sole à la d'Orleans. DeSantis runs his finger down the page of his open book and reads the description.

There is some initial commotion over the presentation. Brian has placed a large shrimp between two cone-shaped paupiettes, with the sauce underneath. Czack says, "This is crazy." But DeSantis argues that it's fine, given Escoffier's description and what they'd spoken about in lecture, and Czack accepts DeSantis's ruling.

The room grows quiet as they taste.

Czack: "Here you can see the forcemeat."

Buchtenkirch: "It's ahead of the last one, a lot better."

DeSantis: "This is tasty. The forcemeat is nice."

Czack: "M-hm."

Buchtenkirch: "It's not awful."

DeSantis: "I like this. It's cooked nicely. Mine's *hot.* The shrimp is cooked perfectly."

Buchtenkirch: "Especially for one this big."

DeSantis: "*Very* good effort."

When the last course, Poulet Sauté à la Catalane, arrives, Buchtenkirch exclaims, "I'm gonna cry. Did you see the chipolatas?" She is a charcuterie instructor and made these small delicate sausages herself.

"I just saw that," DeSantis says. "They're all split right down the middle."

"All he had to do was reheat them. They've lost all their moisture."

Czack has begun to eat and says in a persnickety voice, "I don't know about you, but I am *not* into *pink* chicken."

Brian has slightly undercooked his chicken—according to Czack, a fairly serious error. Other flaws in the dish are noted: The sauce is fatty and a little washed out; the haricots verts aren't properly seasoned. DeSantis says, "I got five beans on my plate." Then he turns to Czack and asks, "Were these menus too difficult?"

"No," Czack says.

The last candidate's consommés arrive, a pheasant consommé from big, silent Steve. DeSantis reads the description in *Escoffier* and then tastes. He smiles immediately and turns to Czack.

Czack, tasting, looks at DeSantis and says, "This is the best consommé we've had."

The entire meal pretty much follows along those lines. The sole is hot and delicious, the textures perfect. Czack is moved by the sole to stand up and walk over to the table where Steve's food has been set. He regards the platter and says, "This guy is cooking. This guy is cooking with some *soul.*"

DeSantis says, "I've eaten it, and my mouth is clean and refreshed. He took it exactly to the right height." When the final course is brought in, DeSantis tastes the starch dish, Risotto à la Piémontaise, and says, "Did you taste this risotto? Oh, *man.*" The risotto is steaming hot. Buchtenkirch tastes and nods. DeSantis says, "Look at this sauce."

"Nice sheen, translucent," Buchtenkirch concurs.

DeSantis says to his plate, "Thank you. Yes, thank you very much. I personally prepared that fond de veau. *I made* it." It's a days-long process to finish fond de veau lié, a double-strength brown veal stock, and he is delighted that someone has treated it so well, kept the fat out, kept it clear and clean. Everyone is quiet, just eating. Then DeSantis says, "This is beautiful food. I was getting worried. I was thinking the menus were too hard."

For another half hour they wander the room, examining each platter, which is set on a table with the appropriate number. At number one DeSantis just stares and says, "Horrible sauce. The carrots show no craftsmanship." His potato dish is lourettes, a type of croquette. "Potato lourette is very specific. You roll it out, the ends are tapered, and you bend it."

DeSantis stops at number three, says, "I put a high score on this fish."

"Pretty decent," says Buchtenkirch.

But DeSantis scrutinizes the platter and finds shrimp that haven't been fully deveined. He doesn't like the knife cuts for the salpicon: should be a dice, not a rough chop. He even rethinks the sauce. "I didn't get any of that light, spicier flavor. All I got was rich. I got some cayenne, but . . ." he trails off.

"The entrée is washed out," he concludes. "This is not master chef level. We're not in Skills here." *Skills* refers to Skill Development One, the first kitchen for incoming CIA students, where they learn how to mince onion and make stock.

Chef Flory enters to deliver his kitchen proctor scores. DeSantis asks how station three was.

"Pretty organized," Flory answers. "At the last minute it got a little hectic." He sits and waits, listening to some of the judges' comments. He knows it hasn't gone well, but he thinks the judges are being overly critical.

For instance, Czack, in checking his numbers against one particular entry, peers into a terrine filled with consommé. He glances at his numbers and says, "The consommé is a zero." But this sounds too drastic, and he reconsiders: "He did put the soup *in* the bowl."

DeSantis returns to his seat and begins the tabulations, adding all the judges' scores, averaging them, then adding them to Flory's score.

Flory increasingly distressed says, "If you *fail* someone, don't make it by *one* point, *please*," and walks out, clearly upset. Later, after learning of the one failure, he whispers to me, "They were up against a tough panel. He should not have failed. I tasted his food."

DeSantis finishes his tabulations, and Neil has indeed failed classical cuisine by three points. When DeSantis tabulates Brian's score, 66.11, he says, "See, my problem with this, come Sunday, they're gonna get the rug pulled out from under them."

The first two candidates, Mark Linden, passing by just one more point than Brian, and Neil Becker, enter and depart, receiving their blows with humility and little surprise. To the seated Neil, DeSantis comes straight out and says, "You did not pass," even before the critique begins, and Neil's straight face doesn't budge except for a noticeable twinge in one eyebrow and a brief, brusque inhalation.

Brian Polcyn, the third candidate, enters and greets the judges, but Buchtenkirch stands abruptly and says she has another engagement. This seems to rattle Brian a little, as though he were somehow the reason for her departure, a small snub. Brian won't get the chance to apologize to her face for ruining the sausages. It's among the first things he mentions when DeSantis asks what he would have done differently. Brian says, "Those beautiful sausages split." He wasn't happy with the consistency with his sauce or the knife cuts for his salpicon, and he thinks he fired the chicken too early and worries that it was slightly overcooked.

Czack begins by ensuring that Brian knows the reason for errors, asking, "What happened to the sausages to make them burst?"

"I should have poached them," Brian says. "They boiled at too-high heat."

Czack then launches into his critique of the last course. The sauce showed quite a bit of fat; the pilaf was overcooked, Brian skimped on the green beans. "And my breast was pink," he finishes.

With a look of distressed surprise, Brian says, "Really? *Under.*"

Then DeSantis, reading from his score sheet, launches into his critique, first with a right, then with a left, numerous jabs and the occasional but effective uppercut. "You went to the trouble to clean the bones, but you didn't get all the cartilage off. Those are the kinds of details that must be attended to at the master chef level. On the salpicon we're looking for some nice knife cuts. Four of your shrimp are not completely deveined."

Brian winces angrily at this. All three chefs in this room know that deveining shrimp was a task likely assigned to the assistant. Brian says, "That's my fault. I checked the ones that went on the plate, but I didn't check all the ones on the platter."

"The sauce." DeSantis continues. "First I thought, 'Oh, this is good.' But as I kept eating, I thought at first it needed a wine reduction, but it doesn't call for that. It needed some spice."

"Cayenne, yes. I've got some cayenne in there. Maybe I could have added some acid."

Looking at another sheet, DeSantis says, "Consommé was cloudy."

"The consommé was clear before I added the barley," Brian says.

DeSantis asks him how he prepared the barley, and Brian says he washed it, blanched it, then cooked it.

Doesn't matter. Cloudy is cloudy, and it didn't taste good either. "It really needed a boost in flavor," DeSantis concludes.

The consommé's flavor was partly a result of the quality of the stock he was given, but all the exhausted Brian can say is, "This was very difficult."

"Details," DeSantis continues without remorse. "You needed more attention to details. The salpicon, it's a nappé sauce, not a reduced liquid. The chipolatas should have been cut in half."

"Really?"

DeSantis peers into the Book and reads, "'Three poached chipolatas cut in half.'"

Brian's lips curl tightly, and he simply nods, taking it. The judges offer virtually nothing positive. It almost sounds as if they'd had to spit this food out it was so bad.

Without more ado DeSantis leans forward and says, "You *passed*. Sixty-six point one one. I wanna be *real* clear about this. You *must* focus on details. You can draw this same menu on Sunday. You really have to build yourself up from here."

Brian stands like a buck private and says, *"Yes, Chef, thank you for the advice. I hope to cook better for you next time."* He shakes their hands and strides out.

Moments later big Steve enters the room and suddenly it's as if the place were filled with balloons and confetti. "You got an eighty-seven point seven," DeSantis says, after some obligatory nit-picking and much praise. "You should feel real good about this."

Steve's eyebrows rise and fall once. "Thank you, Chef," he says.

CHAPTER TWELVE

The following morning, Day Eight, the chefs as always must return to the CIA campus before seven, this time to begin the day with a lecture on beverage management, then the baking section of the test, followed by a lecture on Asian cuisine and the Asian cuisine practical. The four remaining men are exhausted as they wait outside Noble Masi's bakeshop on the second floor of the continuing education building at nine o'clock. Their heads hang, and they stare at the floor. Neil looks pretty well rattled. He shakes his head and mumbles, "All those little garnishes. I don't know, man, I don't know."

I wait with them and ask Brian how it's going. He says, "I'll call you Monday and tell you my opinion."

Sunday is the final and hardest day of the test. Today, Friday, is a relatively restful day. This morning the chefs will demonstrate competence in fundamental baking: soft rolls and bread, two pecan pies, pâte à choux for thirty-two éclairs and the pastry cream to fill them, and tuiles. It's mapped out hour by hour. All the chefs must do is follow directions.

Neil stands across the hall from Steve and says, "On the last day they don't give you a grade on the mystery basket. You go in there, and there's either champagne in the basket or it's empty."

Brian says, "I'm not drinking with them."

Steve says that's not presently his main concern.

Brian says, "It felt good to say it." Then he lifts his gaze from the floor, turns seriously to Steve beside him, and asks, "Did you change the way you cooked because it was classical?"

"No," Steve says, "I just cooked."

"How did you get flavor in your consommé?"

"I had the pheasant."

"Ah," Brian says. Steve was given bones to roast and fortify his stock with and pheasant meat to garnish it with. Tons of flavor. Brian says, "Let's talk about something else."

They spend about an hour in a lecture on baking and then head into the bakeshop. They have moved through seven days of the test. Neil keeps shaking his head as if to clear his vision. He doesn't realize how much yesterday's failure has shaken him until he sets to work once again in the kitchen. His study partner, silent Steve, confesses that the cold he's been trying to avoid this whole last week has finally got its hooks into him. Brian stares into a mixing bowl filled with flour and shortening. It appears as if he's staring into a pond searching for some strange fish. But he says, "That's what this test makes you do. I can't believe I scaled my *pie* dough wrong." It's the most simple pie dough there is: a 3-2-1 dough, three parts flour, two parts shortening, one part water. Today is his youngest son's birthday; Ben is two years old the day Brian reverses his flour and shortening measurements, and this deepens his frustration not just at the dough error but by the fact that he's here at all.

This day and the next are designed to be easy on the chef's bodies, a kind of calm before the storm of Day Ten. Baking and pastry are different from hot cooking. It's not just that the kitchen is cooler, that the pressure is constant throughout and does not build to the crescendo of service. Baking and pastry require a different attitude entirely. One doesn't bang out a prep list and cook like mad, "a lot of hot pans under control." One bakes. Baking. Takes time. Baking. Is slow. Baking. Requires. Patience. Measurements must be perfect. Plating, in pastry, must be exact. Movements are slow. Kitchen noises are soft. An easy hush presides over the kitchen.

After the strain of classical, this attitude shift is not altogether natural for these four chefs, three of whom cook hard pretty much every day in their hotel, country club, and restaurant kitchens. None of them is a pastry chef. (The American Culinary Federation does offer a Certified Master Pastry Chef exam—there are currently seventeen CMPCs—that coincides with the CMC exam, but only when enough chefs ask to take it and can all be in Hyde Park, New York, for those ten days.) So even though it's a break, it's not necessarily an easy break or any kind of breather. Steve, Mark, and Brian have still got two days to get through before the last long day. As for Neil, that may not be the last day. Even if he passes everything else as strongly as he began, he will not earn his CMC title unless he retakes and passes a makeup classical cuisine section after Day Ten, which Dieter will arrange if it is needed.

There are no surprises in baking, and all cruise through it almost on the momentum of seven marathon days. After lunch Asian cuisine begins, another minor category, led by Shirley Cheng, a CIA instructor born and formally trained in China. This day has been billed as "fun" by Dieter, but it's still three hours of cooking followed by service, plating for four and a platter for six. Furthermore, the judges include Buchtenkirch and DeSantis, all but ensuring that the atmosphere in the judging room will be characterized more by Parris Island methods than by Asian delicacy.

Indeed it's a jarring surprise. Neil draws Thai hot and sour soup, sushi maki, and pork with Peking sauce and just barely clears 70. Mark Linden's hot and sour soup, spring roll, and shrimp with cashews *fail*. Mark, utterly unfamiliar with Asian cookery, simply gets off on the wrong foot and never recovers; his menu falls apart. Steve passes, but his cold deepens, and he must take medicine that makes him drowsy and threatens his balance. Brian passes with a wonton soup, Vietnamese fresh spring rolls, and shrimp tempura. He knows his nemesis DeSantis is a judge, so he actually measures his vegetables with a ruler to ensure that his knife cuts are perfectly uniform. DeSantis won't get him on his knife cuts today, goddammit.

Saturday they're up early again for a 7:00 A.M. lecture on pastry followed by nine hours of pastry production, each chef creating a plated dessert for twelve and a torte for sixteen, with one torte piece cut and served.

I left early the day before, not waiting out the results of Asian cuisine. I've begun to lose my focus. I'm not cooking, I don't always attend the dull classroom lectures, I don't have to be anywhere at all if I don't feel like it, no one is evaluating my every move, and *I'm* exhausted. I remain home—friends have loaned us their cottage on a lake not far from the Culinary—to work on notes, sleep, and spend some time with my wife and daughter. I return midday on Saturday once the quiet, patient work of patisserie, like model building, is well under way.

I meet Brian in the hall heading upstairs to the bakeshop, where his desserts (pear and ginger Bavarian with almond tuiles and chocolate-hazelnut torte with raspberry coulis) are in good shape. He takes the elevator—no need to expend any more energy than necessary—and I join him. I ask how Asian went last night. He says, "Fine," as he always replies no matter how fine or unfine it in fact was. Another form of energy he does not want to expend. Once a day has passed, it's gone; dwelling on it can serve only to draw his focus away from the present, which is where he needs to be. But he chuckles—or snorts rather. Hard to tell if he thinks it's funny, inevitable, ironic, or ridiculous.

"DeSantis got me on my knife cuts," he says.

"*What?*" I say.

Brian nods. "They were *too* perfect, he said."

"How can they be *too* perfect?"

"This was a style of cooking that didn't require perfect knife cuts, so time spent on perfect knife cuts is time misspent."

The elevator doors close. The car begins to rise. Brian offers that yesterday was his youngest son's birthday and that he had had a bad night. "I dreamed I couldn't remember Ben's face. I couldn't remember what he *looked* like. It was *freaky.*"

With the birth of each child, the sense of family and familial responsibilities does not numb from the routine and work but rather intensi-

fies Brian's sense of fatherhood. He is absolutely and utterly devoted to
his children and to Julia, and part of him feels guilty to be here, half a
continent away from his home. That he misses Ben's second birthday
enhances the guilt. The dream is self-imposed punishment; he is too far
away, in body and in mind, to see his own son's face.

I follow Brian into the cool, quiet bakeshop, where all chefs are at
work perfecting their desserts. I notice Steve returning at a slow lope to
his station. He stops walking and stands still. His eyelids fall three-
quarters shut. A tight, strong shiver starts at his neck and runs through
his entire body. When it passes, he takes a deep breath and walks to his
station. A fever has apparently taken hold. Steve has been steady throughout eight full days, lumbering through each menu with an unbreakable
and steady stride, perfect at every step. For the first time, having just
seen the tremor, I'm worried about him.

At 4:00 P.M. the first plates are up and delivered to a judging room
across the bakeshop. The evaluation is over by 6:00. The judging is
tough, but the critique is intelligent and informative, and all chefs pass.
Brian thinks it's the best critique so far and seems grateful. He returns
to his station in the bakeshop and opens his notebook. He has drawn
his first assignment for Day Ten. It was possible for him to land an international assignment. He might possibly have chosen the Spanish
menu again: gazpacho, risotto, grilled veg, stuffed squid. He has decided from the beginning not to worry about what he draws. Whatever's in the envelope he can and will do. Neil, as it happens, draws the
Spanish menu.

Brian will perform a classical menu: consommé Portalis, ordinary
consommé flavored with tomato and saffron, garnished with vermicelli,
grated cheese served separately; filets de sole Floréal, paupiettes shallow-
poached in mushroom juices and butter, served on top of asparagus
tips, coated with sauce vin blanc, and finished with beurre printanier;
and finally, poulet sauté Stanley, a white sauté—the chicken isn't browned
but kept pale and is served with mushrooms and a soubise sauce (here
simply cream cooked with onions) spiked with cayenne and curry.

Joe Scully leans on the bench and looks over Brian's menu. "Oh,
man, they gave you *four* garnishes?" he says. In addition to the three

main courses, Brian must serve chateau potatoes, glazed carrots, haricots verts with butter, and crêpes d'epinards. Furthermore, he will have only four hours to complete this menu, not four and half, as he had two days ago.

Brian winces and nods.

"You can complain to Dieter if you think it's too much."

"I'll do it," Brian says angrily. "I'm gonna throw it in their face."

Brian then discussed with Joe various facets of the menu. While everything is written down, there's still room for interpretation and judgment. "How would you do those carrots?" he asks. "Channel knife?" ("Place a slice of grooved carrot cooked in a little Bouillon on top of each Paupiette," Escoffier writes, "and a small, very green sprig of chervil in the centre of the carrot.")

"Channel knife." Joe agrees.

Brian asks about the sauce vin blanc.

"That sauce, you want good nappage," says Joe. "Not like we'd serve at our restaurants. It would stand on your thumb."

"I'm gonna whack it," Brian says, meaning thicken it heavily.

The two discuss the chateau potatoes, how much clarified butter to cook them in, then the cleaning of the chicken joints. Brian draws a diagram of the bottom drumstick joint, then draws a diagonal line through it just above the cartilage knob, showing Joe where he will cut to remove all the cartilage without splintering the bone. They discuss how far ahead to cook the chicken, how to hold it and serve it. When Brian's got a handle on his menu, he packs up his book and his tools and strides out of the building, down the steps to the parking lot, into his Jeep, and flies up Route 9 at sixty miles an hour to his hotel room to prepare for tomorrow.

CHAPTER THIRTEEN

*I*t's 6:45 A.M., Sunday, and Brian Polcyn is all but bobbing on his toes like a prizefighter waiting to enter the ring. His energy is manic-depressive; he moves from euphoric confidence to defensive fatalism all in the same breath.

"I'm gonna kick some ass," he says. "I feel good. I'm a better cook today than I was ten days ago. That's how I feel now. I don't know how I'll feel after I hear what the judges think. The way I look at it, I'm gonna be on the road in twelve hours."

Brian has drawn position two. At seven-twenty he will enter the kitchen, cook hard by the Book for four hours, take an hour's break, and then begin the Day Ten mystery basket, the last and most difficult cooking of the test because of the judges' expectations. As Brian puts it, "For nine days it's solid fundamentals, good cooking principles, nothing outside the baseline. The last day they want Lutèce." His scores today are not like the scores on classical and American cuisine from Days Six and Seven. Today is a day unto itself and will account for 50 percent of Brian's final score. He can't pass classical today with a 66.11 and earn his CMC; his cumulative score is only in the seventies going into today, so he must score better than a 75 on classical (for which he has less time than before) and the mystery basket combined.

Of the four chefs still standing, Brian and Steve are the only chefs who have not failed a single section and therefore the only two who can hope to earn their CMC titles on this day. The best Neil and Mark can hope for is a strong pass today and to make up their failures tomorrow.

Steve Jilleba is in position one and begins cooking exactly at seven. He has drawn a classical menu, the menu Neil failed three days ago. With pain relievers and decongestant he has negotiated a temporary truce with the cold in his body: It can stay, he tells it; just be quiet until this day is done.

Brian walks to his station at 7:20 A.M., and tapes his prep and equipment lists to the wall beside the window looking into the quad lit with spring sun. He tapes plating diagrams to a rolling equipment rack. The equipment list—"Product on Station," it reads—covers two full columns on a sheet of yellow legal paper, items assistant Ezra has already set on sheet trays, including a chinois, rubber spatula, whisk, Japanese mandoline, strainer, perforated spoon, slotted spoon, wooden spoon, measuring cup, chef's knife, tourner knife, boning knife, mini offset spatula, steel, zester, peeler, pencil, timer, and beside these, a Robot Coupe and a blender.

"OK, Ezra, let's go," Brian says. "Here's your list. Check everything with me as you accomplish it." Brian begins by butchering five chickens. He can take a chicken down in the poulet sauté style in two and a half minutes. He brings his consommé up—adding two of his chicken carcasses, chopped up, for more flavor—and then butchers the Dover sole, trimming it neatly and saving the scraps for his forcemeat. Every day of this test he has felt out of sync, but today, at last, he has found his groove. "Rockin'," he says, sliding his boning knife along the flat ribs of a sole. "I'm *geeked*."

It's impossible to know the state of Brian's mind. Is his judgment clear? Has he entered a kind of marathon runner's trance? Is this hypersharp perception, or is he simply deluded from fatigue? It's been a long journey through these past nine days, with much frustration and physical labor, little sleep, and intense psychological stress. The test does funny things to your head.

Dieter Doppelfeld is back in full swing today, having taken most of Friday and Saturday off. He is angry about the judging on Asian, the

DeSantis–Buchtenkirch severity. "They are not Asian *cooks*," he tells me. "If they missed basic cooking fundamentals, they should be nailed. Otherwise . . ." And he shakes his head. "If I had been here, it would have been different. I feel bad about that."

Dieter is neither proctor nor judge today. He says that by this stage he has become too close to the candidates to be an objective judge. He has brought in five non-CIA judges from as near as Connecticut and as far as Texas. Tom Peer and CIA senior vice-president Tim Ryan will also judge.

Neil enters the kitchen twenty minutes after Brian and passes through Steve's station to see how his buddy's doing. Steve's consommé is already up and simmering, and he has chicken and fish stocks in the works. He finishes his forcemeat shortly after eight, pushing it through a tamis into a bowl resting in ice. He begins his quenelles, using this forcemeat, which he will then set upright in small hollowed tomatoes for his filets de sole Rosine.

Brad Barnes, a corporate chef for ITB Restaurant Group in Greenwich, Connecticut, is this morning's proctor. Tall, lean with thick brown hair and wearing a lab coat, he strolls the kitchen, observing and taking notes. He watches as Brian tourners his carrots, then moves off.

The tourner cut—a seven-sided oval—is a difficult cut, especially with hard carrots, and Brian does a sloppy job in his haste; the carrots are of different shapes and sizes. Turning vegetables is time-consuming, and there's a lot of waste involved, so it's unlikely that Brian turns a lot of carrots at his contemporary American restaurant. I ask Dieter how important it is to have perfectly turned vegetables. He shrugs. It *is* important in classical cuisine. But, he notes, "If they don't taste good, who cares? If they're beautiful tourners, but they don't taste good, I say you should have used all that time tournering and learned how to *cook*."

"I'm starting to feel good," Brian says aloud. He has just gotten both his fish velouté—fish stock thickened with roux—on the stove to cook, the base sauce for his sauce vin blanc. He heads to his prep list to find the next items, saying, "Everything is beautiful in its own way."

Brad Barnes finishes marking on his clipboard, thinking to himself, "This guy's pretty nervous," and walks away. Brian can't help noticing the pencil clicking on clipboard, the stranger in a lab coat; he chuckles and shakes his head as though this were too much grade-school silliness.

But already Barnes sees serious errors at Brian's station. His roux is too dry, and Brian doesn't flavor the stock that will go into that roux for the velouté. There's also too much roux. The sauce thickens up so fast that the pasty flour taste and feel won't cook out of the sauce. Each early mistake, always but especially in classical cooking, will stay with you till the end. It's built in, you can't fix it later, as Brian himself said.

The protein in egg whites clarifies a stock into a consommé; to make consommé, you stir into stock a mixture of egg whites and some acid, preferably some form of tomato, as well as lean meat and vegetables for additional flavor. When this mixture heats, it solidifies into what is called a raft; it's a kind of protein net that traps all the impurities for date-on-a-dime-at-the-bottom-of-a-gallon clear soup. But Brian has chosen a pot that is too wide and uses only two egg whites; this means his raft will be too spread out, too thin to be an efficient clarifier. Barnes notes furthermore that Brian hasn't flavored his forcemeat with stock or flavored the cream that went into it.

"You've really got to pay attention to the building of flavors," Barnes tells me.

On the other hand, Brian is working very clean and organized and communicating well with his assistant. This accounts for some points, but nothing the judges will ever taste. His small mistakes will fester.

At the three-hour mark Brian pushes his beurre printanier—a tricky preparation of butter flavored with vegetables—through a tamis, then stores it. He begins the spinach crepes. He hands a finished one to Ezra. "Here's breakfast," he says with deadpan gravity. "I didn't have to do this. I made it just for you." Joe Scully has been watching Brian cook. Dieter sends him on an errand, and Scully leaves the kitchen, saying to me as he passes, "I love that guy. And he's a great cook."

Brian runs down his prep list: "Carrots, done. Chervil, done. Then we have mushrooms." He hustles to get these cooked, garnish for his sole.

At eleven Steve's window opens; his consommé is ready, and out it goes, as do the rest of his courses, cleanly, though it's hectic toward the end. Brian has already begun his chicken and now completes his garnishes. At 11:07 he pulls the chicken, pure white, from the oven. "Let's finish that sauce," he says. "I need those yolks." Ezra has saved the yolks (separated from the whites that went into the consommé), and Brian will combine them with cream to thicken his sauce, a mixture called a liaison. His chateau potatoes are bubbling, submerged in clarified butter. He does not know if they're done all the way through, so he lifts one from the pan, sticks a metal skewer into its center, pulls the skewer out, and touches the metal to his wrist. "Ow!" he says. Then he says, "They're done."

When Steve's poulet sauté à la bourguignonne vanishes into the judging chamber, Brad Barnes strides to station two and says to Brian, "We'll take your food any time, Chef."

"Thank you," he responds, then, to Ezra: "You know what I'm looking for." Ezra will be working on the platters.

"Yes, Chef."

"I shall serve the soup," Brian narrates, adding the vermicelli to the consommé cups, then says to the waiting runners, "Serve the cheese on the side." Out the soup goes almost exactly at eleven-twenty.

Next course, the fish. Time melts away. Brian has pans smoking on the stove, chicken in the oven, potatoes to keep warm, along with the crepes, the carrots and beans. Joe Scully stands back, watching Brian work. The fish is up on his station in serving dishes, and he tastes the sauce before dressing the paupiettes. "This should be hotter," he says, and returns it to the stove. Another minute passes, and he still has to finish four plates, another platter even before he sends his complicated final course out. As he sauces the fish and finishes it with the beurre printanier, in his mind he's already putting the final course together. He sends the plates out as Ezra works on the fish platter. "You have seven minutes, Chef," Barnes says. Brian turns to the stove. The mushrooms are still there, garnish for the fish that is now speeding down the corridor to the judges. He turns urgently to Dieter and asks, "Can I serve them on the side?"

Dieter shakes his head sadly, then shrugs. "You have no other choice," he says softly.

The mushrooms make it onto the platter, and four ramekins go with it to be placed before the judges. Mushrooms on the side.

No time to fret now, must get the chicken out. "You work on the platter," Brian says to Ezra. "I'll start the plates." Everything is ready; everything is hot. The plates come together, but he's really got to hustle. "Put some parsley on the potatoes as I sauce," he says to Ezra. "Put a truffle on the chicken and *go*."

The final plates, poulet sauté Stanley, are whisked away, and it is over. Barnes has already left for Neil at station three. Before Brian can take a breath, Scully is smack in his face like a marine. "Chef," Scully says, "I would just walk away from this. I'll break down your station."

"I forgot the mushrooms," Brian says, earnestly, angrily at Scully.

"I know. I would just walk away from this. Go get some lunch. I'll break down your station."

"I forgot the mushrooms on the judges' plates. How much is that going to hurt me?"

Scully is still right in Brian's face talking like a marine. "Chef, I don't think I can answer that."

Brian smiles. Easily, casually. He says, "I love you, man."

Brian turns to begin gathering his own equipment, and he sees two items on his station, untouched. His body clenches at the sight. The cayenne and the curry powder. He has forgotten to season his sauce for the chicken. Without these spices it's simply a creamy onion sauce, an entirely different sauce. Cayenne and curry are what *make* the dish a sauté Stanley.

In Lecture Hall 2, five judges evaluate the first cooking of Day Ten. In addition to Tom Peer and Tim Ryan (who is CIA heir apparent to Ferdinand Metz and, when he passed at twenty-seven, the youngest to earn the Certified Master Chef title), are three outside judges. Victor Gielisse, chef-owner of CFT/Culinary Fast-Trac and Associate in Dallas, a food consulting business; Gielisse formerly owned the restaurant Actuelle in Dallas and is the author of two cookbooks. Rudy Speckhamp is chef-owner of Rudy's 2900 in Finksburg, Maryland, outside Baltimore. And David Megenis is director of culinary development for Sodexho Marriott Services, a huge food service concern.

The group is an accurate representation of the profession, a mixture of restaurant chefs, culinary educators, and culinary businessmen. Of all the cooks in America, a million or more, only a fraction run public restaurant kitchens. The majority are in the food service business but do not necessarily cook. Some consult. Others work for corporations. Others teach. Many work in administrative capacities or in research and development. These are the chefs that the public rarely sees. Not only does the public rarely see them, but they rarely see one another. This is partly why so many chefs think the CMC test is important; it's a way for them to find out where they stand among their peers. It's a measure of success and achievement in a field that offers few such measurements outside the potential hope of becoming a celebrity chef, a hope akin to a high school athlete's expecting to become an NBA all-star. Of the one million chefs in America, only a few dozen have attained what can be called celebrity.

These five men taste and discuss Brian's food as he and Ezra sit quietly at a table in the East Wing dining room. Brian has turkey on a soft bun, potato chips, and a Diet Coke.

After one hour Brian strides back into the kitchen, squats at his lowboy, and pulls out the sheet trays that Joe Scully has put there, compliments of Dieter Doppelfeld. This is what he finds:

> one whole tilefish
> mussels
> sea scallops
> shrimp
>
> double loin of lamb
>
> two ears of corn
> pattypan squash
> Spanish cantaloupe
> trevisano radicchio

romaine
white asparagus
fava beans
portobello mushrooms
jalapeño peppers
ramps

Israeli couscous
ancho peppers

For a half hour Brian hovers over a legal pad, scribbling possible combinations of these items. He'll use as much of them as possible in a four-course meal for ten. He needs to get Ezra working and has him blanch, peel, and chop tomatoes. "I'm still in the conceptual stage of the salad," he says, "so give me a good concassé. No seeds. I'm gonna make a nice vinaigrette."

Outside, in the hallway, Dieter says that he is "discouraged."

"We maybe get two CMCs this year," he says, "maybe none." He looks at me and tilts his head. "Does *everyone* have to do *every* discipline *perfectly*?" He worries that this exam is becoming too difficult to be accessible to enough chefs to make it valuable. He totters off, looking sad.

In a half hour Brian turns in his menu:

Poached Gulf shrimp, scallops, and mussels with cantaloupe
and jalapeño salsa
Salad of white asparagus, Israeli couscous, romaine,
and tomato vinaigrette
Sautéed Atlantic tilefish on sweet-corn sauce with fava beans
Roast loin of lamb with mustard sauce,
wild leek–and–potato cake with
grilled portobello mushrooms and braised pattypan squash

Once again he is cooking, no wasted movement. So are Steve and Mark. Neil is cooking, but it's only motions. He's become disoriented. He has simply run out of gas. He looks to Darren, his assistant, and says, "You gotta help me because I can't think straight." Neil has flamed out.

Brian just keeps cooking, fast and hard. Five hours later his roast lamb entrée is sent to the judges, and the test is over.

Dieter goes in and out of the judging room. At one point he returns with an official rule book. There seems to be much debate in the room. Dieter looks sad. He waits outside, sits on a window ledge. Another year, another test. Not a good showing this year: a lot of work for one, maybe two, maybe no passes. No one has performed well today, apparently, and you can see it on his face. I too feel oddly depressed. But Dieter's new Continuing Education class, Using Game in Menus, begins tomorrow, and the arrival today of the rattlesnake meat, the boar, and the emu cheers him a little.

The chefs wait outside the judging room, leaning against the wall, heads hanging. This is the worst wait of all for Brian. During the unpleasant minutes before he enters the judging chamber, he retraces the steps of his long day; his errors occur to him as small pings in his mind. The judges' door opens, and ominously, Polcyn, who had been in position two, is called in before Steve Jilleba, position one.

The judges encircle Polcyn beside a table where his platters lie. Rudy Speckhamp begins the critique with the confident, gentle voice of a doctor explaining that the tumor is not benign. "You had so many flavors there it was hard to harmonize them," Speckhamp says, pointing to the poached Gulf shrimp, scallops, and mussels with cantaloupe and jalapeño salsa. "It was too spicy. And the herbed mayonnaise didn't really go." The list of errors continues: "The asparagus were undercooked . . . the vinaigrette was much too thick . . . the sweet-corn sauce did not have a great taste . . . I was most disappointed in the lamb platter: the lamb was undercooked, and so it was tough."

Classical was worse, given the omission of major components. Victor Gielisse says, "I know you. You're a much better craftsman than this," but concludes with a question: "Did you have any curry?"

"I forgot to put it in," Polcyn says.

Tom Peer tells Polcyn his scores: 62.82 on classical, 62.55 on the mystery basket. He has failed the CMC test again.

Polcyn thanks the judges, says good night, and heads for the door, exhaling brusquely once. He pauses only to give a thumbs-down sign to Jilleba and hand his toque to Dieter, who accepts it sadly. In an hour Brian will be crossing the Hudson River in his Jeep, back at work the day after he arrives home. He will soon call Steve Jilleba, executive chef at Sunset Ridge Country Club, to congratulate him, the fifty-fourth cook to earn the CMC title.

Part Two

LOLA

CHAPTER ONE

$\mathcal{L}$ola Bistro and Wine Bar is a loud, happy restaurant. Its floors are hardwood; its ceiling is tin; its interior walls are brick. The bar forms a curving zigzag and is, for half of its length, two deep by eight on Friday night; the other half is the service counter for the open kitchen, where three cooks send out between one hundred and three hundred meals a night. The room is dimly lighted, and when Frank Rogers, the sous chef, flames the wine in a seafood pasta sauce, sending a fireball into the air, heads turn at the flash.

The only voice louder than the crowd noise is that of Lola's chef-owner, twenty-eight-year-old Michael Symon, whose frat boy baritone booms through the din and is followed by an extraordinary laugh. One can say only that it is high-pitched, staccato, lasts about two seconds, and might pass for a mating call for a rare rain forest bird. But there is nothing in city life to compare it with, and it is impossible to render it adequately on the written page, though the laugh and accompanying smile invariably make his customers laugh and smile too. One typically needs to spend only a moment or two here to know if the chef is cooking; that laugh will pierce even the heaviest bank of shouted conversation, swing music, and clanking sauté pans.

But on this Wednesday, a typically busy night, February 11, 1998, Michael Symon works the line silently like a man possessed. When he needs to focus, the laughter ceases, and his hulking frame and Cro-Magnon head, shaved and glistening in the heat, dominate the ten-foot line. Though he is five-eleven, weighs more than two hundred pounds, and wears a size fifty-two jacket, he appears agile and light, a wrestler, weighed down only by the ledge of his brow and his nearly black eyes. Everything he cooks is important to him, but the plates he hovers over now—grouper, spiked with Jamaican jerk sauce, on lobster fritters with whipped avocado and outlined with a red pepper coulis, Great Lakes walleye on lobster pierogies, halibut on artichoke salad—are especially critical because he suspects that the three-top at table P-3 contains an editor from *Food & Wine* magazine, here unannounced to evaluate the restaurant and the food.

A man at the bar with bushy brown and gray hair, a thick mustache, and eyebrows the dimensions of bricks glances over his shoulder at the mysterious table, two women and a man who, to judge from their laughter and smiles, are enjoying themselves. The man at the bar is Stephen Michaelides, sixty-three years old, former editor of the trade journal *Restaurant Hospitality*, well connected in the food world. He is also an indefatigable Cleveland booster and will do virtually anything to promote the town. For the past several years, for instance, he's barraged the food writer and critic John Mariani with letters, badgering him, daring him to come to Cleveland to see what's happened to the culinary scene here. Michaelides has been a fan of Michael Symon's for years, and earlier in the day Michael called him and said, "Stephen, we think that *Food & Wine* might be here tonight. Is there anything you can find out?"

Apparently, a month or so back Michael was asked to fax a menu to the magazine, and this was followed by a casual chat with an editor there.

This indeed is how *Food & Wine* puts together its annual "America's Ten Best New Chefs" issue. Late in the year editor Monica Forrestall sends a letter and nominating form to 250 food critics and food writers throughout the country. She receives the names of some 400 chefs and responses to general criteria: The chef has to head the kitchen; he or she can't have been in the head chef position for more than five years. Also, the magazine tends to favor innovative or cutting-edge cuisine rather than classical cuisine. About 100 of the nominated chefs won't fit the criteria. The editors then gather menus and conduct informal interviews to glean more information without noting their actual intent. Forrestall can then reduce the list to about 150 potential chefs, as many as 7 or 8 in two dozen cities. A food and wine editor then visits each one of those restaurants; the editors who have traveled and eaten return to their offices and debate the top ten. By this point the top ten are fairly clear, according to Forrestall.

Symon faxed a menu. He got a call. He didn't think anything of it. He was just having a good time, cooking all the way, never looking back, always laughing. Michael claims never to have spent an entire day without being happy for at least part of it, even when things were bad.

On February 11 he noticed a 212 area code on a confirmation number in the reservation book. This was curious because there were almost never out-of-town confirmation numbers. Stephen Michaelides suggested Michael dial the number to see who answered. No one did. Stephen then said he'd make a couple of calls, and in the meantime why not check a *Food & Wine* masthead? Maybe Michael would see on the masthead the name under which the reservation had been made, Crow. One of the cook's brothers had a copy of the magazine and scanned the masthead. There it was, way down in the Copy & Production section, "Associate Editor Martha Crow."

Symon informed Michaelides, and lifelong Cleveland-booster that he was—he'd been trying to push the perception of Cleveland restaurants out of the pierogi-and-polka gutter and into the kind of respectful spotlight he thought several restaurants in his town now deserved—he strolled down from his house a couple of blocks away in the artsy urban enclave called Tremont and had a drink at Lola's bar. He sipped and glanced back at P-3, which stands for Platform 3; Michael wanted to break up the bowling alley feel of his long restaurant via a platform, which now held the four tables where VIPs were often seated. Michaelides chatted with Frankie, Lola's ace bartender, and glanced again. The three-top at P-3 continued, by appearances, to be having a swell time. They would order nearly the entire menu before the night was over.

When the woman had gone, Michael went to the basement office, lit a Camel cigarette, and called his girlfriend, Liz Shanahan, Lola's general manager, who was off that night.

"Honey," Michael told her softly and seriously, the laughter gone, "everything I did for them, I did perfectly. Everything was perfectly plated; everything was perfectly cooked. If we never hear from them again, I at least know that I did the best food I could do."

Two years earlier I'd gone to interview Michael Symon. He was then chef at a small chic restaurant called Caxton Café and had recently been featured on the cover of the Sunday magazine of Cleveland's main newspaper, the *Plain Dealer*, which called him the city's "hottest chef" and praised him for bringing cutting-edge fare to a behind-the-times meat-and-potatoes city. And making money doing it. Several chefs had tried and failed. Ali Barker, lionized in New York City for his work at Union Square Cafe and then 150 Wooster, had opened a restaurant called Piperade down the street from Michael Symon but had recently closed after several years of struggle.

Symon fiercely defended those chefs who couldn't make it in his hometown. About Ali Barker and another well-known chef packing it in that same month, he said, "I think it's a fucking crime. I hate it. They're two of the guys in the city, two of maybe six, who have a passion for doing things the right way. I don't even get along with Ali, but I respect the hell out of what he does. He does it right; he doesn't take shortcuts; he doesn't put out bullshit food."

But while other, obviously talented chefs collapsed in Cleveland, Symon vaulted. Wherever Symon's personality could flourish, great food, crowds, and reviews followed. The Caxton Café, where he earned the "hottest chef" label and turned a profit, had foundered before the owners hired Symon. As soon as he left, it would sink like stone. Symon clearly had something that other talent didn't have.

I'd gone to see him and watch him work because he was a graduate of the Culinary Institute of America. At the time I was about to go to the school myself to learn to cook and to write about it. Meeting with Symon, a typical CIA graduate and representative of the most visible segment of the industry at that time, was my prep work.

And he did do good food, fun food, worth noting. His fried calamari were the best I'd tasted anywhere. He wanted to get the flavor of ginger into his calamari somehow. He tried grating ginger into the flour coating, but that didn't produce the right effect. He tried putting ginger powder in the flour, but it resulted in a fake ginger taste. He began to think about batter, how some batters use carbonation as a leavener, such as beer batters. He didn't like heavy batters, but this idea led him to the idea of soaking the calamari in ginger ale and fresh-grated ginger. The ginger-marinated squid would then be coated in a peppery flour and fried. "It came out really nice," he told me. He served it with a smooth green onion sauce.

Michael was playful. He'd been doing a macaroni and cheese dish at the Caxton, pasta with goat cheese, and grilled chicken, serious comfort food. He did a cold-smoked pork tenderloin with a ginger potato cake and hot wasabi fish eggs (flying fish roe spiked with wasabi that are a bright, almost neon green) and called it Green Eggs and Ham, after the Dr. Seuss book. He also got away with serving food that didn't typically fly in Cleveland, items such as duck carpaccio—duck tenderloin, pounded flat and served raw with a port wine glaze—and tuna tartare. Tuna tartare was being served in cosmopolitan cities across the country, but few had dared offer it in Cleveland before. People in this town liked their meat *cooked*. Symon served it raw, and the meat-and-potatoes clientele tried it, liked it, and even felt a little hip.

While Michael and I talked in the forty-seat dining room, Frank Rogers, who had been Michael's dishwasher and had since worked his way to lunch cook, sautéed corn crepes in the kitchen, dozens of them—a basic crepe batter but with chopped corn, corn juice, red and green peppers. Frank had three pans going and several stacks already cooled. He'd been cooking corn crepes for a long time today. They'd be filled this evening with duck confit and barbecue sauce—another Symon favorite. He couldn't take them off the menu they were so popular. It was good food. Nothing fancy. Symon used few meat-based sauces. When he sauced a plate, he rarely used more than an ounce of it. He liked flavors that "popped"—ginger, lemon grass, wasabi fish eggs, fresh herbs, good vinegars—but he stayed true to the tone of the midwestern steel city by offering big chops and creamy pastas. "Simple," he said with a shrug.

"What makes it so successful?" I asked.

"I just do it the best," he said. And the laugh pealed into the air like a bizarre bird out of the jungle.

What was most impressive to me at the time was the kitchen where he plied his trade. It measured fourteen feet square, with all but a U-shaped lane, large enough for one person, taken up by serving areas, stoves, broken refrigerators, sinks, and a dishwasher. Michael and one other chef, his buddy Tim Bando, cooked all the food virtually without moving from their spots. There was no room even if they needed to move. From this cubbyhole of a kitchen Michael and Tim could put out 170 plates in the two packed hours before any Indians game, which took place at the end of the block in Jacobs Field, Cleveland's awesome new ball park. And they could do it with half the equipment not working.

Giving a tour of the kitchen, Michael explained in his resounding baritone, "Two ovens don't work; the grill's not the right height; the fryer isn't the right height. No cooler space. The flattop is worthless; I use it to keep soup warm." He didn't mention that the big refrigerators lining one wall didn't work either; they were used to store hand towels.

But there he was, cooking like a madman six nights a week putting out Cleveland's most interesting food in its hottest restaurant.

"Fire a house!" Symon called, reading tickets that night. "A crepe! Caponata! Calamari!" Waiters squeezed in and out all night, ducking and contorting to get by with full and empty plates. "Carpaccio, mac and cheese, calamari! Jakie! Quit rootin' in my shit!" Jackie, a waitress, dug around in Michael's green onion sauce when she ran low on soup spoons. Usually a few extra could be found there.

Tony, a waiter with earrings, a dark Vandyke, and a subtle sashay in his walk, placed a ticket on the service shelf, saying, "Order in." A deuce has asked for a house salad and an appetizer as their entire dinner. Michael read it and grumbled at Tony. Tony said, "I'm not the one who invited the hillbillies. I didn't take their reservation." As he turned to leave, Tony said, "They're drinking hot water and lemon if that tells you anything."

Frankie, the bartender, who had squeezed into the kitchen for more glasses, asked, "Did they bring their own lemon?"

Michael hooted and said, "Give 'em directions to Pete and Dewey's!" a sports bar around the corner. Michael spooned saffron risotto for the salmon paella into a pan and slid it over a flame, then dropped some fritters into the oil for his "slash and burn" grouper, a fillet slashed open and smeared with spicy jerk paste.

Doug, the biggest of the waiters, pushed in and asked, "Is this my calamari?"

"Yeah!" Michael said, who had four pans working and several in the oven.

"I need the soup."

"I know, I know," Michael said, spinning for soup.

A friend of Michael's poked his head through the swinging door, and Michael, without breaking stride, said, "Slow-WE! Hey, Slowey! You comin' to the West Side with us tonight?"

"What time are you going?"

Michael and his buddy made plans to meet after the kitchen closed. Michael Symon's evening would end in a West Side bar at 3:00 A.M. after too many shots of Jägermeister, and he'd be in by 11:00 the following morning to begin prepping for Saturday night and another packed house.

Mismanagement of the restaurant by the owners forced Michael to leave the Caxton. Within a couple of months the restaurant had declared bankruptcy. When we talked at the Caxton Café, Symon had just turned twenty-six. He'd begun his cooking career at a Geppetto's Pizza & Ribs chain ten years before. I'd asked what he wanted to do in his career, what his goals were. He said he wanted to own his own restaurant. I questioned whether or not he was ready for that, wondered if at twenty-six he'd learned everything he needed to know.

No, he conceded. He hadn't. One of the things he'd like to do, he told me, would be to work under a great chef for a year. Most of his contemporaries had at least one mentoring chef, but not Michael. And if he ever did do this, he said, it would be at a place in California called the French Laundry, run by a chef named Thomas Keller. He believed that Keller was cooking some of the most interesting food in the country. If he were to work again under a chef, he would do it at the French Laundry. Other than that, he preferred to stay and work as his own boss in the city where he'd grown up and where his family still lived.

I'd never heard of the French Laundry or Thomas Keller before, but the unusual name of the restaurant stuck, and so did the fact that Michael Symon had chosen Keller as the only chef he'd want to work for. I didn't write this down in my notes, and Michael mentioned it only once, but I have always remembered that afternoon was when I first heard the name of the Napa Valley restaurant and chef.

Within a year of my first interviews with Symon, he had left Caxton, and he and Liz Shanahan, Caxton's former manager, were searching for a place to buy. Their first possibility fell through, and Symon actually considered leaving town for the French Laundry. A friend in Cleveland named Susie Heller, a friend of Keller's, offered to introduce Michael. Michael spoke with Keller on the phone. Keller asked him why he wanted to give up being a head chef and go to work somewhere else as a line cook, maybe even a prep cook. Symon didn't have a good enough answer, either for himself or for Keller.

At the same time, the space that eventually was to be the home of Lola Bistro and Wine Bar became available, and Michael and Liz pounced. Not wanting to be beholden to investors, they borrowed $170,000 from banks and relatives to refurbish the restaurant, buy new equipment, open up the kitchen, put in a new curving bar and a platform to break up the long, narrow room.

Michael and Liz, who is thirty-six with a ten-year-old son from her previous marriage, had borrowed enough money so that when all the work was done, they'd have a ten-thousand-dollar cushion in the bank when they opened. They intended to open quietly, to work out the wrinkles before they sent out press releases and menus to the local media. They'd borrowed a lot of money; they were nervous and wanted everything to go right. On opening day Michael checked the bank account. It contained four dollars. That and pocket change were all they had in the way of cash. Michael knew that they had to have *some* cash to open the restaurant—people still used the stuff—and he called his father. "Dad, I need to borrow three hundred dollars."

"So go to the bank," his father said, who'd loaned them a good chunk of their capital.

"Dad, we open in two hours. I don't have *time*, please," Michael said. He couldn't bear to tell his father that they'd spent all but four of the dollars they'd borrowed.

His dad obliged, and Lola opened in March 1997. But not quietly. Despite the fact that Michael and Liz had not sent out announcements or even mentioned an official opening, Lola was jammed that first night. It seemed as if the entire city had been waiting to see what Michael Symon would create. The food was the same: fun, interesting, delicious, and affordable (Michael made it a point to keep every entrée under twenty dollars). Forecasting an annual fiscal plan, Michael and Liz guessed they could do at least one turn during the week and two turns on weekends in their sixty-five-seat space, a total of 480 covers. They knew that the check average would be about thirty dollars per person and made a conservative projection that they'd do $700,000 in sales during their first year.

They were wrong by more than 100 percent. At the end of February the following year Lola had registered sales of $1.5 million. That happened to be the month Martha Crow of *Food & Wine* ate there. A couple months later Dana Cowin, *Food & Wine* executive editor, called Michael to say she had some good news.

Michael doesn't recall his exact response, but it was something along the lines of "Quit shittin' me, who is this? Did Slowey put you up to this?"

Gradually it dawned on him that it was true. The popular magazine had named him one of America's ten best new chefs of 1998.

CHAPTER TWO

In February 1996, three months after I'd introduced myself to
Michael Symon and spent some time watching him work in his
Caxton kitchen, I donned for the first time checked chef's pants and a
chef's jacket to enter K-8, a teaching kitchen at the Culinary Institute
of America in Hyde Park, New York. Here Chef Michael Pardus taught
a class called Skill Development I—the first kitchen class in the two-
year curriculum of the most influential cooking school in the world—
to eighteen men and women of varying skills and backgrounds. I
happened to be the only person in the class with a book contract. With
the blessings of the CIA and a loaner knife kit, I intended to move
through the kitchens of the CIA like a student, then write an intimate,
colorful narrative of learning to cook, a lively description of what one
needed to know to be a professional chef. I had been a hobby cook
since fourth grade, and I figured that a nifty perk of this project would
be learning the basics of cookery, the fundamentals as they were taught
by the best cooking school in the country. I figured this was going to be
neat.

It wasn't "neat." For me it quickly became intensely serious. Imagine
a writer joining a crowd of Spaniards for the yearly foot race in Pam-
plona. The writer figures he's going to have a swell trip to Spain, go for
a run, watch some nutty people, and leave with a story, but suddenly he
finds *real bulls* chasing *him*, and he's got to run for his life to avoid
being gored. And he finds it exciting; he likes the danger. Such was my

surprise upon entering the CIA. I couldn't write about people learning to cook without completely engaging myself in the process, and as it turned out, that process was more like a force, one that demands not just your attention for eight hours a day but your whole being; learning to cook at that level changed how you behaved and how you perceived the world. I *changed.*

I learned efficiency of movement to minimize wasted energy and time, and the idea of efficiency of movement extended to intellectual work. I began to value speed of movement more than ever before. Also, precision of movement. Speed without precision is harmful, especially when knives and hot steel and scalding oil are involved. I learned mental flexibility: You can accomplish anything, anything at all, if you set your mind to it. One must adopt a can-do-anything attitude. You were a professional. You didn't say no, not ever. You didn't complain. You didn't get tired. And you showed up, no matter what. You got there. Nothing but nothing kept you from reaching that kitchen.

Also, you accepted the implicit obligation of excellence: Every effort would be your absolute best. Otherwise it was simply not worth doing. At the same time, you accepted that your best was never your best and never could be because you could always work faster, cleaner, more efficiently.

Many of the internal changes a formal culinary education wrought were in one's attitude, a kind of tougher-than-thou stance. I'm tougher than you, faster than you, *better* than you. I'm a *chef.* I work in inhuman temperatures, and I like it that way. I don't have to sleep every day if there's work to be done now; you get the work done. Only got a couple hours' sleep last night, and you've got eighteen more hours of work ahead of you. Good. You like that. You're a chef. You can sleep *later.*

Some people denigrated this attitude as false machismo in a profession famously abusive to women. I bought into it, wore that mantle, because the work was hard and you had to think like that to get the work done. That's all there was to it. Tom Griffiths, one of my instructors at the CIA, told me about his first job, poissonier at Le Cirque in Manhattan. He was so young and naive he had responded to Le Cirque's want ad for an executive pastry chef. Fresh out of the CIA,

Griffiths figured he should get the job. He didn't, but they did have a cook's position available. He butchered fish all day long, six days a week. The work left him so exhausted, demoralized, and depleted that he returned to his apartment every night and wept. On his day off he lay flat, hoping just to recover.

Working in kitchens can be hard. Whatever tools you could forge in your mind and soul to get the work done, you were glad for. You changed.

And you couldn't turn this stuff off. You weren't just like this when you went to work; you were like this every waking second. You were like this in your dreams. It was who you were. You were a chef. Your work as a chef extended to all areas of your life. Dan Turgeon, another CIA instructor, told our class about his first job, a line cook for Jeffrey Buben at Vidalia in D.C., a turning point in his career. One night, mid-service, Buben kicked Turgeon off the line because he wasn't fast enough. Turgeon was taken out of the game. *Off the line—you're not good enough!* But he wasn't fired. Turgeon had one more chance, and that next day something clicked in, a new gear engaged, and Turgeon *hustled.* "From that day on," Turgeon told our class, "I *ran* everywhere I went."

In his restaurant he put that kind of pressure on you. His was the last class in the CIA curriculum, the American Bounty restaurant, and I spent every day in a kind of controlled panic. There was no way I could get everything done, and that's what he wanted you to feel because he, like most chefs at the CIA, wanted to remind you that you could never be fast enough and you could never be good enough. You had to hustle *all* the *time.* You couldn't stop. A couple of days I took five minutes to bolt a quick lunch. But the main thing I felt all day long was fear that I was not going to be ready at service.

Then I left the CIA and returned home and began to write about learning to cook at the Culinary Institute of America. I had four months to write the book. Before my culinary education I wouldn't have thought you could write a book in four months—I couldn't any-way—but I didn't think that way anymore because I had *changed.* If I had four months to write a book, that book would be written in four months.

I remember this exchange between a chef and his bachelors class in the CIA's four-year degree program:

Chef: "How long does it take to make rice pilaf?!"

Class: "Twenty minutes!"

Chef: "How long does it take to make pilaf if service is in sixteen minutes?!"

Class: "Sixteen minutes!"

You got it done. No matter what. Write a book in four months? You bet. Not getting enough sleep? Too bad, sleep later! Can't come up with the words, writer's block? Too bad, come up with words now, come up with double what you need! Other obligations pressing in, family, say? Meet those obligations in full and still get your work done.

You *like* it this way. You're a chef.

One afternoon in the grocery store the check-out girl said to me, "Why are you always in a hurry?" From her cash register she could see me running through the parking lot every single day I came to get groceries and then running back out, bags in hand. I told her I could get more done that way.

It was true: While I wrote the book, I *ran* everywhere I went. Life in a kitchen—life, period—was a race. You against the clock, every day, every year. Whoever does the most the best wins. Period.

So what happened to your head at the CIA—or what happened to my head—translated from the kitchen to the desk. I was using the attitude taught young chefs to get my book written. And I grew to believe that the methods and standards of kitchen work would translate well to a lot of other professions.

But people who weren't chefs—construction workers, financial consultants, social workers, even some *chefs*—didn't understand the true demands of kitchen work, and so didn't have the same ideas about efficiency, speed, hustle, getting things done, perfect work, and so don't understand chefs. When such people encounter chefs, they call them crazy, temperamental. Chefs don't understand *them* either. Construction on the new restaurant kitchen not done? *What do you mean not done?* the chef asks. The ovens aren't installed, says the construction head, the floor's not in, the wiring's not hooked up, parts didn't come in. Sorry, you'll have to wait.

A chef cannot *fathom* this. *What?* Would one of his line cooks at five-thirty say, "Sorry, Chef, not ready for the service"? Or when the chef called, *"Fire a lamb shank,"* would a cook ever dream of saying, "Sorry, Chef, didn't get around to braising the shank today. I'll try to get to them tomorrow"?

Of course not. You would either get some shanks *now*, or if you really screwed up so badly that you had no shanks already cooked, you might just fire *yourself* on the spot.

I was with a good chef recently as he asked a construction man to come back and fix a problem that the guy had claimed already to have fixed. The chef had to argue with the man, who only grudgingly admitted that the machine was still broken, and he was obviously hoping to avoid returning at all. The chef left shaking his head, saying, "I don't understand. How can people work like that? Can you imagine running a kitchen like that?"

Chefs, I found, really were different. They worked *hard*, often in incredibly hot places with no daylight for long stretches. It could make anyone a little zooey. Not long after I finished the book, I got a line cook job at a French Mediterranean restaurant that could get fairly busy. During the year before I came, two line cooks at different times left the line in the middle of service saying they had to go to the bathroom and never returned. This is firing yourself, but it won't make you a lot of friends on a Saturday night. I worked grill station, over both a stove and a wood-burning grill. I had to keep that grill really hot or the fish would stick to it and make my life miserable. I left a thermometer out on my station. It hit 150 degrees during service, which lasted on a Saturday from five-thirty to eleven. On most Saturdays you hit the ground running, and you do not stop moving until close. You're not just standing there, bearing the heat for five and a half hours after spending all day prepping your station. You're moving like an athlete. This is your court, your field. You're focused, you're thinking hard, you're organized, you have a dozen different dinners going on every second and they're going out that door and they've got to be perfect, they've got to look beautiful and that plate has got to be clean. One hundred fifty degrees. Let me tell you, that's hot. You can cook *yourself* that way. And I think some chefs really do cook themselves. Their brains get a little too hot, and they get a little *whacked*.

I saw this at the CIA. Yes, people had observed that chefs could be driven, temperamental, a tad stressed, but no writer I knew had been for so long under the same roof with so many chefs as I had at the CIA, long enough to see the patterns of chefness. I didn't intend to make blanket generalizations. Every chef wasn't a madman. Most weren't, in fact. But many were and are, and the very best chefs, I knew, as I wrote my book at what my chef, Chef Pardus, would call production speed, were a little twisted in the dark spaces of their brain. They had to be. They worked in a different world with different rules. They had to play by those rules in their own kitchens but everywhere outside their kitchens those rules no longer applied. It made some chefs angry. The world is not a kitchen. People move too slowly and too inefficiently outside a kitchen. They don't get things done, and sometimes they don't get there at all.

I don't understand, the chef said. *How can people work like that? Can you imagine running a kitchen like that?*

While I was writing my book about a culinary education, I found a book called *But Beautiful: A Book About Jazz* by a writer named Geoff Dyer. In a way it seemed more that the book found me, or maybe that Providence had sent the book my way as a conversation topic between it and me. Dyer's book is a semifictional account of famous jazz musicians, and a meditation on jazz itself, but the things he says about jazz happen to be the very things that hooked me on cooking.

Dyer notes the high early death rate and high incidence of drug abuse by the great jazzmen such as Charlie Parker and then suggests not that high-risk personalities are drawn to jazz but rather that there is something dangerous in the form, something dangerous in jazz itself. It wreaked havoc on those who played it, Dyer writes.

Cooking professionally in a first-flight kitchen has the same effect.

Lunatics and madmen aren't drawn to cooking; chefs become that way because of the conditions of the form, conditions you could measure; in hours, in actual degrees Fahrenheit. *I* had changed, hadn't I? I worked in 150-degree temperatures in a daylightless, cavernous kitchen, I ran through parking lots—I ran *everywhere* I went—and I got angry when the world moved less quickly and efficiently than my kitchen expectations. I'd changed in a *year.* Imagine the changes that happen over a *lifetime* of cooking!

My imagination was clearly out of balance. I had been living in and writing about a world that was a kind of imitation of itself, almost to the point of parody. The chefs at the CIA were actual chefs, but they were also playing at being chefs, projecting their chefness; they were not only teaching cooking but personifying their profession for their young and sometimes not so young students. So what I was seeing was the professional chef almost in caricature. What I'd witnessed hadn't been inaccurate, but it had been only one version of a vast picture.

M. F. K. Fisher, who got most things right about food and cooking, also achieved the balance I needed when, in 1949, regarding a remark by James Whistler, the painter, that "a good cook drinks," she wrote:

> If Whistler meant that all good cooks drink to excess, his quip is only superficially amusing, and is part of the grim picture drawn by statistics which show that in many great prisons there are more cooks than there are representatives of any other one profession. Most cooks, it would seem, are misunderstood wretches, ill-housed, dyspeptic, with aching broken arches. They turn more eagerly than any other artists to the bottle, the needle, and more vicious pleasures; they grow irritable; finally they seize upon the nearest weapon, which if they are worth their salt is a long knife kept sharp as lightning . . . and they are in San Quentin.
>
> On the other hand, some of the best cups I have ever downed were in the company of good cooks, men (and a few

women) who were peaceful and self-assured, confident that they were artists among their sincere admirers.

This was an accurate statement about the extremes chefs reached (I'll ignore the "artist" business, which I don't believe in). I knew chefs who weren't lunatics and madmen. I knew chefs who were. I knew gentle and sane chefs. I knew chefs who weren't stressed and crazy and angry that the world didn't operate like a professional kitchen.

In fact, the more kitchens I visited, the fewer examples of the chef as madman I could find. And in these kitchens the cooks themselves did not seem to hustle as hard as I'd hustled in Turgeon's American Bounty class. In fact I didn't recognize any of the qualities and attitude that I'd written about and witnessed at the CIA. Kitchens were messy. Plates were sloppy. Sanitation was not bad, but it was lax. People didn't hustle.

What's more, some of my most basic tenets of cooking were by appearances nonexistent. I would walk into many kitchens and see a stockpot boiling away like mad. This was unthinkable to me; you cook stocks at a low, low temperature, 180, 190 degrees, just hot enough to produce a bubble every now and then. This was the first fundamental you learned in class, but in the "real" world, chefs were cooking the bejesus out of their stocks and doing just fine.

Chefs worked hard, but they didn't *run* everywhere they went, for crying out loud. They didn't put on a tougher-than-thou show. Some were downright mellow. Some never moved fast. During my brief months on a hot line—the restaurant was called Sans Souci; its chef, a dashing Frenchman named Claude Rodier, had worked under the French chef Roger Vergé—I even used a chicken stock *base* (a heavily salted paste to which you add water, like a boullion cube). But, the chef explained, when I confronted him, we didn't use enough chicken stock to make the effort of fresh stock worthwhile. Chef Claude wasn't around much anymore, having taken over all the hotel cooking in which our high-end boîte was housed, but every now and then he'd walk the line before service spot-checking. And when he did, you made damn sure that your station was clean, that you were ready, that your sauces were perfect, just as you'd been taught in school. I saw what happened when you didn't. Angel, on sauté next to me, was not having a good day. His station, as usual, was a mess, and his sauces were gunky. Claude started screaming like a deranged Frenchman. *"What is zees? Merde! You must skimming, skimming, skimming all zee time! [Unintelligible French raving.] Merde!"* He did everything short of smacking Angel in the back of the head. Now this is more like it, I thought. And then, repairing Angel's sauces, Chef Claude turned to me and screamed, *"This is why we don't make chicken stock!"*

I'd had a glimpse then of what I expected from a real kitchen with standards as high as the CIA expected, but the next day Claude was back in another part of the hotel running banquets for nine hundred people. He scarcely cooked anymore. Probably the city's best chef, as far as talent, experience, and knowledge went, buried in banquet food. Fillets par-cooked and stacked in speed racks, thirty pounds of spinach cooked off in advance, chicken marked on the grill and cooled. A gold mine for this Marriott operation, and Claude was no doubt duly compensated. When he wasn't in our kitchen, things were mellow, and the restaurant still got great reviews and was booked solid every weekend.

So while I knew that what the CIA taught was valid and maybe existed somewhere, it wasn't the norm. Standards and expectations varied enormously throughout the country. And only rarely was it the stuff of my imagination, created in that bell jar–perfect atmosphere of the CIA.

But how could I reconcile all those things I'd learned by becoming a professional cook myself and studying the work of the professional kitchen? I had changed, but were the changes counterfeit? Was my entire attitude a kind of lie? Did I *really* need to *run* everywhere I went?

When I read in the local paper that my old acquaintance Michael Symon had been named one of America's ten best new chefs of 1998, I wrote him a note of congratulations and told him he'd be hearing from me.

One of the ten best new chefs in the country, huh? OK, let's see this. Michael Symon ran a loud and happy restaurant, the hippest place in the city, and now had earned some national recognition. This was not a Chef Turgeon or Chef Pardus kitchen. Michael Symon's kitchen, open to the whole rollicking room, was *fun* to work in. People liked it here.

He was serious about food, but there was always laughter. When he overheard Frankie, the bartender, tell me, "I'll never work for anyone else," Michael said to me, "He's blowin' smoke up your ass!" and let his laugh rip. Frank Rogers, former dishwasher, now sous chef, said, "I'm a Michael Symon lifer." These guys liked it here, the food was *happ'nin'*, the place was alive, and Symon had just gotten a ten best award. Most of the other chefs on the *Food & Wine* list ran expensive white table-cloth restaurants. The check average for the others was between forty-five and seventy dollars per person. They used luxurious items that warranted the high ticket, truffles and foie gras and beluga, products that impress foodie magazines but that don't make money. Michael Symon earned a ten best award doing thirty-dollar check averages and not a single entrée over twenty bucks.

How was he doing this? What was happening at Lola? What did it say about the nature of a chef and what it meant to be a chef in the real world of contemporary restaurants? And was he still making those in-credible calimari, those corn crepes filled with duck confit?

CHAPTER THREE

*L*iz stops at Michael, who's standing beside the bar with Jimmy, his heating and cooling guy. Michael turns toward her and says, "Liz, I could just kick myself for not—"

Liz has been walking hard in his direction. She has straight, long, red-moving-to-black hair and wears dark burgundy lipstick, which, with her black clothes, gives her the aspect of an urban femme fatale, a parallel to the hip urban neighborhood called Tremont, where Lola anchors one corner of the Literary Road and Professor Avenue intersection. She has stopped Michael dead by holding her palm to his face and saying, "Let me just." Seeing that Michael has clammed up, she continues: "We're missing a *million* invoices. All invoices that come in, go directly on that clipboard. Especially Ohio City Pasta."

Michael's dark brow knits, his full lips purse, and he nods quickly and seriously. "OK."

When he doesn't say more, Liz says, "I *know* where they are. They're all in your jeans pockets on the floor at home."

Michael's lips remain pursed. Given how hard it is to shut Michael up, Liz is obviously not exaggerating. When a voice over the intercom says, "Michael, Carole Chandler from Channel Three," he seems eager to get to the phone. Liz heads to the reservation book. Michael takes the call at the bar. It is a routine day. Matt Harlan shapes pierogies at his station on the line. Sous chef Frank Rogers sautés corn crepes and works on the soup of the day. And Courtney Churchin spoons angel food batter into individual-portion bundt molds, while sheets of phyllo, buttered, sugared, and sprinkled with nuts, bake in the oven.

"This is Michael," he says, taking a barstool seat. "Thank you. . . . Correct." The laugh. "Absolutely. . . . Fantastic." More laughter. "So you'll be here around. . . . See you then."

Michael doesn't look tired, but he claims to be dragging today. Last week was the *Food & Wine* celebration in Aspen, Colorado, where he cooked and served eight hundred portions of his lavender shortcake in two hours, racked by leg cramps from dehydration in that high, dry air. He hasn't quite caught up from that trip. Matt was off last night, so Michael worked the station, which got hit hard. Just when he thought it was going to be an easy night, Frank called orders for thirteen walleye, firing ten immediately, and the night went downhill from there.

The walleye's a big seller: herb-coated fillets served atop lobster-filled pierogies with a truffle-butter sauce. Matt made seven hundred pierogies the first month the dish was on the menu. Because it's the recipe Michael gave to *Food & Wine*, it will likely stay on the menu. Michael had to fight with the editors on his choice. *Food & Wine* wanted the slash and burn grouper. But Michael was the only midwestern chef on the list, so he argued for a midwestern dish. Thus a fish from the Great Lakes and pierogies, a kind of potato-pasta ravioli famous in these parts, his granddad's recipe (flour, potato, egg, chives, and sour cream). The editors relented.

Lola's kitchen serves from 4:00 P.M. till 1:00 A.M. on weekdays and an hour later on weekends, so nights are late. On the ride home he and Liz talked about how to tighten service to meet expectations heightened by the award. Michael usually sleeps five hours, but he slept nine and a half hours, not stirring even when Liz's alarm went off to get Kyle to camp and herself back to the restaurant.

Yet it's all part of what has become a normal day at Lola. By four o'clock he's put a chef's jacket over his T-shirt and gets behind the line to help with the prep. He'll work the line, and when it slows, he'll say, "Frank, give me five to schmooze?" When the line gets hit hard, he'll jump in to help get the food out. By six o'clock the room begins to fill, and the noise increases. By seven, when TV reporter Carole Chandler and cameraman Peter Miller arrive, most tables are seated—the first turn—and have begun to eat.

Carole, a short, sprightly blonde with vivid blue eyes and a complexion so blemishless and even as to seem unnatural, is twenty-four and a new reporter for WEWS, Channel 3. She finds Michael, who's schmoozing the crowd, introduces herself, and explains the drill, which begins with shooting B-roll, general footage for the story. They'll then do the tease and a brief interview, after which they'll leave and return at eleven for a live tease and then a live introduction and live conclusion. Or, as Carole describes it, "Live intro, tossed to a package, live out."

Michael strides toward the back, pushes through the swinging doors into the dishwasher's sink room, really just an aisle, and pushes back through two more narrow swinging doors into the open kitchen, which contains a tall, upright broiler, a deep fryer, and a Vulcan range with eight burners. Next to the burners is a small prep area for Abby, a high school student working the raw bar and garde-manger station this summer, desperate to go to culinary school. During service she opens oysters, plates the shrimp cocktail, mounds the salads, and fashions the desserts. There's scarcely room for a cameraman too, and Abby scoots out of the way while Peter, tall as a construction crane with the enormous video camera on his shoulder, films and interviews Michael, now rigged for sound.

Michael beams at the camera, puts his arm around Frank, and says, "This is Frank, my sous chef." Frank, twenty-eight years old, wears a beard and mustache but shaves his enormous cheeks. Ninety percent of his head seems to take place below his eyes, an impression accentuated by the slim black Lola's baseball cap concealing his thick brown hair. Frank sends the camera a toothy smile.

"And this is Matt," Michael continues; it's his nature to introduce his friend to a guest. "He's one of the cooks. We call him Chatty Matty because he never shuts up." Michael laughs, and so does Matt. Matt Harlan is twenty-two. He wears an earring and a neck chain and shaves his entire head, but frequently wears a Lola cap too, usually reversed. He's a skinny boy who might never have gotten into cooking if he hadn't been jumped at a party a couple of years ago and got his jaw broken. The broken jaw mandated a liquid diet. With slim nourishment, he got dizzy on the job, which at the time was roofing. Roofs were not good places to get dizzy in summer heat, so he found work of a lower order, grilling burgers and cooking pastas at a restaurant not far from his home in Lakewood, a suburb abutting Cleveland. His sister was good friends through Lakewood High School with Frank, and Frank told him that a spot on raw bar had opened up at Lola, and Matt took it. He'd work grill one night a week, when Jill, the grill cook, was off. Jill soon left for another restaurant, and Matt took over grill station full-time. Chatty Matty's come a long way fast, and Michael has high hopes for him. Matt is curious and eager to learn; fish butchering and sauté stations are the learning priorities now. Frank, on the other hand, just likes the job, and when I ask him what his goals are, he says, "I just want to ride this one out." His hope is that Michael will open a second restaurant and put him in charge. After a few moments he says, "When you ask a question like that, should I say, 'I just want to be the best possible cook I can be'?" Frank laughs. He's a solid cook, and Michael says he'd be in trouble if he lost Frank.

The cameraman never stops looking through his camera, even as he's conversing with Michael. He asks about Lola, and Michael gives the rote response: "Here we do American food with a Midwest slant . . . all very simply prepared but using very good ingredients."

Then the ticket machine begins to chatter, and a flurry of orders arrives. The cameraman departs to let Matt, Frank, Michael, and Abby get the food out. In the meantime he wanders the restaurant, shooting more B-roll and MOS footage. Given his size and the equipment and spotlight on his shoulder, he's not exactly inconspicuous. When a white stretch limousine pulls up to the corner, he pops outside to film. Inside, he asks waiters to halt so he can film the food they carry. "Can you stop for a second?" he says to a waiter balancing four plates of food and moving at a steady clip. When the waiter sees the cameraman blocking his path, the waiter says unequivocally, "No, I can't," and squeezes past, hot plates branding his forearms.

When the push of meals slows, Carole asks to film her tease. She stands before the service counter where finished plates come up, her

back to the cooks. Her designated word for tonight's tease is *And.*
Sometimes it's *Also,* sometimes *Plus,* and occasionally *Then.*

"*Aaaand,*" Carole says into the microphone. "I'm Carole Chandler.
Where can you find one of the hottest chefs in the nation? Right here.
In the city of Cleveland." As directed, Michael slides two finished plates
onto the counter: tuna, encrusted with coriander seed, seared, sliced
and served very rare over a seaweed salad, and the walleye with pierogies. He smiles sweetly, apparently embarrassed, at the camera.

"OK, stand by," Carole says.

Peter says, "Michael, work. I'm rolling."

Carole says, "Let's try it one more time."

Michael removes the plates from the service counter.

Carole takes a breath. "*Aaaand.* I'm Carole Chandler. Where can you
find one of the hottest chefs in the nation? Right here. In the city of
Cleveland." Michael slides the tuna and the walleye onto the counter,
smiling again, a little more embarrassed this time.

Carole thinks that one went pretty well and gets a nod from Peter,
but she says to Michael, "Let's try it one more time."

"I can't do it one more time," Michael says. Carole doesn't say anything, but waits for Michael to explain why not. "This is a table's food.
If we do it again, it'll be *cold.*"

Carole and Peter seem to have forgotten that they are in a restaurant
in the middle of service. They think for a moment and then say OK,
they'll go with one of the two they have. Michael shouts for a waiter to
run the food. Carole, Peter, and the camera equipment depart, and the
restaurant returns to normal. Almost. Michael has done this before, and
the effect is common. The commotion has distracted all the diners.
They've been slow to order and to eat, having stopped to watch the reporter and cameraman with his big camera and spotlight. The second
turn will arrive before the first is through, and the entire evening will be
out of sync.

By eleven o'clock, after two full turns, Lola bustles. Almost nowhere
else in the city has a kitchen that's still open, and none of this caliber,
but Lola is cranking (his colleagues told him he was crazy to set those
kinds of hours for his staff; no one will eat that late in Cleveland, they

said). Carole and Peter have returned. She'll do a live tease and then the story, a good package all in all, she thinks.

Michael has been miked, so when the story opens on local TV shortly after 11:00 P.M.—B-roll footage—his voice is distinct: "Hey, Frankie, will you get me two raviolis?"

Frank hustles to the freezer downstairs for ravioli. Carole's voice: "It's seven o'clock on a Wednesday night." The scene cuts to Michael jiggling a sauté pan for the ravioli dish, and he says, "The sauce for our potato and truffle ravioli is asparagus, fresh morels, a little bit of stock, salt, pepper, a little bit of truffle butter."

Carole: "But it may as well be Saturday. The reservations at Lola are booked, the guests are parading in, and everything receives the *once-over*. Because Michael Symon *knows* that every *meal* must hold up to the hype."

The story is quick. A short interview addressing why he returned to Cleveland (the city, still low on self-esteem, is ever-suspicious of people who remain here despite success), to which he responds with a crowd-pleasing answer: "I missed my home, I missed my friends"; more MOS shots, women disembarking from the stretch limo, happy customers with their impossible-to-get reservations, Carole's voice: "But once you're *in*, let the feast *begin*," and then to the live out: Michael slides two hot entrées to the counter, salmon with a horseradish crust, grilled and served on a red and gold beet salad with a horseradish vinaigrette, and grilled halibut on a roasted artichoke salad with red peppers, basil vinaigrette, and preserved lemon.

The bar is packed, and the crowd noise is strong, so Carole speaks loudly as the camera trains on the entrées to finish the live-out: "In simplest terms, because I am no chef, this is salmon over beets, and over here we have halibut with artichokes. Just two of the many dishes. And you know, he's really a modest guy. He credits the award to the whole Cleveland area, and saying that because there are so many fine restaurants popping in, day in and day out through the months and years, that Cleveland's developed, that that's why he got so much attention, with *Food & Wine* and other national press that's been coming to him as of lately."

Cut away to the anchors, snug in the studio. Carole choked on the live tease, and she more or less choked here. She knows it; her tendonitis is acting up, and nothing's gone right with this story. Judd Hambrick, the handsome anchorman, smiles warmly at his coanchor and says in a deep, sugary voice, "Well, he may be modest, but that food you just showed us speaks *volumes*."

"Oh, yeah."

"Thanks, Carole," says Judd. "Well, it sure makes you hungry, right? This next story should spoil your appetite for a late snack, though. More than half . . . ," and in comes a story about America's obesity. The story preceding Michael's concerned a one-year-old child who was found alive beneath a pile of garbage in the backseat of a car parked in the Cleveland Metroparks. Local news.

When an event such as this is done, Michael will usually head downstairs to the office for a Camel (cartons are provided free to the restaurant, along with Camel bar napkins and matches, so just about everyone employed here smokes, and smokes Camels). Frank can always shout down for Michael if there's a sudden rush. Frank has likely taken a cigarette just before Michael. The downstairs feels very much like the basement of a World War I–era building. The office is just past the grease trap and directly below the bathrooms—the white pipes and stack are visible above the desks—so there's always a little something in the air to make you glad for the cigarette smoke. Often Michael will smoke and take a look at the computer, which registers hour by hour what items have been ordered and bought, how much money has come in, how the bar is doing. It's a computerized version of the night, like a game or blueprint. If he wanted, he could simply watch the computer, and the night would unfold for him like a baseball game. He could see for instance, that by nine o'clock, forty-three walleyes had been ordered, and he could say, "Man, Chatty's gettin hammered!" Or, "Look at all the meals being served at the bar; no one's drinking." The computer has changed restaurant work dramatically. Shortly after Michael returned from Aspen and back at a station, two women spoke to him as he cooked.

"Mazel tov," said the first, referring to the *Food & Wine* award. "Sweet *stuff*."

The second woman said, "Congratulations!"

"Thank you," Michael called to them, then turned to lean out over the counter. "You know," he said, "without the computer, none of this would have been possible."

You'd think he was joking, but not after you see the computer.

So smoking and the computer provide the short breaks during the long nights. But often visitors arrive. On a night before the Channel 3 news story, Michael was reviewing the year's profit-and-loss statement when a loud voice bellowed, "O solo mio!" and heavy footsteps pounded the steep wooden stairs to the basement. The door flew open, and in barged a large, ominous figure in black: long black hair in a ponytail, black beard, long black leather blazer, black pants, and black shoes with tread about an inch thick.

It was Michael's vegetable guy, Tony. Beans and berries, and fancy mushrooms. Tony Anselmo, Anselmo produce, family business. Tony's been at the bar with his wife and some friends.

"Lemme see your new menu," he says after initial banter.

Michael tilts back in his chair and finds a loose sheet of legal paper on which he's written in block print produce items for the new menu. "Beets," he reads, "golden beets, cucumber, watercress, mesclun, arugula, red onions, peeled potatoes, ramps, portobellos, morels, haricots verts, red pepper, berries, carrots, basil, rosemary, chives, sage, truffle."

"No problem," Tony says. "Easy. So that and the basics." Tony pauses and then asks, "You wanna try any sauces or peppers out of a jar or anything like that because I know a—"

"I buy all the stuff fresh from you and make my own," Michael says with a smile. Michael asks how the morels are, they on their way out? Tony tells him about a man in Louisiana who grows them year-round, small and dry and perfect. Then Tony describes a company in New York called Urbani with all kinds of interesting items he can get for Michael: French foie gras, and truffles and various truffle-related products, truffle paste, truffle powder. "Man, if I could shit truffles," Tony says, and his face lights at the thought.

"Truffle powder?" Michael asks.

"Yeah."

"Let me see this list. Truffle powder." Michael tilts back in his chair, hands on head. "I wonder what would happen if you mixed it with flour. You mix it with flour, and you dust a piece of fish with it. I bet that would taste fucking *good*."

"They sell truffle flour."

"Lemme see this list. And I wanna see *prices* too."

"There's gonna be a big black Magic Marker line right down the price list!" They both find this uproarious, and in the middle of the laughter a server appears to inform Tony that his wife is leaving with or without him, so Tony scoots. Michael watches happily; he loves that guy. As he will tell anyone, Tony is one of the reasons he can keep every entrée below twenty dollars. He says that about most of his purveyors. They become his friends.

These are the two worlds, upstairs and downstairs, that Michael Symon straddles on his accelerating rise in the restaurant business. What he doesn't know at this point early in the summer of 1998, shortly after his *Food & Wine* award and an onslaught of local media coverage, is that it's about to become even more exciting. The bushy-haired man who often walks down the block from his house for a couple of Dortmunders, Stephen Michaelides, is hatching a plot to lure the prominent food writer and critic John Mariani to town, and Lola's going to be a prime draw. Cleveland restaurants have never before had any real national attention, and Michael has never cooked for a national food critic and writer, one who covers the entire United States and a good deal of Europe as well, someone with that kind of depth and perspective. He's received nothing but gushing praise for virtually his entire cooking career.

CHAPTER FOUR

*W*hen I returned a year and a half after I'd first watched him at Caxton, Michael Symon had become an enigma to me. Everything about him ran counter to what I'd learned and believed in about cooking, both the food itself and the method and intensity of the mind producing it. I believed all that I'd learned, absorbed into my heart, during my time at the Culinary Institute of America and all that had followed from there. I loved the classics. My favorite sauce was Sauce Robert, essentially a rich brown veal stock flavored with white wine, shallots, and mustard, perhaps the oldest sauce still in existence. Food didn't get more classic than that. I developed an appreciation for veal stock, an understanding and respect based as much on what you could do with it as with the idea of it, this neutral but potent essence, and this appreciation for veal stock soon became the kind of adoration usually reserved for great literature or symphonies. I believed in professionalism. I had been taught and believed in cleanliness and working clean. I believed in uniforms and uniformity. I believed in the relentless drive toward perfection under extraordinarily difficult and uncomfortable situations. I believed in the madness of chefs, a madness that was in fact an exaltation, born of high heat, hard labor, and unrelenting stress during work with beautiful, delicate, even sublime natural materials.

While he wouldn't have denied me my romantic vision of the profession, Michael Symon, a big, rumbling, hilarious fullback of a chef, seemed the antithesis of this and the antithesis of the CIA, despite the fact that he'd come out of that world and had loved the school and had graduated in the top 5 percent of his class in 1989. His first Cleveland employer remembers that Michael was rigid with CIA dogma; Michael remembers, "I was arrogant." But the CIA had given him what he needed to learn the rest, and learn it exclusively on his own; he had no chef mentor and likely never would. He had gradually but inevitably moved beyond the institute's rigors and regimens.

He was by his own admission a slob when he worked. There were no uniforms, and little uniformity, at Lola. Chatty wore a short-sleeve chef's coat that looked like a bowling shirt. Frank wore whatever was available on the wire hangers downstairs. You could wear whatever pants you felt like wearing. And tennis shoes were just as at home on the rubber mats of the kitchen as black leather kitchen clogs.

As for the food, almost nothing Michael did anymore relied on the classical French tradition. He didn't like meat-based sauces, sauces created from reduced veal stock, because they were both expensive and too heavy for his tastes. He made veal stock but used it in atypical ways (plain veal stock over roasted sea bass for instance—veal stock on fish!—just for a little moisture and flavor on the plate; a ladle to reheat and fortify risotto; a veal stock and cream combination for pasta sauce base). For meats, he favored vegetable coulis and vinaigrettes, reduced balsamic and port—and not much of them at that—concoctions we now call modern sauces. His roasted chicken, sometimes served on roasted potatoes, sometimes on whipped root vegetables, was just that: half a roasted chicken, which he bought boned and which he stuffed with mushrooms, nestled right down on those potatoes or root vegetables. The sauce? A few teensy squirts of reduced balsamic vinegar. Good twenty-year-old vinegar and powerfully flavored but less than a teaspoon of it on the plate.

This seemed crazy to me. One of the things you learn in culinary school and working in restaurants is that everything, but everything, gets a sauce. Nothing is complete without a sauce. You will never at a good restaurant be served a piece of meat until it has been sauced. Appetizers, salads, pastas, entrées, and desserts always, always got some form of sauce. Sauce is so pervasive sometimes it's the *only* thing you get, in which case it's called soup. Sauces are a big deal, the main flavor enhancer, the seasoning, the moisture, the counterpoint. Because meat-based sauces, sauces that begin as stock, are not easy and are easily ruined or bad—thick and pasty, tasteless, gummy, gunky, muddy, scorched, oversalted, underskimmed, fatty, greasy, wrong consistency, wrong color, insufficiently strained, cloudy—because so much could go wrong with a sauce, sauce was the true test of the cook, proof of the chef's subtlety and grace. As the chef and teacher Madeleine Kamman once said to me, "You know what, the sauce makes the cook, OK?"

So everything wanted sauce, but especially bland American-grown chicken. Serving chicken with a squirt of balsamic was ridiculous. And to be so antisauce generally, as Michael Symon seemed to be, was fool-hardy. The words of Chef Ron DeSantis, Polcyn nemesis and one of my instructors, to this day rings in my ears: "No dry food, OK, guys? Gotta *see* liquid."

Every now and then I'd make fun of Michael's plates by telling him they looked a little dry. He would say, "I know, we sell more wine that way!" and his laugh would rip through the air.

I hung out at Lola to watch and take notes. Sometimes I put on my chef's jacket and worked. I tasted food components and sauces (such as they were) all the time, and everything tasted good. But the plates just looked a little sloppy to me, a little dry, a little unconventional. I liked classical cooking, and if it wasn't classical, I at least wanted it to be *moist.*

One night at Lola I'd had as much observing and talking and note taking as I had energy for. It was about eight; there was a healthy but restrained crowd. When a seat opened up at the bar, I took it and decided to have some dinner. This way I could tell myself I was working when really I was just eating and drinking at the bar. Willfully, defiantly, hopefully, and skeptically I ordered the chicken, the roasted, sauceless chicken. Frankie the bartender made me feel at home, poured me a big zinfandel to try, then tapped the computer screen with his index finger, sending my order to the kitchen three feet to his left. Lola was warm and lively—as always fun to be in with Michael cooking and laughing and schmoozing, Chatty getting hammered on grill, Frank holding down the line.

Then Frankie the bartender set a napkin and silverware before me and delivered my dinner. It looked like the scores of other chickens Chatty sent out every night, tonight sitting on big cubes of roasted red-skinned potatoes, artichoke salad on top. But I focused on the chicken: Was it cooked perfectly, done but juicy? It was. But lo, what was this? At the bottom of my plate was a pool of mustard-colored liquid. I began to eat. I glanced up at Michael, who was on the line cooking.

He saw me and asked, "How is it?"

I said, "Perfect." And I thought, I'll be a son of a bitch. This was ingenious, a little mystery on a plate. Chatty didn't sauce this thing but with a squirt of vinegar. I'd watched him. So where did the sauce come from?

First, the potatoes. Courtney roasted them early in the day and cooled them. When the chicken was ordered, Chatty fired it, plopping the boned half chicken onto the grates of the broiler behind him (raw to perfect in ten or twelve minutes), then reheated those precooked potatoes with some red onion and arugula in a sauté pan into which he poured a little cream, some salt and pepper. The liquid helped reheat the potatoes evenly and added some moisture and the fat that made potatoes good to eat. When the chicken was done, cooking away on the broiler grill behind him, he poured the potatoes into the center of a hot plate and placed the chicken atop the pile, gave the plate an artful squirt from the balsamic squeeze bottle, and off it went.

By the time it reached me, the diner, the chicken had rested a few minutes, the juices redistributing themselves in the chicken; but it was also losing juices, and when you cut into it, plenty of juice ran out. The bird was stuffed with chanterelle, shiitake, and chicken-in-the-woods mushrooms, which are loaded with juice, and as they rested, they dumped their liquid. The chicken and mushroom juices fell over the potatoes, which were generously coated with seasoned cream. The falling juices and cream were then offset by the acid sweetness of the balsamic reduction. And there it was, a dish that sauced itself—with all the familiar components of a classical sauce: meat and mushroom juices, cream, and acid component. Not only was this ingenious, but it was light (the primary components were the natural juices of the chicken and mushrooms) and practical. From a service standpoint, it reduced for the cook the number of steps needed to finish the plate. You're in the weeds, got a million orders called, potatoes, chicken, vinegar, boom out the door. No dipping a ladle or spoon into sauce and pouring. This was not insignificant, and Symon strove for this kind of efficiency. "If I can't finish it in two pans, I won't do it," he told me about his rule for all dishes; everything on the menu could be cooked and readied for service in two pans or fewer. This impacted not only on the cooks and how many meals they could cook at once given eight burners and two ovens but on the dishwasher too, as any dishwasher will appreciate (and as any good chef will tell you, that dishwasher is one of the most important people on the team, so it's a good idea to appreciate him or her). Lastly, it affected Courtney, the day cook who prepped the base items for practically the entire menu. If that chicken had its own separate sauce, she'd have been the one to make it, and she had plenty to do as it was.

So this little self-saucing dish, and the ideology behind it, had a big impact on Lola. It also described for me one of the elements of Michael Symon's success. The products and the flavors were there, but they were enhanced by ingenious *mechanics* as well. The business of cooking was a craft—you worked with tools and materials—and he was mechanically versatile. He used to do a classical crème brûlée—adding fancy flavors like orange and ginger—but it was a traditional brûlée in concept and served in the traditional ramekin. Those ramekins kept chipping and breaking, though, and this was annoying and expensive. In order to get rid of the ramekins, without denying customers the popular crème brûlée, he came up with a crème brûlée napoleon: crème brûlée (cooked in the afternoon and spoonable as pudding at service) layered between sheets of crispy phyllo (baked along with the custard). Ramekin problem solved.

The goat cheese and leek tart was delicious, but a pain in the neck and took up too much space in the cooler, all those tart shells lined side by side. So he thought to wrap goat cheese and leeks in phyllo for a popover. Same elements, crust and filling, but the popovers were simple to make, they could be stacked so they took up no room at all, they were up for service in a snap, and they were delicious, with the crispy buttery phyllo, the hot goat cheese creamy inside, on top of watercress and portobellos and balsamic glaze.

Michael used his scraps beautifully, not just to use them. Scraps from salmon, grouper, and halibut, along with shrimp and mussels, became a black pepper linguini with a seafood puttanesca sauce, and because he did so much fish, these scraps were always very fresh; they were delicious scraps. Tuna scraps from seared tuna became tartare. The duck carpaccio he served at the Caxton Café—a duck tenderloin removed from the meaty breast, pounded paper thin—originated out of the need to use scraps. "I get a duck in that I'd have to sell for twenty-two dollars a portion," he explained, "but if I can pull off a tender and get seven bucks a carpaccio, it balances out. That's how you make money."

Many of these tactics were learned at the Caxton Café, where he first attracted city-wide attention. Only half his equipment worked; there was virtually no space to prep in and just barely enough room for one other cook during service. He *had* to learn ingenuity and versatility.

Unless you really read the menu carefully, you didn't spot the repeated items. The "Roasted beet salad with watercress and horseradish vinaigrette" was a starter, but place a horseradish-encrusted salmon fillet on top, and it became the salmon entrée. He offered "Goat cheese wrapped in prosciutto with artichoke salad," but replace the prosciutto with halibut, and it became "Grilled halibut over a roasted artichoke salad with red peppers, basil vinaigrette, and preserved lemon."

"With this space you've got to do stuff like that," Michael explained.

Yet I knew there was more to him than this kind of mechanical practicality. His restaurant was a booming success. The *Food & Wine* award said a lot, not only that his food ranked among the best in the country as far as new or little-known restaurants went but that it ranked that way serving inexpensive, easily prepared food. Thirty-dollar check average.

I watched a man and a woman, both dressed in pricey business clothes, approach the bar for an after-dinner drink early one evening. Frankie, with a ready smile and polishing a glass with a dry cloth, asked how the meal was. The man swirled his cognac and said, "I had the halibut. It was out of this world. Most expensive thing on the menu. Nineteen ninety-five. 'Gimme the most expensive thing on the menu.' *Nineteen ninety-five.*" The man chuckled and shook his head, then, noticing a little rack of Camels on the counter behind Frankie, said, "Hey, are those cigarettes for people who don't smoke but want an after-dinner cigarette?"

"They can be," Frankie said, and offered the man a cigarette and a light.

Lola was a friendly place. And it was distinctly American. Michael Symon was a distinctly American chef, unencumbered by the legacy of classical cuisine, mentored by no chef after he left cooking school, and serving the kind of food Americans liked to eat simply because it was how he liked to eat, achieving wonderful effects without the classics. He even went easy on the salt. He preferred things a little underseasoned. Every chef I'd met was a salt *maniac*, had to pull himself back from the salt like a drunk from the bottle. I'd never encountered a chef who went light on the salt, didn't even think one existed.

Courtney, the day cook, described Michael's food perfectly. "It's the kind of food you can do at home," she told me as I worked beside her one day. And yet to her it was completely new. "I never would have thought to put halibut on an artichoke salad," she said, referring by way of example to one of her favorite dishes.

A *Food & Wine* ten best award for serving "do-at-home" food. I took some ideas home myself. After my chicken episode I tried the idea with big pork chops. You don't want to serve them really rare, but you still want them juicy. So fill them with sautéed mushrooms, bread them, panfry them, and serve them on another simple sauce I'd made at Lola, leeks sautéed till tender, cream, mustard, salt and pepper, reduced till it's a nice consistency. Serve the pork chop on top of this. It's fantastic, and the mushrooms keep the pork extraordinarily juicy on the inside.

This was the style. Simple. He liked to use specialty items when he could; he loved sweetbreads and foie gras. And he put fancy things, such as herb oils, in squirt bottles. But whereas most high-end chefs will tell you to blanch the basil fifteen seconds for basil oil, shock it, puree it with oil in a blender, let it sit overnight, then strain it through cheesecloth, Michael instructed Chatty to puree a lot of basil with a lot of oil. And that was that. Yes, on the plate the oil wasn't bright, bright green, and there were specs of herb in it, but the plates at Lola were dark, the oil tasted great with the food, and Chatty had time to get other things done or to chat. Taste was what mattered. Michael served oysters on the half shell but didn't serve them with lemon juice and chili sauce. He made a special sauce that went deliciously and originally with the oysters. He called it his Asian Love Sauce: scallions, ginger, cilantro, sesame oil, vegetable oil, lime juice, and rice vinegar blended together. That's all it was, salad dressing, but it was great. Try it at home. Safe for children.

So, largely because he was the antithesis of everything I knew and had learned yet was also phenomenally successful (with the media, his customers, and financially), he was worth watching. Here might be a vision of what the culinary future was in America, this clamoring, lusty multiculture that so loudly lacked its own cuisine and a country so vast that even "regional" cuisines had to be subdivided. Not to mention a changing world and global access to farmers who could provide beautiful raspberries to American chefs in January, rendering two commands "Cook seasonally" and "Use local ingredients" at best obsolete and at worst adhered to with phony integrity. Certainly there was still logic and wisdom in cooking seasonally and using local ingredients (especially for home cooks), but what had once been dogma among America's best chefs was no longer so. America was still learning as it went, redefining itself continually. As was Michael Symon. He was a quintessentially American chef.

"Whenever I do a new menu," Michael Symon said. "I always go back to James Beard. He's so American."

Michael grinned. His big, Beard-bald head shone. He was behind the counter in the middle of a weekday afternoon, prepping and also thinking about the new menu, which he revises every two months or so. Beard is the man Michael always returns to for inspiration, ideas, and guidance. He loved the tips he'd pick up from Beard, such as adding a mashed hard-boiled egg to cake and scone batter to keep them moist. "It's weird, but it works," Michael said.

"So I've been trying to figure out a way I could do lamb," he continued. "Beard, every lamb recipe he has béarnaise with it. He says the things that go with lamb are watercress, eggplant and potatoes," all of which are common items in Michael's kitchen. "I could do a double-cut chop, a piece of lamb liver, and lamb kidney." Michael paused. "I'd *like* to do a béarnaise. I'm thinking I could whip some goat cheese into it." He nodded, thinking. "Then do a kind of potatoes Anna and stack it with eggplant. Béarnaise, maybe some mint oil."

On his legal pad he wrote:

LAMB THREE WAYS ROASTED GRILLED CHOP + LIVER + KIDNEY

EGGPLANT POTATOES + H_2OCRESS

MUSTARD BÉARNAISE + MINT OIL

Because it was out of context, perhaps, I didn't note that offal, potatoes Anna, and béarnaise all came straight out of classical French tradition.

And a few lines down, just floating:

LOBSTER LOUIS

An American classic popular in the seventies, crab or lobster salad with Thousand Island dressing.

It was the beginning of a new menu and would be developed over a few weeks. I watched it the way you watch new buildings go up, shapes emerging, details coming into view, friezes becoming distinct.

During this time his hardback copy of *James Beard's American Cookery* floated from the upstairs kitchen and bar to the office and back up again throughout the menu writing. It was always around. Michael read aloud how Beard liked his duck, flamed with gin. "Flamed with gin!" he bellowed with glee. "That's why I love this guy." Michael would laugh and say, "Listen to this." And he would read aloud from the book, Beard's words on creamed asparagus: "For some reason this used to be considered a rather dressy dish. Actually it is a waste of asparagus. Nevertheless, if it is to your taste, here's how you prepare it." Michael loved that the man would include the recipe for a dish he thought was a waste, because maybe somebody would want to know, maybe that was your taste. Beard allowed for all kinds of tastes. There was no French chef snobbery and absolutism about what was good and what was not, no European rigidity. Beard was as huge and generous as America itself.

In the essay on James Beard, published in her 1983 book *Masters of American Cookery*, the lively Betty Fussell compares him with the folk hero Paul Bunyan and the great American poet Walt Whitman, all in the same paragraph. Both comparisons are apt.

The man was big. A whopping thirteen and a half pounds at birth, in Oregon in 1903, he grew to be six feet four inches tall and weigh between 260 and 310 pounds. Fussell, describing Beard, quotes Whitman: "I am large, I contain multitudes." She notes that M. F. K. Fisher called Beard the literal and spiritual giant of the food world. And she herself says that Beard "has probably done more than anyone else to reshape the American palate to the freedom and largess incarnate in his own girth."

Beard laughed off purism and anyone who took food too seriously. Like his contemporary, the giantess of the food world Julia Child, who liked to say she took the la-di-da out of French cuisine, Beard encouraged people to have fun. "It's something you enjoy and have fun with, and if you don't, to hell with it," he said. His credo: "In my twenty-five years of teaching I have tried to make people realize that cooking is primarily fun and that the more they know about what they are doing, the more fun it is." Fussell concludes: "Like a good showman, Beard boosts the future of American cooking and believes that we are about to recover the gastronomic excellence into which he was born, but which declined rapidly in the industrialization of food before the war."

Beard died in 1985, but he would have been in ecstasy at the state of American restaurants and American cookery at the turn of this century, at the interest and enthusiasm about cooking generally, interest and enthusiasm that he helped initiate. A channel that airs food shows twenty-four hours a day? He would have emceed the entire twenty-four hours!

He would have been to it what Jerry Lewis had been for the muscular dystrophy telethons. He never would have left the set. He himself had the first-ever commercial cooking show on network television. Had he lived long enough, the TV Food Network might well have been called the Beard Network.

It was to this man and his book of American cookery that Michael Symon turned half a dozen times a year, a book that included recipes for cocktail snacks (cheddar cheese log), vegetables (potatoes fried with suet), entrées (boiled ham and cabbage, broiled squirrel), and great American desserts, such as baked Alaska. Beard's work would endure not only on the home cook's shelves but also in hip American restaurant kitchens.

CHAPTER FIVE

*C*ourtney Churchin arrived at Lola at 8:00 A.M. on Tuesday. She had wanted to get here earlier because Tuesdays were usually busy; the restaurant was closed Monday, so many of the big preparations had to be made fresh, and since she was off Sundays as well, most of the food she was responsible for was depleted. But the stultifying heat had lifted in the night, and this June morning was so lovely and cool that she stayed in bed late, just to enjoy the air. Courtney, like most Lola employees, lived near the restaurant with a gigantic chocolate Lab named Guinness. She tied him up outside her home when she left for work and could see him from the restaurant's back patio.

Courtney, twenty-six years old, dressed in a white T-shirt and black cotton overalls with white pinstripes. She wore heavy black lace-up boots. A black Lola cap contained her thick brown hair. Her eyes were large and warm and brown. She was six feet tall, her arms were extraordinarily long, and she worried that they looked too muscular; they were muscular, but with muscle spread out across that length, they just appeared solid. She had the body of an athlete, perhaps developed out of necessity growing up behind two towering brothers.

The first thing Courtney did in the morning, every morning, was clean the exhaust hood vents, which Matt had put in the sink and covered with water before he left at 2:00 A.M. Sunday. She scrubbed these down, then scrubbed the steel wall behind the stove, and lastly she climbed atop Matt's upright broiler and disappeared into the exhaust hood with a rag and can of stainless steel cleaner, only her lower legs and black boots visible, to finish the grease removal hour of her day.

Grease was the bane of restaurants. If you weren't after it constantly, it coated everything and then collected more of itself between layers of dirt. The color of this kind of grease, the grease that is simply omnipresent in the air, like pollen on a severe hay fever day, was black, but it was so fine and elusive you couldn't see it until it had solidified like tar on surfaces. It was especially at home in cracks. Sauté pans in virtually every restaurant kitchen in America describe the true color of grease best. These were not the kinds of pans you found throughout America's home kitchens. These were the kinds that turned black as pitch on the bottom from fired-on grease and carbon and were so bent and rippled from the heat and abuse of the cooks and dishwashers that there was not one flat square inch on the entire surface. Few rested flat, and some were as concave as miniature woks. That was your basic restaurant sauté pan. They were everywhere and contributed to the impression of the dark filthiness of restaurants that we have all come to accept, even perhaps prefer as "the real thing." This was what a professional restaurant was supposed to look like. Golly, some serious cooking must go on here; just look at how black, dirty, and dingy everything is. It was like this in the open Lola kitchen even though Courtney got after that grease every day. Grease was so elusive and tricky that there was even something down in the basement called a grease trap. Grease was wild.

When Courtney replaced the exhaust hood vents, shining, she could at last begin to work.

Courtney had been cooking for fun since she was six, professionally since she was fourteen, and had worked a variety of jobs at various types of establishments: a gourmet soup-and-sandwich joint, a butcher shop, an Italian restaurant, a caterer's. One of Michael's closest friends told her about an opening at Lola just when she needed a new job. She began on raw bar the next day. (Raw bar was where new cooks begin; this gave Michael a chance to watch new cooks work where they could do the least damage if they turned out to be bad eggs.) Courtney took the job, then moved to the line, then to day prep, which she liked. It gave her a half day of solitude and autonomy and space. She had

wanted to go to culinary school but found that the only desirable options, such as Michael's alma mater, were too expensive. So it had been
learn as you go for Court, the way most of the nation's one million
restaurant cooks learn the trade, a trade Courtney inclined toward even
as a child. Her divorced mother was a waitress when Courtney was
growing up, and, in the morning, while her mom slept, when her
brothers roused themselves, she would take her mother's dupe pad and
tray into her brothers' room to take their order. They would order
steak. She would return with carrots on the tray and call them soufflés.
Soon she was cooking for real and looked forward all week to Sundays
when she made omelets for the entire family. Now she cooked all day
for a living and in her off hours provided a local Cleveland bar with
happy hour food and tended bar down the street a couple of nights a
week.

But daily at Lola, she started in on the basic building blocks of the
restaurant's menu. After checking the walk-in and the coolers at Matt's
and Frank's stations, she wrote her prep list:

> Beets
> Wash arugula
> Apple pear
> Angel food
> Pudding
> Phyllo
> Lamb
> Goat ap
> Roast red peppers
> Grill chix
> Penne 2x
> Roast garlic oil
> Puttanesca
> Polenta
> Root mash
> Chatty mash

Tater mash
Stuff chix
Grill portobellos
Greek beans

A typical eight or nine hours of work. The problem today, however, was not that she had a lot to do, but rather that none of the day's deliveries had yet arrived and the walk-in coolers were bare. The lamb on her list was the lamb shank; she had to sear about thirty of them, then braise them, then cool and store them—a long process she'd tired of (she does it almost daily)—but the shanks were not here. She had to make all the desserts today, but the dairy delivery was late; without cream, eggs, and butter, dessert was tricky. The chocolate pudding and the angel food cake would have to wait. The polenta cooked in milk, so she couldn't start that either. About thirty beets must be roasted, cooled, peeled, and sliced for the beet salad but they weren't here either. The chickens that were to be stuffed lay frozen beneath a thin stream of running water in the dish sink. "I never know what I'll be able to do when I'm here," she said, heading back down to the dark, dank basement.

She began to gather a variety of pots, giant stockpots and smaller saucepots. Into a small one she measured out three cups of sugar, a cup of cocoa powder, and some cornstarch—chocolate pudding once the eggs and half-and-half arrive. She dragged a white bucket of peeled potatoes out of the cooler, then filled the tub with parsnips, turnips, carrots. She could get the root veg cooking. She could also start cooking the mashed potatoes that were used for the pierogi filling and the crab tater tots. Outside the cooler was a huge tub of red onions. "Michael uses red onions for everything," she said. "I've never seen him use anything but red onions." She loaded a half dozen of these into the tub. She gathered a dozen apples and pears each, a case of Roma tomatoes. The tomatoes she'd blanch and peel for the puttanesca sauce. The apples and pears must be peeled, cored, sliced, and stewed in a wine enhanced with fresh-chopped rosemary and pepper, later in the day to become dessert tarts.

Frank was off today, so she also had to make the soup of the day. She paused for a moment, thinking, then filled another pot with black beans.

Having gathered all the materials that were available, she began to haul them upstairs to the kitchen.

In addition to cooking the soup, the root veg, the puttanesca, the shank, she'd wash arugula, which would be sautéed with bacon and served as a bed for both the sweetbreads and the calf's liver. She would roll delicious thin slices of prosciutto around small handfuls of goat cheese. At service Matt grilled these and served them on the roasted artichoke salad; Courtney roasted, peeled, and cleaned a dozen red peppers, which were a component of that artichoke salad. She grilled a couple of dozen chicken breasts for the penne pasta—chicken, cream, goat cheese, and rosemary—the mac and cheese. She'd also cook off two batches of penne. Early in the day she threw a few dozen peeled cloves of garlic into a bain-marie, filled it with olive oil, and set it on a low back burner; when the garlic was the color of caramel, the oil would be a garlicky olive oil and would be poured into bottles of fresh herbs, dipping oil for bread. She'd grill portobellos, served with the polenta she'd made and the arugula she'd washed, for the sautéed calf's liver entrée. Finally she'd make the crumbly tart crusts to bake her apple and pear filling in, then bake two large sheet pans of layered phyllo dough for the crème brûlée napoleon. These last items would be in the oven when the kitchen opened for service at four, by which time Courtney would have prepped components of two-thirds of the menu's appetizers and entrées and all the desserts.

She did this day in and day out, winter and summer. Only occasionally did the routine vary. For instance, last February, the pilot light in the stove had gone off, so when she turned the oven on to full bore, it did not light. A couple of hours later, with the burners on the stove lighted, she opened the oven door. The flame from the top burners ignited the gas in a single terrifying rush, blasting Courtney three feet back and three feet into the air so that she landed, seated, on the prep counter. She immediately took off her chef's jacket, which she wore in winter because the basement was so damp and cold, filled it with ice from the machine downstairs, and packed her face in the ice, removing it only to call Michael and Liz (unreachable), then Rob, one of the waiters, who rushed to the restaurant and got her to the hospital. It treated Courtney's first-degree burns and told her she'd been smart to pack her face with ice.

In nine days she was back cleaning exhaust vents and searing lamb shanks. It was the life of a cook.

Most days Matt and Frank arrived around noon. On the day of their first annual evaluation meeting with Michael and Liz, the first thing Frank did was make himself a quick mac and cheese. This annoyed Courtney because she was trying to work on the same stove. Matt entered the cooking area, but he mainly chatted, and the talk was so banal and pleasant as to not be worth writing down or even remembering, like most words uttered here. He was just chatty. Michael explained to Liz that day, "He needs an hour of social time before he can begin work."

Courtney was smack in the middle of her day, and the two-man commotion threw off her momentum. "I work hard all morning, and then you guys come in here all in a good *mood*," she told them. They continued to chuckle and make banal and pleasant cracks. And Courtney continued to be annoyed and to work. They were like brothers and sister.

Matt and Frank sat at the center table, B-4 (bar four), a tall table with high chairs and banquette for two facing the bar and kitchen. They chatted some more as Frank finished his mac and cheese.

"OK," Michael said, striding into the main arena. "Who wants to go first?" Matt was nervous about this meeting, so when he and Frank looked at each other to decide, both shrugging, Matt let Frank go first. Matt waited it out, began to gather some of his product, check his station. He knew he was just learning; he was still a wiry little twenty-two-year-old who barely had his foot in the adult world. He cooked like mad five nights a week, but he didn't know the first thing about food, couldn't tell you what mayonnaise was, for instance, or that the meat he cooked every night, hundreds of portions of it, continued to cook even after he had taken it out of the heat. And yet he was humble and eager to learn these things. Frank, while a more skillful and experienced cook, making more money, and the man in charge when Michael and Liz were gone, just wanted to "ride this one out."

Twenty-minutes later Frank wore a grim face as he sent Matt into the evaluation meeting. He nervously dried his hands with a side towel as he stepped into the dining room where Liz and Michael sat before a large plate glass window, both of them smoking Camels. Matt sat, and his first words were: "Skip the bad stuff. Go right to the good stuff." He chuckled, clearly anxious.

These were the first evaluations Michael had done. He initiated them as a way to take stock regularly of where everyone stood, to address skills and compensation. He didn't want someone coming to him four months from now asking for a raise; now was the time to discuss it. Few problems would be aired because Michael addressed problems as they arose day to day. Matt was nervous nonetheless. He woke ambitious and shaved his head clean, so it was round and shiny as a cue ball. He wore a T-shirt beneath his cook's shirt, the retro fifties' bowling shirt look. He had a ring in his left ear and a thin gold chain around his neck.

Michael, seated in the banquette against the brick wall, folded his hands on the table, white paper covering white cloth. Liz sat in a chair diagonally opposite Michael, one leg over the other and tapping her cigarette in the ashtray.

"There's not a lot of bad for you," Michael said. "There's not a lot of bad for anyone. But the first thing is, when Liz tells you to shut up—"

"He's already learned that," Liz said quickly.

"You know that part OK?"

"I learned that part real quick," Matt said, nodding and laughing, and everyone laughed.

Michael finished laughing himself, extinguished his cigarette, and said, "Matt, I think that since you started here, seven, eight months ago, you've taken tremendous strides. You're a very teachable person, you ask questions, you pay attention. I'm very happy with how far you've come. Essentially being a guy who could barely cook a hamburger to working the line here and doing a fantastic job with your presentations and your temperatures and everything else."

"And you've got a great temperament," Liz added. "You never get flustered, that I've seen. You produce. And you can still talk to *me*."

"And I can't," said Michael, laughing. "I get in the weeds, I'm like"—Michael screwed up his eyes and pushed out his lips—"'Liz, shut up!' When I get weeded, I cannot carry on a conversation."

Liz took offense and said, "Hey, I don't come up and say, 'So, guys, what's goin' on?' It's important."

"Like I said," Michael continued, "I'm thrilled at the progress you've made. I think you still have a long way to go, but I think you'll progress as quickly as you want to." Matt nodded gravely as Michael talked. "As I was telling you guys yesterday, when Liz and I open a second or third spot, you will be a sous chef, like Frankie is here, there. I truly think you'll progress to that point. Now that you've got your station down, I want to start cross-training you on sauté, so that once you get comfortable with the new menu, we'll move you over a day or two a week. When you're completely cross-trained, then you should start learning some of the more prep-intensive things, like how to butcher fish. It's important that you know that."

Matt nodded quickly and said, "That's what I wanted to learn next, fish."

"And the next big step for you, I think, is sauces, sauce work. I spoke briefly about this yesterday, but on nights when we gotta make stock, as soon as it slows down at ten o'clock, we gotta get the bones roasting and ready to go, or else we run into what happened the other day: We're rushing the stock, we can't get it to a boil and skim it properly before it starts cooking all night. Then we get a cloudy stock, and the flavors are all right, but you can't fix the clarity. On that kind of stuff you guys gotta focus a little more at the end of the night. I know on Saturday night when we do two hundred fifty, two hundred eighty covers, the last thing you want to think about is making sure the kitchen is cleaned perfectly before you go home. But it's important that Courtney comes into a clean kitchen in the morning and there's not shit all over the place. You forget to do it for a day or two, and all of a sudden you've got an hour project on your hands." He paused, then concluded, "That's about it. Some people, it might annoy them that you talk so much, but it really doesn't bother me."

"My mom likes it," Matt said, and they laughed.

Liz said, "We're bumping you up."

Michael nodded and said, "We're putting you up to twenty-three five. You're at twenty-one now. It's another hundred dollars every pay period. And the other thing is I know you owe us some money."

"We're wiping the slate," said Liz.

"For your first seven months of hard work. So every pay period you don't have to say, 'Mike, I'll give you the next one.'"

Michael and Liz laughed and joked. When Matt needed money to visit a girlfriend in L.A., Michael and Liz gave it to him, and today they reminded him that when he needed to get laid, they were there for him. Michael and Liz laughed some more at this, and Michael added, "And we don't want to hear it when you haven't been!"

Michael smashed out another cigarette and said, "As we mentioned, we're working on a benefits package. You want to get it, you can start paying it."

"We'll match you fifty percent," said Liz.

"And next year you'll have been here almost two years, you'll get benefits."

Matt looked mildly awestruck and said, "I haven't had benefits since I was in high school."

"Me either!" Michael laughed. Then he said, "And that's about it. We think you're doing a great job."

"Frank got me scared for no reason?" he said.

"That's it."

Still seated, Matt said, *"Cool."*

Michael said, "Now hurry up and make some fucking pierogies. We're gonna get hit at five."

Matt stood, bowed his head, and said, "Thank you," before hustling off.

Michael pulled out another cigarette and said, "Thanks, brother," and they waited for Courtney.

When they told her about the raise and about how they were wiping *her* slate clean—she too owed them money—Courtney's mouth dropped open. And then, apparently mystified, she said, *"Why?"*

Liz grinned and said, "Because we *can*, you gotta problem with that?"

In the dank basement Matt got to work on the pierogi dough. He stood before a large plastic salad bowl. He had put three cups of sour cream into it, three-quarters of a pound of butter, cracked a half dozen eggs into it, handful of minced chives, salt and pepper. He slid his hands around in the goop to mix it. Then he added twelve cups of flour in four cup increments. Pierogi dough.

The recipe was now perfected and consistent, but at first Michael couldn't get it to work, so he called his grandfather, who'd given him the recipe, and said, "Gramps, this dough isn't coming out."

Gramps said, "You put flour on your board?"

"No."

"One of the ten best new chefs in the country and you don't know to put *flour* on your board?" Gramps asked.

Somehow, when Michael tried it again with a well-floured board, the dough came out great. "I'm not very good with recipes," he admits. "When I try to follow recipes, I get so focused on the recipe that I lose all my common sense."

Matt made several batches of dough in the same quantity—seventy-five pieorgie batches—because the dough came out perfectly that way; when he tried to double it, it didn't work. He or Milton, the Honduran dishwasher and indefatigable prep cook, would roll the dough out after it rested, then cut it into circles and form the pierogies into half-moon shapes around a potato and lobster meat filling. (Milton stood for hours peeling crates of tomatoes, peeling and slicing hundreds of beets, and shaping thousands of pierogies, before service started and he got really busy. When I asked Milton what his least favorite job was at Lola, he didn't understand. His English was not perfect. After I rephrased the question in various ways, he shook his head and said, "Nothing. I like to work." On his one day off, he said, he liked to drink beer. He used to like to drink beer all day long, but it was a new year, he said.) The potato dumplings he and Matt made would be boiled and then reheated in a sauté pan with a truffle butter sauce.

Frank meanwhile whipped up some corn crepe batter. Fresh corn, red and green bell peppers, blended in a food processor with a standard crepe batter of flour, milk, eggs, and butter. He'd make about a gallon of it to last a few days. Then he'd take it upstairs, and last thing before service he'd cook off some crepes. They would be filled with shredded duck confit (Michael confits his duck with cinnamon, cumin, and a little brown sugar), scallions, and his own barbecue sauce. It was a great dish. His barbecue sauce was, he said, "the best." He made a fuss over the secret ingredient, which he wouldn't reveal, and then confided that it was espresso beans. The crepe itself was a great vehicle for rich meats. He'd been doing it for years and began by filling it with chorizo.

The corn crepe never left the menu. The day I met Frank a year and a half earlier, he was making corn crepes. He was still at it, and probably would be for as long as he worked for Michael, which he predicted would be for life, the life of a cook. We made some rough calculations. Frank was very near or had already surpassed the ten thousand corn crepe mark. He smiled proudly when we arrived at this number. The Cal Ripkin of corn crepes.

Summer days continued pretty much along these lines. Winter days continued pretty much along these lines too. But with the local press following the *Food & Wine* award, in addition to normal business, Lola remained booked solid during prime dining hours and grew progressively busy in off hours. They could offer just about anyone a four o'clock dinner reservation or an eleven o'clock reservation. They were serving so much food that by Friday of that week even Frank got a little quiet as the ten-hour service approached, "thinking," he said, "of all the things I've got to do and the time I've got to do it." The open kitchen was crowded at three on Friday. Michael butchered a whole salmon. Frank sliced portobellos that Courtney grilled earlier, then stirred the soup, thanking Abby aloud. They had too much grilled chicken left over, and when Frank asked what kind of soup he could do with it, Abby suggested chicken chowder. As Abby moved through her mise en place, Frank quickly diced potatoes and dumped them into the creamy soup, stirred again, then asked Michael to taste. Michael had salmon all over his hands so Frank spoon-fed him as Court waited for room to get at the oven. Michael burned his tongue on the soup, and now couldn't tell what it tasted like. He threw the head of a salmon into the garbage. Courtney squeezed behind Frank to pull out two dark sheet trays, shaking her head. "I burned the phyllo." It had been a good day, but then everyone else arrived, she lost her momentum, and the day slipped away. She turned with the hot sheet trays, and set them down on Frank's chopping surface at the exact moment Frank turned to the stove—as though they were connected at their backs. There was no room for Matt, but it didn't matter because he was on the other side of the counter eating Kentucky Fried Chicken and chatting. He was in good shape, just a few more pierogies to do and the vinaigrette. When Courtney squeezed past with the sheet trays to dump them steaming into the dish sink, Frank pulled out a plastic tub of batter and got to work on the corn crepes.

An hour later Michael was in the office playing with the computer, checking last night's numbers. Twenty halibut and thirty-one walleye (with ninety-three pierogies) were the top sellers in a night that served 180 people. Not bad for a Thursday night. Matt entered the office and said, "Gimme the vinaigrette, bro."

Michael squinted and looked at the ceiling. "Cup a horseradish," he said, pausing for Matt to write it down. "Four ounces white wine vinegar, four slices of beets, couple egg yolks, eight ounces of olive oil."

A few minutes later Matt returned to the office with a food processor bowl containing what appeared to be pink soup. "It looks loose," he said.

Michael dipped a finger in to taste, then said, "It's a little sharp. Add some more oil. That will help thicken it up too." Matt paused staring dumbly at the bowl. Michael saw that Matt didn't know *how much* oil.

Michael began to speak, but Matt shouted over him, "I'll figure it out," and he departed.

Michael called out to the other room, "Drizzle in about six to eight ounces of oil."

"I'll figure it out!" Matt shouted over him. Then to himself but loud enough to hear, "I figure six to eight ounces of oil, see how that works."

To Michael's right, on the desk, among cigarettes, matches, magazines, loose phone messages, a Rolodex, and a phone was a yellow legal pad containing the burgeoning new menu, written in pencil, all caps in Michael's uniform print:

APPS RAW
—OYSTERS ON THE ½
—SHRIMP   NEW SAUCES
—BELUGA
—TUNA TARTARE W/TANGERINE OIL
—LOX TEQUILA CURED W/OHIO CORN RELISH + LEMON CREME FRAICHE

APPS + SALAD
—CORN CREPE (SAME)
—PAN-SEARED SWEETBREADS W/FIG COMPOTE + ARUGULA
—KNUCKLE (SAME)
—HOUSE SALAD (SAME)
—CRACKLING SALAD???
—

MAC + CHEESE
—POTATO TRUFFLE RAVIOLI W/BROILED LOBSTER, CHANTERELLES +
    LOBSTER BUTTER
—PENNE PUTTANESCA W/SHRIMP, MUSSELS AND SEAFOOD

He lit a cigarette and hovered over the pad, staring at it. Liz entered, dressed in black, and said, "Michael, Del Spitzer is here. They say they made reservations, but there's nothing there, and the book's filled." Del Spitzer was a famous car salesman in Cleveland. In the seventies and eighties you couldn't turn on the television without seeing a commercial for his Dodge and Chrysler-Plymouth dealerships. Now the Spitzer name was attached to an Auto World, Buick, Chevrolet, Ford, and Mitsubishi establishments, among others. Del and family were regular customers and Friends of Lola. "Can you call Doug and see if they'll come a little later?" Liz asked, wanting to squeeze the Spitzer four-top in. He nodded, picked up the phone to call Doug Petkovic, a general manager of another popular Cleveland restaurant called Moxie.

"Peanut," Michael said softly to Doug's wife, "it's Michael." He talked some golf, the usual opening subject before getting to the point. "Could you and Doug come about a half hour later?" Doug wasn't back from golfing yet, so it would work out perfectly. Michael relayed this to Liz, who was grabbing a quick smoke. Then he said, "Honey, I was thinking of doing the potato ravioli with chanterelles, and lobster, and I'll mount the lobster stock with a little truffle butter."

"Mmm, that would be excellent" Liz said, then departed to seat the Spitzers.

Michael loved the truffle butter, a good high-fat butter loaded with chopped truffle. It's the perfect substance with which to finish an elegant sauce.

Michael headed upstairs to see how the night was starting. The room was only half full, but Fridays always seem a little out of sync for reasons he can't explain. "Fridays are weird," he says. "It's like amateur night." A couple of no-shows, and several tables that asked to be seated on the patio left the dining room open. As Michael leaned on the counter to speak with Frank, Del Spitzer, seated at the VIP platform table, center of the restaurant, called out to Frank, "Hey! Is that fella bothering you?" A request for Michael to pay them some attention. Del chuckled heartily. Michael smiled happily and walked to their table, laughing and saying hello and shaking hands and asking how everyone is this evening. One of the women at the table uttered the perpetual question, and Michael answered with glee: "Nothing's that good, but we try very hard!" And his laugh pealed through the room.

He returned to the office, sat and thought, then wrote, "PEA SHOOTS, TOMATOES, XTRA VIRGIN." He said, "I gotta think what kind of noodle I'm going to put with it." He wrote, "LAMB BOLOGNAISE." He said, "Grind down my scraps." He paused. "If I get my lamb frenched, it brings down my price." He crossed out "LAMB BOLOGNAISE." An hour later he wrote, "LAMB BOLOGNAISE W/ WHIPPED RICOTTA QUENELLES."

The phone rang, and he answered. With a voice that seemed almost docile, he said, "Lola. . . . What night are you looking for?" He sent the call up to Stephanie, the hostess, who presided over the reservation book. Calls were typically either that or requests for directions. The entrances to the Tremont district were odd, and most of the city seemed to know where it was but had not a clue how to get there. The men usually called for directions from their cars after they were lost. Once Michael had two needy drivers on different lines at the same time. After determining the location of the first, he instructed the driver to make a U-turn on the Lorain-Carnegie Bridge, go back to the first light, make a left, then another left, then a right on West Eleventh, a left on Professor, and Lola was on the corner. He clicked over to the next driver, who, in explaining which bridge he was on, suddenly cursed loudly and said, "Goddamn car just cut me off to make a U-turn!"

Michael shouted, *"Follow that car!"*

Michael wrote "TRIO OF LAMB GRILLED W/CHOPS LIVER + KIDNEY W/EGGPLANT POTATO ANNA + GOAT CHEESE." At seven-thirty another item appeared: "GRILLED SALMON IN SWISS CHARD OVER ASPARAGUS W/CHANTERELLE + SMOKED BACON."

Later in the evening the man with the bushy hair appeared: Stephen Michaelides. He arrived with his wife, Jeanne. Jeanne—with final *e* pronounced, Jeannie—was tall and slender with legs that didn't end, a head of beautiful brown curls, enormous brown eyes, and a gigantic smile that was all shining white teeth. She was a bombshell. She played the dizzy broad, but she was really smart as a whip. They asked for a seat on the patio and ordered drinks. They'd eaten at a different restaurant tonight, but they were looking forward to next weekend. Stephen had made reservations here at eight on Saturday night. And he would be bringing John Mariani, the famous food critic and food writer. His letter campaign had worked.

CHAPTER SIX

$\mathscr{S}$tephanie Joy Thrun, Lola's hostess, bolts awake the following morning thinking about the reservation sheet. Stephanie's hair is dyed orange in patches; with clips, she arranges it into bizarre patterns, kind of like a shifting mountain range. She wears neon-colored formal wear, platform evening shoes. Green eyeliner extends the curves of her upper and lower lids, crossing to form a fishtail. "I'm not the suburban type," she explains. Michael doesn't mind the wacky outfits; they fit the Tremont scene, and he says all the old Jewish ladies from the suburbs adore Stephanie's clothes. Stephanie is the soul of confidence, and no matter how busy the night gets, she never changes her long, lazy stride. But today, she confides to Liz when she arrives at work, she's nervous. Liz too admits that she couldn't sleep, thinking about the reservation book.

Amy will join Frankie at the bar. Amy's a twenty-nine-year-old classical dancer. She used to live in New York, danced and taught at a dance school in Portland, Oregon, for a couple of years, then decided to move back to New York. "Where else can you wake up on a Sunday morning, read the paper, and then decide to take a flamenco class?" she asks. She returned to her hometown, Cleveland, "to regroup," and she never left. Last night while working the bar, her contact lens popped out, so today she wears her thick black Elvis Costello–style glasses. When she hears Stephanie and Liz mention the reservation book, she confesses that she *dreamed* about it last night.

The book has never been so full. Four complete turns are scheduled tonight for all tables. Some tables have five turns.

The kitchen is empty at four o'clock. All the cooks are downstairs. Courtney arrived early because she had so much to do. She's just finished braising the shank. Michael is already in his chef's jacket and Lola cap, and he's hustling. Moments ago he walked into the office and found sous chef Frank seated, rocking back and forth, his face in his hands. Some gentle questioning reveals that Frank's crepe batter wouldn't hold together. It is in fact a crepe crisis: Lola is now open for business, and Frank has no crepes for one of the most popular items on the menu. Together with everything still to do, he feels overwhelmed and has had what might be called a small mental breakdown.

"I'll make another batch," Michael tells Frank. Frank stops rocking and, dazed, looks up at Michael as if from an abyss.

Outside the office, next to a thrift shop couch on a table with a food processor, Michael scribbles a quick recipe on a paper napkin: corn, 1½ cups flour, 2 cups milk, 4 eggs, butter. He's added a little more flour and an extra egg to the typical batter. He suspects humidity is the problem. The restaurant is very warm. Over the July Fourth weekend, Jimmy, his heating and cooling guy, will install a twenty-thousand-dollar air-conditioning system, but until then cooks and diners have to sweat it out with the old, insufficient unit.

Michael stops, squints, and turns. "Courtney, what smells funny?" He starts poking around in some used pans that people leave in the middle of the black concrete floor until Benny, the pot washer, can get to them.

"The pan I did the shanks in?" she asks. "It always smells like that."

He pokes around in the big six-inch-deep hotel pan the shank cooked in. Some thick brown sauce has stuck and burned on the bottom. He winces and goes back to the crepe batter.

By four-thirty Matt, Frank, Michael, and Abby are on the line. Servers finish their side work. The restaurant is quiet and as serious in tone as it ever gets. The first tables are seated. Frank finishes a cream of tomato soup, pours it from the pot into a six-inch hotel pan that fits in an electric steamer. Michael sautés crepes. "*My* crepes are *perfect*," he says. Frank shakes his head and groans. No one likes to get beaten by crepe batter. Michael, working two pans, flips each, then slides one after the other onto an overturned sheet pan to cool before stacking them in the cooler at his station. The printer chatters, and the third ticket of the night scrolls out of the machine. Michael tears it off, reads it, and slides it into the ticket holder on the oven shelf above the burners. He runs his fingers over the two tickets already there, then says to Matt, "Fire two salmons, medium. Fire a salmon and a walleye; that's three salmon and a walleye all day."

Turning away from the line, Michael calls to a server, "Joe, get all the servers together real quick." When they gather at the service counter, Michael explains the soup of the day and a new dessert, a root beer float. He wasn't going to serve it yet; the root beer isn't quite ready. A man who owned a local microbrewery walked into the restaurant asking Michael if he wanted to develop his own Lola brew. Michael said, no, but can you make me a root beer? He hopes to develop a root beer spiked with ginger. It is not quite there, but the weather is so hot he thinks the dessert will do well. He instructs the servers how he wants it served—ice cream in a glass, a full bottle of root beer on the side—and dismisses them.

"Hey, Dori," Michael says. Dorian Reminick is the twenty-one-year-old busser, dressed in a short-sleeve black body T-shirt. In appearance he's a kind of cross between Sal Mineo and Dracula. "I was born in Ethiopa, raised by Cubans, and live in Cleveland," he says, nodding and smiling, knowingly. When you ask him his last name, he says, "It means saddlemaker in Russian," and smiles knowingly. "Dori," Michael says with emphasis, "every table that's cleared, tell me. We've got four turns tonight."

Matt has put up three salmons and a walleye, and Michael calls for the server. Tickets arrive gradually now, and the room is not yet full, but Michael's got to keep everything moving just as fast as if the room were full; he can't allow slack on any tables even though the restaurant is calm and quiet. They figure an hour and a half for the first turn, because early diners typically don't take as long as later ones, who tend to drink more and linger longer. The temptation at this hour is to take your time, go easy—what's the rush?—but it's critical that these early tables turn as scheduled or every other turn will be late; they'll never catch up, and the last turn will be an hour off.

Now that they're open and serving, Liz smiles easily, schmoozing with the customers. Everyone has been so worried about the reservation book that they've overprepared. That's how it always is, they agree. The nightmares come without warning. The nightmare is the surprise surge at midnight on Friday or nine on Wednesday. All is smooth tonight. The ominous sounds of the band Morphine end and a jazzy Billie Holiday disk engages.

By six-thirty the first turn is finished. Michael, Frank, Matt, and Abby have cooked perfectly. Michael shakes Frank's hand and heads downstairs for a cigarette. By seven he's back working the line, a row of tickets on the oven shelf fluttering in the rising heat of the burners. The room is filling, and the volume increases. A woman and her companion, a dapper gentleman, take a seat at the bar to wait for their table and have a drink. They made reservations ages ago but have since heard so many good things about the restaurant they're excited to be here. The woman asks her companion which one of the four people cooking is the chef. When told who it is, she watches with interest, then says, "He's *so* serious."

When Michael's hanging out, prepping, or working the room, he is all loudness and laughter. But when he's cooking—as he is now, working several pans and expediting—he's *focused.* The woman sips her wine, continuing to stare. She says, "He kind of looks like Billy Bob what's-his-name."

"Thornton," says her companion, nodding.

In addition to his broad shoulders and enormous back, Michael's head is likewise big, as well as round, completely shaved. "I got a perfectly shaped head," he argues, but then, noting his prominent brow bone with heavy dark eyebrows, he'll concede, "I'm a little Cro-Magnon; I got a little bit of an overhang." Then he will laugh like Tigger the Tiger and say, "I haven't *evolved* yet!" and laugh some more.

At seven-thirty the restaurant is full, the bar is two deep, and a crowd gathers at the door, waiting to be seated. Michael pauses for a moment to look at the room, the bar, and the crowd at the door, as if evaluating approaching weather. Then he says softly to himself, "Oh, boy. We're gonna get *mushed*."

He finishes a few dishes, slides the tickets to the right end of the ticket holder so they're organized, and leaves the line in Frank's hands. A good friend has just arrived with a blind date. He'll greet them. Among the diners at the door waiting to be seated are Michael's mom and dad, sister and brother-in-law. He'll greet them too, and he and Liz will take them to the VIP platform table.

At eight o'clock Matt hustles downstairs with an empty plastic container to restock on walleye. "I think this is where we go down," he says. In the dining room and on the patio every table is full. But no orders are in. Frank surveys the crowd and says in a near whisper, "This is going to be the hardest hour we've done."

And then the ticket printer starts to *chatter*, pauses, *chatter*, pauses, *chatterchatterchatter*, pauses, *chatterchatterchatter*. The orders arrive in steady, relentless waves, but the three young men and one young woman cook hard and fast and well. The room pulses with conversation as servers move food with balletic agility through the crowd. The tickets are evenly spaced, the servers are in good form, and no one station gets clobbered.

But then the tickets don't stop. It's nine o'clock, and suddenly the chatterbox starts cranking out more orders. And more. It's as if they were coming from a second restaurant somewhere. *Who's ordering all this food?* you want to ask. *Everyone already ordered!* The machine's chatter just keeps on coming, and soon there is a whole new row of white tickets bunched together along the ticket-holding shelf, lifting and falling in the heat of the flame below as if waving to the crowd. Michael, Frank, Matt, and Abby are in constant motion, turning-crouching-turning-cooking-turning-plating, a stationary dance.

Then Michael halts and stares at the tickets. He's lost. He doesn't know where he is, which tickets have been fired. "Fire a halibut, three walleye, a salmon, and a steak! Fire two sweets, a goat cheese, knuckle sandwich, and a crepe!" The tickets keep coming.

Behind him a server named Matt shouts, "Michael!" Michael has to stop cooking and expediting to lean over the counter to hear Matt because the crowd noise is so loud. It's like a huge party in here. "Whaddaya mean why isn't it on the menu?!" Michael shouts. "Pepper's in everything!" Matt tries to explain that the woman at B-3 wants the walleye but doesn't want pepper. "The pierogies have pepper in them already; the sauce has pepper in it! I can grill her a piece of walleye!" Matt hustles away, and Michael keeps cooking. That's the kind of thing that can really throw you off.

Rebecca Yody, thirty-two years old, former rhythm guitarist with a local band, now jewelry maker and waitress, is never flustered, never not at the top of her game—she's too smart—but somehow, the six-top squeezed into B-1, the smoking section, has become trouble. There are three six-tops squeezed into smoking, in addition to the one four-top—an unusual situation. They've all been seated at about the same time and therefore want to order at the same time. Rebecca is handling by herself what amounts to a twenty-two person banquet. Lola is out of every bottle of wine B-1 orders, and they're giving her hell for it. "Eighty-six the Steele pinot noir," Frankie, the bartender, shouts to her as she heads back to their table, shaking her head.

The line is still cranking, and the room is packed, the bar four deep. "Matt, fire a flank steak medium rare on the fly." Michael tears a new ticket off the chatterbox and turns back to the line, calling, "Order but do not fire two mac and cheese VIP." The sea of tickets keep fluttering. By nine forty-five there's no slowing down. Michael's parents have finished dinner and are ready to leave. His father, Dennis, tall and thin, with light brown hair and a mustache, and his mother, a tiny woman of Italian-Greek ancestry with fiery eyes and bright smile, stand to the side, watching. Mom's so proud of her baby. But it upsets her to see him like this; she watches with concern. The first time she saw him burning and turning like a maniac on the line, at one of Michael's first jobs, she bolted the restaurant, and when she reached the parking lot, she burst into tears.

She's looking for just a quick glance from Michael to say thank you and good-bye, but Michael is a blur. Everyone on the line is a blur. She decides to approach the service counter for a quick good-bye anyway; she'll shout it next time he puts a plate up and then be gone. Matt approaches, holding a large plate of the pasta puttanesca. He's got another problem customer, a customer who wants his pasta cooked till it's mushy. "Tell them we cook—" His mother is trying to lean in over the counter. Michael sees her leaning in, holds a flat hand almost against her nose, and shouts, "I can't talk now!" Mom nods once as though she'd been scolded and walks quickly toward the door. Michael shouts, "Tell them we cook our pasta al dente! If they want it cooked farther, we can *do* that!" He refires a pasta puttanesca, with overcooked pasta.

Everyone on the line is buried. Michael turns to the tickets, lost. He's at least five tickets behind and he doesn't know where he is and there are so many things to cook he can't afford to just *stand* there *staring* at the tickets figuring out where he is. He's got to get this stuff *cooked*. He covers the puttanesca with a sauté pan to make it cook faster. He slams sauté pans down on every burner. As soon as he *does* figure out where the hell he is, he wants pans *hot*. "Fire a salmon, a chicken—make that three salmon, a chicken, and a steak!" he shouts at Matt. "Frank, I need a crepe, this table's going out!"

"I got it," Frank says, but Frank's working half a dozen other items.

Another server passes and calls to Michael, "The steak rare that just came in, they want that very rare. Can't be too rare, said just wave it over the flame." Michael asks Matt if he got that.

Michael completes two appetizer plates, and Matt gets his up, and Michael asks Frank, "Where's the crepe?" The table is already way late. The food is up, and the server is waiting, but Frank has yet to fire the crepe. Michael sees this, grabs a pan, squats at the lowboy, and hammers the pan into the floor in anger. Then he lays a crepe in it, sprinkles some shredded duck confit on it, stands, gives it a squirt of barbecue sauce and slides it into Matt's oven, which is the hottest one they have.

It'll be done in two minutes. Michael turns to the line and throws more pans onto burners; two tumble off the shelf onto the stovetop with loud clanks. He takes a grouper off the flame and slides it into his oven, then slams the door so hard that it falls back open against his legs. He kicks it shut with such anger it's surprising his foot doesn't punch through it.

Serious weeds.

At ten-fifteen, nearly three hours after the tickets began, it's over. The last meals from this seating are sent out. Three tickets flutter lazily on the shelf, but nothing is fired. Almost everyone in the restaurant is eating. Michael doesn't know what happened. Matt's customer sent back the second pasta puttanesca. Pasta still wasn't cooked enough. Plates never come back. And then *another* plate came back. The very rare, couldn't-be-too-rare steak . . . was too rare. Michael smashes out off the line and through the narrow swinging doors, heads to the basement. He pounds down the narrow stairs and, panting heavily, falls into the chair at the desk, lights a Camel, then slides the mouse and double clicks, his eyes fixed on the computer screen. "Twenty-five *hundred,*" he says. "No wonder I was so fucking weeded."

Twenty-five hundred dollar's worth of food has just been ordered and cooked between nine and ten. It is Lola's most lucrative hour ever. But it is too much. Liz arrives to see how Michael's doing; she knows he's had a hard time, so she doesn't say anything, just lets him talk. "That was too fucking much," he says. Then sad, almost pleading forgiveness from her, he says, "*Liz,* we were on the brink of putting out food that . . . it didn't matter." Liz nods. "That was the busiest hour we've ever done. I feel like someone's beaten me with a stick." He pauses and looks to Liz. "That was too much."

Michael's teeth grit, and he shakes his head. He draws on his Camel.

The evening doesn't end there. It's only half over. At one in the morning Michael will be staring out at his restaurant, incredulous at the sight. Frank, Matt, and Abby still cooking hard, the bar packed, and tables filling up *again* for dinner. At one in the morning. In Cleveland. This does not happen in Cleveland.

It is Lola's most lucrative night ever. A typical weekend night, a good busy, packed night when the kitchen really cranks and Frankie and Amy work the bar like magicians, brings in between seven and eight grand. Never before have they brought in more than ten thousand dollars in a single evening.

Michael will be in tomorrow to work sauté so Frank can play softball and break his finger. Monday the restaurant is closed, and the room and stoves and bar rest. They have the following week to get ready for the Mariani visit. Once Michael's rested, he begins to look forward to it. "We'll smoke him," he says. "He'll love the food."

CHAPTER SEVEN

"The AC's down, Milton got deported, Mariani's coming Satur-day. It was eighty-five *degrees* in here last night. *Great* day at *Lola*." This is as stressed as Michael Symon is likely to get in the middle of the afternoon on a Thursday, and even with the heat, even with los-ing his ace dishwasher and prep cook to immigration authorities, he's still laughing and mouthing off. (Truth is, he's a good deal more chatty than Matt.)

"When are we changing the menu?" Matt asks.

"I don't know," Michael says. "I'm still working on it. I'm having writer's block."

He hasn't done much work on it because the week has been so busy. This morning he's already had a photo shoot with the *Plain Dealer* and a local magazine. And they're packed again tonight.

The following day, Friday, begins in summer heat trying to haul up to the roof an enormous air conditioner, a six-thousand-dollar tempo-rary unit he needs till the new system goes in next weekend. Sous chef Frank and Frankie, the bartender, were up early in the heat to help drag it up to the roof with ropes but couldn't do it, and Michael has to spend another five hundred bucks to bring in a crane. But the good news is that Milton is not being deported. He owes a thousand dollars in court fees before authorities will let him go back to work. Michael picks up the cost; Milton is valuable. The other dishwasher, Benny, is valuable too; Michael bought him a car so he could get to and from work.

Matt's got to hustle today. He got hammered last night: forty walleyes. He ran out of pierogies and found himself rolling dough at eleven o'clock—not what you want to be doing at that hour after seven hours of cooking.

Michael is in a good mood once the AC is in. It was hot in here last night. "I think I saw a camel walk through here at eight o'clock!" he says. "It keeled over!"

And they move through their Lola day as usual. Things just keep getting a little busier every week, it seems. Big prep day, but the night should be steady. As the tables fill, Michael heads downstairs concerned about the heat and the air conditioner, and mad that the patio lights suddenly went out; the patio will bring fifteen hundred dollars when they can open it, but they can't do it without light. He hovers over his legal pad to focus on something different, the emerging menu.

"I'm taking the tuna off," he says. "I'm going out on a limb."

The tuna is not only one of the most popular menu items, but also Michael's favorite dish. A block of tuna, thoroughly coated in freshly ground coriander, seared on all sides, sliced thin—he doesn't like the tuna in a big chunk, cut on a bias into two chunks as many chefs do; too much raw meat that way, unpleasant to eat—and he serves the slices on a seaweed salad with pickled ginger, green wasabi fish eggs, and a citrus reduction (OJ, ginger, and rice vinegar). But he's getting tired of it, and Frank, who cooks most of them, is tired of it too. A main benefit of the new menu is that it prevents your cooks from burning out. He still wants to do a seared tuna, and the tartare, but maybe he'll put both with olives, neo-niçoise. "I love tuna and olives," he says. "Maybe puree them and add a little tangerine oil."

He puts his head down and begins to write quickly in precise block capital print with a mechanical pencil, saying, "I'm going to do a calf's liver with caramelized onions and apple. I think that would be really good." He counts the number of entrées he's got, only eight. "What am I missing? Vegetarian entrée." He picks up a fancy cheese catalog. "I'm rollin'," he says. "I'm gonna do a smoked mozzarella, a napoleon of polenta and smoked mozzarella, summer squash."

A voice over the phone's intercom says, "Michael Symon, Doug Petkovic on line one." He reaches for the phone, hits line one, and says, "Hey, fat ass! . . . It was invitational only. . . . Oh, my fuckin' God unbelievable. I shot a ninety-three; it was a hard course." They continue to talk golf.

Michael has committed to putting filet mignon on the menu and has written "GRILLED FILET OVER A WILD MUSHROOM RAGU W/BLUE CHEESE RAVIOLI" on his legal pad. He doesn't like doing this—filet mignon has no flavor, and it's the most expensive beef you can buy, forcing him to surpass his self-imposed twenty-dollar maximum entrée price—but his customers keep requesting it. He asks himself, "Who's more stupid: them for eating it or me for not serving it when they ask?" To keep all the entrées under twenty dollars, he may charge by the ounce, with a minimum of six ounces.

Doug has to put Michael on hold, and Michael continues to write: "NAPOLEON OF POLENTA W/SUMMER SQUASH + TOMATO COULIS." Liz enters the office and stands at his shoulder, reading the items on the legal pad as he writes. He says to her, "I'm unconscious. I'm like Larry Bird in the zone." He continues writing appetizers and entrées. "COD WRAPPED IN PROSCIUTTO W/RATATOUILLE OF SUMMER SQUASH." Doug returns to the line, and Michael tells him, "I gotta go, Liz is ridin' me like a dog." He hangs up and says to Liz, "Don't break my roll."

Liz picks up the legal pad and reads items aloud skeptically, and Michael says, "Will you stop that? It's not a finished product!" He grabs for a Camel, lights it, takes the legal pad back, and continues to write.

"You don't have any tomatoes on here," Liz says.

"Am I *done* yet?" He looks up irritated at the phone, which no one is answering. "Hello, Lola," he says in his soft, docile voice. "Yeah, absolutely. . . . No concert T-shirts or torn jeans."

When he hangs up, Liz, reading, says, "Ooo, lamb sampler with goat cheese béarnaise. *That* sounds good." He looks up at her, half smiling but gritting his teeth. "No," she says, "I'm serious. It sounds good." His teeth remain gritted, and he shakes his head. She's ruining his roll.

Liz sits in a chair beside Michael, who continues to hover over the legal pad, pencil in hand. She finds the cheese catalog and flips through it. "I think we need to make a cheese-buying trip through France," she says.

"Wanna go now?" Michael laughs. "You can go now, just be back by tomorrow night when Mariani comes." He's found out through his friend Michaelides that Mariani was in town Wednesday, then in Chicago, then back to Cleveland tonight and tomorrow night, eating at Moxie (where his buddy Doug works), at Sans Souci (my former employer), and at Fat Cats, a new restaurant down the street from Lola. Lola will be Mariani's last stop in Cleveland. Michaelides, the instigator of the visit, has also orchestrated it. It takes some doing. *Esquire* will pay for Mariani to visit only first-tier cities. So Michaelides has had to arrange for all the restaurants to pick up Mariani's airfare; he's gotten the Renaissance Hotel (where Sans Souci is located, a chain owned by Marriott) to comp a room while Mariani's there. This is partly how Mariani is able to visit and eat in twenty-five cities each year.

Michael tells Liz a story Doug told him about Craig Summers, Moxie's owner, and Mariani: "Craig goes to Mariani, 'You been to Lola yet?' Mariani said, 'I'm going Saturday.' And Craig said, 'Michael Symon's a good cook, but his golf game is terrible. And if you ask me, your golf game is much more important than being a good chef.' And Mariani just looked at him and said, 'Really?'"

Michael and Liz discuss Mariani's Cleveland jaunt. They understand the reason Michaelides chose Moxie and Sans Souci. "Why did Stephen take him to Fat Cats?" Liz wonders.

Michael says, "Because he wants to show off Tremont. I don't know why he's coming *here.*" Michael glances at the legal pad, then back to Liz and says, "Probably needed someone else to help pay for the airfare." His laugh rings through the office.

Michael heads back upstairs, and Liz watches him leave. "It's almost bad that he knows Mariani's coming," she says. "Too much time to think." He's better working impromptu, she says. He's not a planner. They didn't know *Food & Wine* was coming ahead of time, and he cooked straight off the menu and did so perfectly. It's a good menu. Tomorrow, she says, Michael's not planning anything special. He's going to cook straight off the menu again; he's just got to do it perfectly.

The night is smooth, and before long Michael returns to the menu.

By the end of the night the last of the new menu items come together. He really wants to get foie gras back on the menu, especially now that Hudson Valley, one of two foie gras producers in the country, is back up and running after an expansion. He's going to offer something Cleveland rarely sees, a whole roasted foie gras. He'll do it for two. A special item like foie gras, he'll work into the menu twice, in a "surf and turf" dish. He'll get the seared tuna in here. Sautéed foie gras with seared rare tuna. Tuna has the meaty rich quality of filet mignon, which is sometimes paired with foie gras. Tuna and foie gras—surf and turf. And accompanying it, a mango salad, mango and roasted radicchio. "Foie gras and mango will blow your mind," he says. "It's one of those things. Foie gras, mango—I don't like fruity things—and a little balsamic reduction is *great*."

He's toying with doing a foie gras terrine too, a way to use the scraps. And he hopes to get beluga caviar on there.

At the end of the night the final item appears. He almost forgot! "SAGE PAPPARDELLE W/BRAISED RABBIT, TURNIPS, CARROTS + AU JUS." He wanted to do a pappardelle, and rabbit will work great. He loves rabbit. He used to be allergic to rabbit. First time he had it, as a student at the Culinary Institute, his head blew up like a balloon, and it was hard to breathe. But he liked the taste so much he just kept eating it, first in small, then in increasing doses, until his head didn't blow up anymore and he could eat as much as he wanted.

Over the weekend he'll write the menu out clean and see how it reads.

RAW BAR

—HOUSE CURED GRAVLAX W/PICKLED ONIONS, H_2OCRESS + CROSTINI

—TUNA TARTARE W/TANGERINE OIL, CHIVES, BLACK OLIVES + SHAVED
   FENNEL

—OYSTERS ON THE ½ SHELL W/LIME VINAIGRETTE + PICKLED JALAPENO

——POACHED SHRIMP W/APRICOT COCKTAIL SAUCE
——AVOCADO + CRAB SALAD W/OHIO SWEET CORN

APPS
——CORN CREPE W/DUCK CONFIT, BBQ SAUCE + SOUR CREAM
——PAN SEARED SWEETBREADS W/FIGS, ARUGULA, BALSAMIC
——PAN SEARED SCALLOP OVER RISOTTO W/ENGLISH PEAS, PROSCIUTO +
   TRUFFLE OIL
——KNUCKLE SANDWICH W/LOBSTER, SMK BACON + FONTINA ON
   FOCACCIA
——GOAT CHEESE WRAPPED IN PROSCIUTTO OVER A ROASTED ARTICHOKE
   SALAD
——HOUSE SALAD W/JICAMA, TOASTED SESAME + BALSAMIC VINAIGRETTE
——VINE RIPENED TOMATOES W/ARUGULA + SMOKED MOZZARELLA
——FOIE GRAS TERRINE

PASTA
——MACARONI + CHEESE W/ROASTED CHICKEN, GOAT CHEESE +
   ROSEMARY
——PENNE PASTA W/EXTRA VIRGIN OLIVE OIL, VINE RIPENED TOMATOES +
   SMOKED MOZZARELLA
——POTATO RAVIOLI W/ROASTED LOBSTER ASPARAGUS + TRUFFLE BUTTER
——SEAFOOD LINGUINI W/SHRIMP, SALMON, MUSSELS, HALIBUT +
   GROUPER IN PUTTANESCA SAUCE
——SAGE PAPPARDELLE W/BRAISED RABBIT, TURNIPS, CARROTS + AU JUS

ENTREES
——PAN ROASTED SALMON OVER FRIED OYSTERS W/ROASTED CORN +
   MUSSEL RELISH
——SLASH + BURN GROUPER OVER CRAB TATER TOTS W/WHIPPED
   AVOCADO + PEPPER COULIS
——HERB CRUSTED WALLEYE W/LOBSTER PIEROGIES + TRUFFLE BUTTER
——SURF + TURF SEARED RARE TUNA W/FOIE GRAS
——PAN SEARED HALIBUT OVER A ROASTED ARTICHOKE + RED PEPPER
   SALAD W/PRESERVED LEMON

—LAMB SAMPLER OF GRILLED CHOP, KIDNEY + LIVER OVER POTATO +
EGGPLANT NAPOLEON W/GOAT CHEESE BEARNAISE

—SAGE + LEMON ROASTED CHICKEN OVER WHIPPED ROOT VEGETABLES
W/ROASTED ARTICHOKES

—PAN SEARED CALF'S LIVER W/CARAMELIZED ONIONS + APPLES OVER
SAGE POLENTA W/BALSAMIC

—GRILLED FILET OVER A WILD MUSHROOM RAGU W/BAKED BLUE
CHEESE RAVIOLI

—POLENTA + SUMMER SQUASH NAPOLEON W/BRIE + A CHARRED
TOMATO COULIS

—ROASTED FOIE GRAS FOR TWO m.p.

CHAPTER EIGHT

*M*ichael had gone home early last night, the day before the Mariani dinner, to take a nap. He'd been at the restaurant since 9:00 A.M. and planned to close for Frank, who asked to leave early on a date; Michael agreed to cover for him. When Michael woke from his nap at 3:00 A.M., he quickly called Frank, who was already starting to close. "Sorry, brother," he said to Frank.

But it meant today he was well rested! When Abby, soon to be a senior at Lakewood High School and now working raw bar, made a crack about Michael's not returning to the restaurant, Michael said, "You're too young to be lippy. When you're twenty-one, you can be lippy. Till then keep it zipped." He chuckled. Michael has quietly confided his hopes for Abby. She was the real thing, he said, and thought that she'd be a great cook.

It was a good day today. The place actually felt *cool;* the AC was working. Everything was going right, business as usual. Rebecca Yody wandered in at three-thirty to begin her day. Doug and Tony walked the room with the reservation sheet and pencil, making sure each table was properly set for the first turn. Michael polished wineglasses and up-ended them on a clean cloth napkin on the bar, then left to take a phone call. Frankie and Amy prepped the bar, and Amy, at the register, said, "Frank, what's this payout for?" Courtney, at the stove, called, "Phyllo dough"; they'd run out, and she had to cross the street to buy a

couple extra boxes at the deli. Courtney headed downstairs to crack egg
yolks into the tater tot mixture and get the egg whites whipping for the
angel food cake. Matt was down there too, working on three consecutive batches of pierogie dough. At four-oh-five, Del Spitzer and friends
arrived for an early supper. Liz sauntered into the room at four twenty-
four and stopped by the Spitzer table first thing to say hello. The customers at the bar wore shorts and T-shirts and caps, refugees from
Cleveland's 9–5 loss in the eleventh inning to Houston. The room was
filled with sunlight, a bright summer afternoon. But as more and more
customers arrived, the room gradually began to darken. Clouds rolled
in, and rain began. The storm took hold, and wind slapped rain into
the windows. Lightning flashed, thunder cracked, and all of Lola's
lights flickered. They'd already lost power once this summer, middle of
a weekend service. Michael's stomach clenched, and he looked at the
lights. *Not tonight,* he thought. *Don't have the power go off when Mariani's here.* The first turn was smooth, Matt, Frank, Abby, and Michael
all on the line. By seven-thirty the storm had passed. The room was
again loud with conversation and the sounds of cooking, a ball of flame
rising out of the seafood puttanesca linguini when Frank flamed it,
lighting the dark room and turning heads. Most tables were arriving
now for the second turn, and the bar was full.

I am one of the people at the bar. At seven-forty Stephen Michaelides
arrives with his wife, Jeanne, beside him, and Michael Sanson, editor of
Restaurant Hospitality. Behind them is John Mariani.

You know immediately it's Mariani. The guy has presence. At first it's
visual; the man is tall, six feet or more, the very last inches composed of
very white, fine hair over very black eyebrows and large dark-rimmed
glasses. So striking is the contrast between his white hair and black eyebrows I'd wager that even color photographs of the guy appear to be
black and white. White in that dark restaurant, snow white and
combed in a preppy part just off center.

Michaelides has asked me to join them tonight, and I'm grateful for the opportunity. First, I've been reading Mariani's by-line for years; he's all over the place. *Esquire's* critic. He pens columns for *Wine Spectator, Eating Well, Diversion,* and numerous other publications, including *Restaurant Hospitality* (a trade magazine whose former and current editors will sit beside each other at the central circular VIP table tonight). In all these publications Mariani's prose seemed to me always very clean, knowledgeable, with no nonsense and no foodie fluff.

But more than that, this guy ate at more restaurants in more cities each year than just about any other food writer and critic I knew of. There may be a couple of others, Florence Fabricant, perhaps, who writes for the *New York Times* and *Nation's Restaurant News,* certainly seems to cover a lot of ground throughout the year. Ruth Reichl, when she was restaurant critic for the *New York Times,* was the most powerful and watched critic in the country. Alan Richman, also based in New York as *GQ's* restaurant critic, has won best magazine restaurant critic from the Beard Foundation so often it should just retire the category in his name. There were also legions of critics throughout the country who were talented and knowledgeable and brought great diligence and balance to the tricky business of reviewing and writing about restaurants. But Mariani was really the preeminent *national* critic. No one covered as much territory as he did for such visible publications, writing with such authority.

Mariani, who earned his Ph.D. in English literature from Columbia, was an intellectual, a former teacher who had trained his sights on food. In 1977, while in his early thirties, he and his wife set off across the country to travel; he fell into writing about food then, and he has been traveling the country eating and writing ever since, penning not only articles but also numerous books—cookbooks, gastronomical history, and food dictionaries. His *Dictionary of Italian Food and Drink* was about to be released in the fall.

The man, simply by virtue of the number of cities he covered year after year, could bring some perspective to my observations of Lola. Thus I was eager to meet him and watch him eat Michael Symon's food and hear what he had to say.

There was another element to my interest. Food critics and media were increasingly important to the restaurant scene; indeed an entire book, called *Dining Out,* by Andrew Dornenburg (a bona fide chef) and his wife, Karen Page, was devoted to restaurant critics and criticism. Mariani was a prominent member of this group of critics, and I was curious about how he worked. I'd never eaten with a famous food writer and critic. How did he order? How did he eat? I was also a little skeptical of his methods. My first job out of college was copyboy at a big-city newspaper, so I was reared with newspaper ethics. The idea that restaurants would pay for Mariani's flight, feed him an enormous dinner (no check, of course), and then he would maybe write something nice about them was a technique from a different planet from the one I'd been raised on.

Liz shows us to the center table. Tony, one of Lola's best waiters ("I'm not the one who invited the hillbillies"), who usually works the platform on weekends, hands menus to all.

Not only is Mariani visually striking and substantial in reputation, but his voice likewise is so loud and clear as to seem a kind of tool or lever. Everything that comes out of his mouth has an air of absoluteness, even when it's a question. He glances at the menu, just long enough to see the categories, and says to Tony, *"Do you just want to give us five appetizers, five entrées, some pastas?"* Tony nods. Tony, who is never nervous, is clearly nervous, hemming and hawing about taking the menus or leaving the menus; his entire demeanor is strangely tentative and uncertain. He leaves the menus—they're big, eleven-by-seventeen-inch single printed sheets—on the table, no one looks at them, and he departs as Mariani says to the table and to the diminishing Tony that he eats anything, anything except oysters on the half shell. Those he can't eat.

Excellent, I think, after this first round. This is by far the best way to eat at a good restaurant. Mariani clearly knows what he's doing. Why waste time reading a menu? He can get that later. Bring on the food, all kinds of it. Let's see what ya got. Let's try as many different things as is comfortably possible. *Give us your best!*

Liz hands Mariani a wine list. This he does read, apparently carefully and very quickly. He seems to be favorably impressed. He names his choice, Liz departs, and with the authority of a Supreme Court justice handing down a ruling, he says, *"Nothing like a Sancerre to open up the palate."*

I shall never forget those words, so absolutely were they spoken. If ever in the company of people I want to impress, I shall begin a meal with Sancerre because now I knew, sure as the sun will rise, that nothing *but nothing* opens the palate like a Sancerre.

Pleasant banter follows: Stephen, a ribald conversationalist, describing a novel he's working on titled *Condom;* wife, Jeanne, all teeth and gorgeous eyes, playing dizzy and delightful, a starlet from 1920s Hollywood; Michael Sanson, the young savvy magazine editor; and Mariani, *the* Mariani. I get right to the personal stuff and ask straight off how does he operate.

Mariani explains that he lives outside New York City with his wife and two sons, the older of whom was soon to start college. He doesn't like to be away from his family, so he prefers to travel in two- to three-day pops. Tonight, exhausted, he concludes a six-day trip; six days are too long for him. *"That's why I never go to the Far East,"* he says. In order to hit twenty-five cities a year, he must travel an average of every other week. To choose his destinations, he relies on friends' recommendations throughout the country, and he reads broadly.

He explains that *Esquire* picks up expenses, but few of the other periodicals he works for will. If he were to fly to twenty-five cities a year and pay for it himself, not rely on others to help him get him to these places and put him up while he's there, he would have to spend extraordinary amounts of money on airfare and accommodations alone.

(He explained later—I didn't want to get into a tricky discussion here of whether or not the practice on which he based his livelihood was ethical—that it was up to writers to make their own decisions about how they worked, decisions that were largely governed by the publications they happened to be writing for. He had to work this way, and because he wrote for magazines about the best spots, rather than as a newspaper restaurant review critic, the ethics of being flown in and accommodated were not compromised.)

There is something intimidating to me about Mariani, but I can't figure out exactly what it is. Maybe it's just me, because he is to this point, and will be throughout the rest of the evening, nothing but friendly, engaging, generous, and open.

After fifteen minutes of chat, our palates Sancerre–wide open, five first courses arrive. I recognize four; they're on the menu: the corn crepe with duck confit and Michael's barbecue sauce, sweetbreads with bacon, balsamic, and sautéed arugula, a roasted beet salad with horse-radish vinaigrette, and goat cheese wrapped in prosciutto over the arti-choke salad. All of these dishes are on-the-money, confirmed, tried and true winners, simple good flavors—delicious starters, as always. But Tony sets a plate in front of Mariani and says, "And this is lobster with morels and asparagus with a truffle butter sauce."

Michael has gone off the menu. I turn to glance over my left shoul-der at him, illuminated by the overhead kitchen lights in the otherwise dimly lit restaurant—he's bright as a stage actor, his bald head flash-ing—as he plates another dish. Then I rise several inches out of my seat to look at the new dish. There before Mariani are half a lobster tail and one claw on a bed of asparagus and morels.

Perhaps everyone at the table is waiting for Mariani to say some-thing, or perhaps all finished listening to Tony describe the dishes and are pondering, but for whatever reason the table is dead silent.

Mariani spoke: *"Where's the rest of the lobster?"*

This is jarring. Is it a criticism? Is it a joke? What does he mean? Why did he say that? Tony doesn't know whether or not to answer, and of course there is no answer.

Mariani suggests we all pass to the left, clockwise, and then we dig in. Everything is delicious. Michael's impromptu lobster-morels-asparagus starter is very tasty indeed. The table returns to conversation as we bite and pass.

I have been writing about cooking and food and chefs, studying the work, working in restaurants, and scrutinizing cooking exclusively for what is nearing three years, and I have often wondered if they have been years well spent and how long I would, I should, continue to do it. Writing about food and cooking is fun—you bet—but really, in the long run, isn't it a little self-indulgent and shallow to spend a lifetime doing it? Shouldn't one return to more serious matters than pleasing one's mouth and body? So I ask Mariani, who has been writing about food and cooking and chefs for more than two decades if he has ever been bothered that the subject, while interesting, might be in the end a shallow concern to devote one's entire working life to.

He says he *has* thought about this. While he doesn't respond either way, he notes that even after Italy's unification in the mid-nineteenth century, the country could scarcely converse with one another because all the regions spoke various dialects. Then a guy named Pellegrino Artusi published a book called *The Science of Cookery and the Art of Eating Well,* written in formal Italian. The book was extraordinarily popular, and people from north to south, east and west read the thing and as a result created a common language for the entire country. Though an Italian man or woman was likely to speak in the local dialect after the book was published in 1891, the cookbook may be credited with determining the language that a century hence all Italians would speak. If a cookbook could determine a country's language, Mariani suggests, then perhaps cookery and the art of eating well are not so shallow and self-indulgent as they may at first seem. (At least to a shallow, self-indulgent person such as myself. I am grateful for Mariani's observation and will never again feel guilty that I am not off in Bosnia or the Middle East, writing books there, or exploring our country's prison system or HMOs or campaign finance reform.)

After our plates are cleared, Mariani orders a second bottle of wine, a Barbaresco. Tony returns with it, dead serious, perspiration beading beneath his long dark sideburns. He shows Mariani. Mariani nods. Tony uncorks the bottle, pours a couple of ounces into Mariani's glass. Mariani tastes it, considers it, then says, *"That's good."* Tony nods and is moving to fill Jeanne's glass when Mariani says, *"if it could just be a little colder."* Tony nods again and departs (he'll fly downstairs and plunge it in the ice machine and twist and turn, twist and turn; Liz will personally chill the next bottle of red that's served). Mariani and Sanson lament aloud the temperatures restaurants will serve red wine at these days—if they even think about red wine temperature at all.

Once the wine has been chilled from warm to cool and poured, the pasta course arrives. Michael has sent penne pasta with the puttanesca sauce to the table in one large bowl, enough for five small portions.

Once again the table goes quiet. Once again, Mariani renders a verdict with sonorous authority, a ribald comment suggesting the pasta is overcooked.

You can see that the pasta *is* overcooked. The penne is bloated, and a few that are visible throughout the tomato-based sauce are split open. By this point I know I'm rooting for Michael because I'm so disappointed. Stephen laughs at Mariani's remark, but he's disappointed too. We're all rooting for Michael. He's the local boy up against the big-time critic. And he's just served something that doesn't look great to eat. Jeanne offers to serve and does. It tastes exactly how it looks: OK.

Stephen says to Mariani, "How do you like it?"

"I'm not crazy about it," Mariani says. *"There's too much sauce. He doesn't understand. There's a* reason *puttanesca is served with spaghetti."*

For better or worse, Michael has served a classic Italian pasta preparation to the man whose book *A Dictionary of Italian Food and Drink* is about to arrive in bookstores all over the country. The guy, we may presume, is an Italian food *expert.* In his book Mariani defines *alla puttanesca* this way: "'Harlot style.' A robust southern Italian tomato sauce. Usually made with tomatoes, onions, garlic, chile peppers, capers, olives, anchovies, and oregano. The reference to prostitutes supposedly suggests that this was a sauce quickly made by such women between clients. It is most often associated with Naples and Calabria, although versions are found throughout Italy." Mariani discusses the derivation at the table as well as how much sauce Italians put on their food.

Sanson defends Michael. "Michael doesn't claim to be a classic Italian restaurant," he says. "Who cares what the experts say the proper way Italians serve puttanesca? What matters is that he pleases his customers. He knows his market; he knows how to price his menu; he knows what the customers expect and want when they order this."

Mariani's not buying. *"He just doesn't get it,"* he says again.

Michael has erred, and you can point to the exact moment when it happened: when Michael, at the last minute, decided to go off the menu.
Moments before, trying to come up with a new first course, Michael
made a foie gras mousse pierogie, but when he tasted it, he said, "it
tasted shitty." So, on the spot, he combined lobster, morels, and asparagus. This has consequences no one at the table realizes and Mariani
can't possibly know. Michael's best pasta is the potato ravioli with
morels and asparagus in a veal stock and cream sauce that is hit at the
end with a healthy dose of truffle butter; it's light and delicious, rich
with the truffle flavor, the earthy morels, and their classic companion,
asparagus. The pasta is perfect; Michael makes the filling with
marscapone, truffle oil and chopped truffle, cream, chives, salt and pepper, and delivers it to his friend Gary Thomas at Ohio City Pasta, who
puts the ravioli together using his own fresh Ohio City pasta. It's a great
dish—*the best pasta he makes*—but he can't serve it. He's already squan-
dered the asparagus and morels on the impromptu lobster dish.
Michael wouldn't dare send Mariani *more* morels and asparagus right
after the lobster. So he opts for his second favorite pasta, pasta puttanesca, which he makes with fresh tomatoes and excellent Greek olives
that are packed not in a brine but in olive oil.

It's the middle of a Saturday night, the restaurant is packed, and the
whole line is really humping; Michael isn't cooking just for our table.
The whole line is getting clobbered. But Michael focuses on the pasta
dish for Mariani. He pops the raw seafood into a sauté pan and last
adds the shrimp, which cook in about two seconds. He drops to the
lowboy and pulls a portion of the thin, long black pepper linguini Ohio
City Pasta makes fresh daily. But when Michael turns to drop the linguini into the pasta water, he sees that it's lost its boil; everyone's cooking pasta in it, and Chatty dumps pierogies there. This fresh uncooked
linguini will take too long to cook in water that's not boiling; the
shrimp are already in the pan and will be rubber if he cooks the linguini. So he's forced to substitute the penne; the penne is precooked al
dente, cooled, then simply reheated at service. But when Courtney happened to cook this batch, a food delivery took her away from the pasta

and it overcooked. Michael half notices this, but the line is so crazy he tosses the penne into the sauce and dumps the pan into a large hot bowl and sends it out. No time to stop.

The meal continues, and there will be no decisions on the level of the puttanesca boner. Conversation is breezy. Mariani remarks on how lively the room is and then, looking around, observes that no one is drinking wine. He's so astonished by this he actually stands to scan the tables. Lola does a lot of sales in wine, so this is unusual. Mariani keeps saying he can't believe it. Five entrées arrive.

Mariani is served the calf's liver, sautéed over grilled polenta with portobello mushrooms and arugula. Mariani says: *"What is it? I can't even see it?"* The room is dark. He tilts the dish toward the single votive flickering in the center of the table. He applauds Michael for offering liver, but he seems really annoyed that he can't see what he's eating. He keeps bending over the dish, poking, tilting his head, tilting the plate. Conversation resumes; plates are passed. Jeanne, seated next to Mariani, is served what Michael knows is her favorite, the seared tuna with the coriander crust. I begin with the midwestern dish of walleye and pierogies, Michael Sanson gets the shank, which he loves, and Stephen receives the crowd-pleasing slash and burn grouper. Desserts follow, culminating in a shared root beer float, which everyone is very pleased to see and taste. It transports me straight back to boyhood summers, and I think what a great idea, this root beer float; how apt and right this idea is in this restaurant. Simple, American, delicious, and fun. That's what Lola is all about.

After the entrées have been served, Michael comes to the table, shakes hands with Mariani, laughs and jokes and hopes everything is all right. Then he makes the rounds of the other tables and shakes hands and talks, that laugh ripping through the noisy din of Saturday night. Mariani watches him for a while, apparently marveling at Michael in the crowd.

Mariani says, *"He's so exuberant."*

This energy he seems genuinely to admire.

As the meal winds down, Mariani excuses himself to hit the men's room. Michael is off the line at the service counter, and Mariani stops to thank him. It has been a very tiring trip, he tells Michael, and this was a delightful way to finish it.

When it's over, Mariani drops a single bill, a generous gratuity, onto the table. Neither I nor the others leave one red cent. Mariani thanks both Liz and Michael for a wonderful meal, and he reiterates that it was a great way to finish off his trip. He hands Michael his business card and tells Michael to send him a list of everything he'd eaten to-night. Then John Mariani, beneath his fluffy cloud of locks, departs the restaurant.

I linger behind, and as soon they're gone, Liz clutches my elbow. We are going downstairs to the office, and I don't have much say in the matter. I drive a bargain—a large glass of Dewar's on ice—which she concedes. In fact Liz herself asks for a glass of red wine; she never drinks during service, never, but she's so tense from the Mariani visit that she's going to indulge. When we arrive in the office, Michael is smoking hard and rubbing his forehead. He already knows the pasta was a serious error, and you can see from the way he's smashing his palm into his forehead and squeezing his temples that he's mentally beating himself up.

Liz says, *"Tell us everything."*

And I do, what little there is. He seemed to have a good meal; he liked the exuberance of the place; he thought it was too dark. I tell him about the pasta remarks. Michael winces; he will not forgive himself for that. Then Stephanie's voice over the intercom says, "Michael Symon, Claude Rodier is here to see you." Chef Claude, my old boss, has stopped by hoping to catch the Michaelides party for an after-dinner sip. Michael goes upstairs to greet him. Claude cooked for Mariani earlier in the week. Already Michael is telling Claude about his limp pasta and what Mariani said about it. Laughing at it, howling. His laughter, once again, peals through the room. He's having a ball.

A few days later I e-mailed Michaelides asking what Mariani thought of the meal at Lola. He e-mailed back, heading the missive "Let's hear it for viagrapasta": "Dropped Mariani off at Hopkins [Airport] Sunday morning; asked him what he thought of Lola dinner. He said, 'Terrific, but could have used more light.' He didn't elaborate; I didn't ask him to. Perhaps I should have. Later."

CHAPTER NINE

The following week Lola was back to normal: loud, happy, undistracted by national critics, as if nothing had happened. In fact Mariani's visit was becoming business as usual in a successful restaurant. Things like this were going to happen more often in what was becoming, increasingly throughout the country, a high-profile business. The Cleveland Indians would finish the summer at the head of their division, for instance, and host the great and hated Yankees in the American League championship. At one in the morning on a Friday night during the series, television commentators Bob Costas and Joe Morgan, actor Billy Crystal, and Yankee manager Joe Torres arrived at Lola for dinner. The choice of Lola was perhaps inevitable: Except for all-night diners, Lola was the only place open for dinner at one in the morning. People who had laughed at Symon for staying open so late in a bed-by-ten city weren't laughing now. Joe Torres ate at Lola every night he was in town, happily, one would presume, as the Yanks went on to conclude one of the best seasons of any team in baseball history.

The restaurant closed for the Fourth of July weekend, the new AC unit was installed, as were new kitchen and bathroom floors, and proper uniforms were ordered for the cooks. The week after July Fourth, Michael gathered the entire waitstaff around the bar and cooked for them, discussing each dish of the new menu that would be put into effect on Tuesday.

And the final bit of news in this happy cruise called Lola was that in the fall, after four years of living together, Michael and Liz planned to marry.

Only a trace of anger lingered in Michael Symon, anger at himself for not being perfect. He had had words with Courtney about over-cooked pasta. She claimed she was usually on top of the pasta when she cooked it, except for that one time; a delivery needing to be checked in and signed for had called her away from the boiling penne and it had overcooked. The casual atmosphere at Lola can easily lull waitstaff and cooks alike into such complacency, and Michael has to stay on top of them, in this instance, on top of Courtney. He tried to explain calmly but clearly that she should *never* overcook pasta. She tried to explain about the deliveryman. Michael told her the deliveryman wouldn't go anywhere, he could wait, cook the pasta right.

Courtney, feeling slightly ridden, said, *"I can't be perfect all the time."*

Michael leaned into her, like a boxing trainer, smiling a smile that wasn't a happy smile. His eyes were slivers. He nodded very quickly and said, *"Yes, you can."*

True. This was the goal, this was what a good chef—not even a great one, but a good one—had to strive for at all times, even in the casual hilarity of Lola Bistro and Wine Bar.

A few days later, on a calm weekday evening, I headed down the steps to Lola's basement, walked past the ice machine and the grease trap, and stood in the doorway of the office. Michael, alone and at his desk, was more or less balled up over his dinner. He sponged the last bit of sauce and a remaining asparagus tip from the bottom of the bowl with a scrap of bread and finished it off. He looked like a miser, the way he hunched over that bowl, lowering his big bald head to take the last bite out of his hand, rather than raise his hand from the bowl. I knew what he had been eating. The potato ravioli with roasted garlic, asparagus and morels, the sauce enriched with truffle butter, his best pasta dish. I also knew why he was shaking his head at the bowl. I could *see* what he was thinking.

I decided to ask anyway: "What's the matter?"

"I'm pissed off," he said.

"Why?" I asked.

"Why didn't I give this to Mariani?" he said, gritting his teeth and shaking his head at his empty bowl. "Fucking idiot. Stupid. *Idiot.* This is my *favorite* pasta."

And so some regret and anger at having not been perfect all the time remained, even here at casual Lola, with scratched plates, not enough light, and hardwood floors that always felt gritty under foot no matter how well swept they were. It bothered me, this sloppiness. I was never a clean cook myself—I too was sloppy by nature—but I wasn't a chef with a restaurant pulling in 1.5 mil, nor was I one of the ten best new chefs in the country. I thought cleanliness and neatness and sanitation should mean something to such a restaurant and chef like Lola and Michael Symon. So when I saw him plating a shrimp cocktail, working raw bar because Abby was off, I couldn't help being judgmental.

As always the flavors in this dish were excellent: Abby poaches the shrimp in water spiced with Jamaican-made jerk paste, which Michael buys by the case (one of his rules is that if he can simplify things without diminishing quality, he will; he used to make the jerk paste, but, he says, "I was working my ass off making jerk sauce from scratch, and it's not even as good as something I can buy"). He spreads this paste inside his grouper. Michael has fashioned an original sauce, which looks like your standard cocktail sauce—people in this city want to *see* cocktail sauce—but his is based on a tomato and ancho chile combination, and the dish also includes a good seaweed salad, which he also buys. He sold the shrimp for $1.50 each, and the starter I watched him make was for two. He pushed some seaweed salad into the bottom of a small glass, squirted some cocktail sauce on top, and then, after staring at the glass and the plate on which it sat, put the shrimp into it, the tails sticking out, regarded it some more, and shrugged. Sauce pushed up and dribbled over the edge. It looked messy even without the sauce slopped over the side. I stared at it and kept staring at it. I didn't want him to serve it like that; at least wipe the glass, I thought. He looked at me and said, "Shuddup, Ruhlman."

"But there's sauce falling down the side," I said.

He said, "I wanna give the impression of *abundance*." He laughed and called for a runner.

What I didn't realize at the time was that sauce on the glass didn't matter, nor did it matter that the plates were spotted, the floor gritty. That's not what mattered here. All that mattered was that you felt good the instant you walked through the door. Liz had that cool, urban look, and she welcomed you as if she'd invited you to Lola herself and was glad you could make it. And there was Michael, laughing and gabbing with the regulars and cooking up awesome sweetbreads and liver, grouper and halibut—"do at home" food. For me there was no revelation to Lola's success; rather it slowly permeated me. Mariani had seen it immediately. *"He's so exuberant!"* Mariani had said after Michael had said hello to the table and was making the rounds. Exuberant. That was it. This guy's personality absolutely filled the place. As Zona Spray had said about her dinner with *Food & Wine* editor Martha Crow, after Michael had made the rounds and stopped by their table, "You just couldn't help but fall in love with him." He made that room feel packed and rollicking even at four-thirty when only two tables were seated. His personality drew people there at one in the morning for dinner. If he served even mediocre food, would he still have this following? I bet he would. There is sauce dripping down the glass, you can't see your food, but you are having a great time and feel lucky to be here.

And, yes, taste, everything did *taste* really good; everything was perfectly cooked. But that was not half so important as Michael's personality, which was big as Ohio itself. James Beard, I'd bet, would have been right at home at Lola.

John Mariani dutifully wrote his stories. In the November *Esquire*, under the title "A Reason to Go to Cleveland," he covered hotel restaurants in Memphis, Louisville, Scottsdale, and Lake Buena Vista, Florida, among a dozen or so cities in all. "I had a spirited meal in Cleveland last month at the Provençal-inspired Sans Souci in the Renaissance Hotel," he wrote. "Executive Chef Claude Rodier and chef de cuisine Mark Morton demonstrate enormous finesse in dishes like grilled swordfish with citrus romesco sauce, and I've never tasted better beef than their grilled strip steak with leek and lentil gratin." I used to work grill station here, which was responsible for that leek and lentil gratin and that steak; the beef was nothing special, just good strip, but we used to soak it for days in olive oil and garlic and black pepper, which accounted for its awesome flavor.

And *Plain Dealer* food reporter John Long wrote a small story excoriating Mariani for his methods: "[S]everal restaurateurs flew Mariani to town, wined and dined him and put him up at the Renaissance.

"Rather than being a restaurant critic, it sounds more like Mariani was working at what is often referred to as the world's oldest profession."

Mariani apparently did not like to be referred to as *puttanesca* himself, and there ensued a series of irate phone calls between Mariani, John Long, and *Plain Dealer* editors.

Meanwhile *Esquire*'s December issue was already set and a month later appeared with Mariani's annual recap of the year's best new restaurants, citing Cleveland's Moxie in the long list.

"About once a month," Mariani wrote, "I get a letter from a Clevelander indicting me for not writing about his city's restaurants. A charge to which I admit guilt. . . .

"But that's past tense, thanks to the elegant Sans Souci, the funky Fat Cats, the eclectic Lola, and the hot new Moxie out in Beachwood." He went on to praise Moxie's food and style and concluded, "A substantial wine list, hot chocolate desserts, and fleet-footed waiters help Moxie live up to its name. Now, no more letters!"

Thus ended the Mariani drama.

Meanwhile, beyond the fray of restaurant criticism and restaurant-criticism criticism, Michael Symon and Liz Shanahan, aloft on their own good spirits and generosity, were married at Pilgrim Church on November 1, two blocks from Lola, a black-stone church with a central dome as gorgeous as Tiffany. A barrel-chested African-American minister with a resounding voice and an inspirational mien, performed the ceremony. Kyle, Liz's son, now eleven years old, bore the ring. Liz almost couldn't walk the aisle, weeping-laughing on her father's arm from nerves and happiness. It was a Sunday; they'd worked late the night before (if you own a restaurant, you don't marry on the busiest night of the week). The crowd, a hundred or so, threw rose petals as they descended the stone steps on the cold, slate-colored day. The reception was held at Moxie, under the culinary direction of Michael's contemporary, Doug Katz, the restaurant run by his buddy (and today usher) Doug Petkovic, affectionately known as Fat Ass. The food was perfect (if you want good food, let me tell you, go to the wedding of a chef), Chet Baker tunes played, and Michael and Liz filled this room too, as completely as they fill Lola.

The following day they left on their honeymoon. Michael and Liz did not go to Paris, or Italy, or anywhere in Europe. They did not flee to a beach in Hawaii or the Caribbean. They went instead to the Napa Valley, to Yountville, and the French Laundry.

Thus, in November 1998, ten years after he'd eaten at Thomas Keller's Rakel as a culinary student, ten years after Keller received a ten best from *Food & Wine,* and the year he himself received his own, Michael Symon finally ate at the French Laundry. Upon his return he told me, "It was the meal of our life." Then he said, "Michael, it was the strangest thing. We couldn't stop laughing."

Part Three

JOURNEY TOWARD PERFECTION

CHAPTER ONE

I'd finished my book, a narrative of a culinary education, but in the same way that actual culinary graduates are in effect newborns to the industry, pink and bald with wrinkled little hands and feet, needy, inarticulate, but healthy and primed for the world, I was too. How could I stop? I'd just arrived on the culinary scene and had so much more to know about the world of professional cooking, chefs, kitchens. I hadn't reached the core of this work, and I knew I would keep writing about it until I did. I knew, furthermore, that I needed to write about the big guns, the famous chefs working today, spanning the country, chefs like Jean-Georges Vongerichten and Daniel Boulud, Charlie Trotter, and, of course, Thomas Keller and the beguilingly named French Laundry, whose mystery in my mind had only sharpened after I saw that the Beard Foundation had that spring named him the country's best chef.

I'd watched the Certified Master Chef candidates by then, and that surely was a fascinating and instructive lesson in attempts at technical perfection and great stamina, a lot of cooking under difficult physical circumstances. But that in the end wasn't what being a chef was all about; the CMC could be useful one day as a valid certification process if it were available to more people and more people knew what it measured. Indeed I'd found the test enormously educational in describing how cooking can be evaluated along fairly objective criteria. Was a sauce cooked out enough? Did it leave your palate cleanly, or did it hang around a little too long? Was the consommé perfectly clear? Were your beans cooked through? Did you know how to make a proper galantine and terrine? Did a forcemeat feel smooth on your palate? All these small questions—asked and answered by knowledgeable chef-judges—added up to a big picture, mainly accurate, about who one was as a cook. On the other hand, the test I saw was like a mountain that needed to be scaled, a personal achievement of mental and intellectual skill rather than the cooking and serving of food to people, daily work that came out of your heart, work you devoted your life to because it was what you loved and you had no other option but to cook. How can a test measure that?

Michael Symon had seen the CMC exam close up as a student assistant to a CMC candidate. When he read an article I'd written about the exam, which described Brian Polcyn's errant slice of the duck terrine, he said of the test, "I think it's horseshit. Like that duck terrine. If it tasted great, what difference does it make if the cut was just a little off? I could see if he mauled it, and it didn't eat great, but if it eats well, I don't understand. What does that test have to do with food?" he concluded. "What does it have to do with cooking?"

Neil Becker, who'd crashed and burned the final day, failing both international and the mystery basket on Day Ten, headed straight back the following year to take it. Lynn Kennedy-Tilyou intended to take it again as well. "My heart tells me I have to do it," she said more than a year after taking the dive on Day Six, American cuisine (hard red beans, undercooked artichoke, Dieter's raw scallop). Brian Polcyn still rankled; that test annoyed him. He knew in his heart he was a better cook than a lot of CMCs. Other CMCs he worked with—he now held down two jobs, teaching and lecturing on butchery, forcemeat, and charcuterie technique at his alma mater, Schoolcraft College in Michigan, and running Five Lakes Grill, a minimum seventy-hour workweek—told him this. He was the only non-CMC teacher on a staff of six, and these consoling chefs just made the anger worse. He wasn't going to take it again. He was going to take it again. No, he wasn't. He didn't know, dammit. Brian didn't much like CMCs generally, yet it pissed him off that he had failed. Twice.

On an intellectual level Brian maintained that this exam should be important and valued, and he lamented that his friends in the industry derided it. Brian consulted for Northwest Airlines with numerous chefs, critically and commercially successful ones with popular restaurants and cookbooks: Todd English from Boston, for example, Waldy Malouf from New York City, Mark Peel from L.A., and others, all of whom were quick to praise Brian behind his back. They got together occasionally to eat and plan food for Northwest. After one such gathering in San Francisco, Brian called me. He had brought up the CMC exam; he had wanted to talk about it with his successful and charismatic colleagues. Didn't they think that the CMC exam was at least *potentially* a good idea? To have an organized method of determining quality in the industry?

"They turned their backs, man," Brian said, of their response. They dismissed it out of hand, thought the subject was unpleasant. Brian didn't understand this. With genuine anger, dismay, and confusion, he said, "The CMC exam and adhering to the regimen of classical cuisine hold no admiration among the 'popular' chefs. Go figure."

While I personally understood and agreed with Brian's lament, the CMC test as it stood was not by any means the end of a search for me personally, even though it did embody for me the importance, permanence, and greatness of classical cooking. It tried hard to measure true excellence; if the cooks didn't live up to it or even come close, that was not the test's fault. And the raison d'être of the test, its ultimate aim, was to create and measure a standard that would be recognized by the entire food service industry, so that the CMC credential would mean something, in the way that, say, the words *Harvard M.B.A.* mean something. In an industry whose standards ranged from excellence to deplorable, this was not a small thing. And yet, given its present impact and the types of chefs who valued it, I was not surprised that Michael Symon denigrated the test. It was antithetical to his personality: big, laughing, generous, sauce-over-the-edge, Ghost of Christmas Present Michael Symon and Lola Bistro.

Michael Symon of course would never be the end either, no matter how much I adored his style and admired his mechanical genius. I had seen the importance of personality in a restaurant at Lola, how a single chef's personality could fill a menu and fill a room, but it was one young man cooking—smart, talented, generous, original—and he was not yet Daniel, not Jean-Georges, not Trotter.

Even these guys, the big names, the Michael Jordans of their industry, weren't representative of it. If anything, they were anomalies. Wolfgang Puck was more a business mogul than chef, what with his scads of successful high-end restaurants and line of prepared foods, and yet he was a chef, no doubt an excellent one. Charlie Trotter had built a broadcast studio–test kitchen next to his restaurant. Can one imagine an André Soltner, the iconic French chef of Lutèce, a chef's chef who never left the kitchen, building a broadcast studio? But even Soltner was a one-of-a-kind talent and spirit. Where were all the rest of these chefs, one million of them, according to the federal Bureau of Labor Statistics? They were working the line and sous-chefing across the country, yes. But they were working in country clubs too. Cooking and managing food programs at state universities. They cooked in nursing homes. They cooked in prisons. They cooked at home and delivered their food to working parents who paid for preprepped meals. They wore coat and tie and lab coats in R&D at big food companies. They worked in sales; they developed cooking Web sites. They were corporate chefs for Cuisinart and Calphalon. They worked in the test kitchens of food magazines and the Food Network, and they cooked in front of the cameras. They taught. They cooked on cruise lines and clipper ships. And they cooked for corporations like General Motors and the New York Times Company.

But it was the restaurant chef who was most dynamic, the creature that I was most interested in and that most people were interested in, the successful entrepreneur, showman, superlative craftsman, and food talent.

I had no idea how I was going to explore this level of cooking, but I had heard about Susie Heller and had once interviewed her for a local story. Susie was a cute forty-something divorcée with two grown children. She'd run catering companies and restaurants in Cleveland, yes, but she was also, Michael Symon had told me, one of the best-connected people in the food world with regard to knowing great chefs. In addition to her work in Cleveland, she was regularly on the production team of her friend Jacques Pepin. When Jacques teamed up with Julia Child for a television series, they called Susie. When Charlie Trotter needed recipes tested, he called Susie. When Jean-Louis Palladin wanted to put a new book together, he called Susie ("I always say I want a boyfriend who touches me the way Jean-Louis touches food," she says. "There is no chef who touches food the way he touches food. It is so sensual"). And when a talented young Cleveland chef wanted a stage— unpaid work in order to learn—at a big New York restaurant, Susie called her friend Jean-Georges, and it was done.

I thought it would be a good idea to introduce myself, given that I needed to write more about chefs and professional cooking and she knew a hell of a lot of chefs.

She also lived with a chef. Her business partner and companion was a cook's cook named Charlie Saccardi, who had cooked all over, most notably perhaps as a sous chef at Bouley in Manhattan. He'd met Susie and was ready to move out of the intense world of New York City kitchens and into a nice house on the rural outskirts of Cleveland with plenty of land. Susie and Charlie opened a barbecue joint, called Stix, presumably because that was where it was in relation to the city. They wanted a low-key restaurant that would serve big portions of meat to hungry midwesterners, something easy and profitable. Stix was highly regarded by both the meat-and-potatoes crowd as well as the city's food intelligentsia. It was to this restaurant that I drove to introduce myself to Susie in June 1997. When she saw me, she said, "Oh, hi!" in a manner that I soon found customary of her easygoing, friendly, chatty personality. You couldn't not like this person immediately unless there was something wrong with you.

I'd brought, as evidence of my worth, a copy of my first book (nothing to do with cooking), some reviews of it, and the catalog copy of my forthcoming book about learning to cook at the CIA. I would tell her that I was fleshing out a potential book on chefs and professional cook-

ing and ask for her thoughts. I planned to find work as a cook with the
best chef I could find in Cleveland, and I wanted to ask her advice on
possible kitchens.

We sat in a booth with a large plate glass window looking into the
parking lot. Susie glanced at my materials, turning the one published
book in her hands. We talked a little about what I was up to and where
I was headed. Then she began to read the catalog copy for *The Making
of a Chef,* and she said these words, words that had that soprano lilt of
hers, that easy, chatty, friendly grace, but that sounded in my ears like a
kettledrum: "I'm doing a book with Thomas Keller at the French Laundry, and we're looking for a writer. We were going to go with a cookbook writer, but Thomas wants a real story, so we were thinking about
getting a real writer."

I said nothing or nearly nothing. Perhaps I said, "Oh, yeah?" I don't
know because suddenly there was noise in my ears like a jet engine and
I couldn't hear a thing.

Susie continued to read the catalog copy. At the bottom of the page
was what may have been the clincher. A very generous reviewer of my
first book had likened my "manner" to that of John McPhee, and my
publisher had dutifully trumpeted it in bold italics in the catalog copy:
in the manner of John McPhee.

Susie saw the name and said, "Oh, John McPhee. That's who someone suggested we get to do the cookbook."

I chuckled. John McPhee, the nonfiction writer's nonfiction writer,
the literary journalist's icon, hero, guru, unreachable deity toward
whom one could only strive.

Susie looked up abruptly when I laughed and said, "Yeah, that's what
our agent did too."

The agent was Susan Lescher, who was one of the first agents to specialize exclusively in food books and who represented some of the best
chefs, writers, and cookbook authors in the industry, such as grande
dame M. F. K. Fischer, Alice Waters, Marcella Hazan, food journalist
Molly O'Neill, chef Charlie Palmer, and now Thomas Keller.

Susie set my materials to the side of the table. I don't think I actually
stood on the seat and waved my arms, but I do recall that to my sur-

prise my hand had risen involuntarily into the air: *Hello, call on me! Here I am! Exactly what you're looking for! Poor man's John McPhee— everyone's always saying that! Cut-rate, work like a dog, damn good writer, says so right there in the catalog, read for yourself! I'M YOUR GUY!*

Susie and I chatted some about the project; we chatted more about my work (oh, I was the soul of casual. Take it or leave it, come and go as I please, all the same to me, one way or the other). But before I said, "Good to meet you, I'm glad I introduced myself," I told Susie, for the record, I would like to be considered to serve as a writer in any capacity she might need with regard to the French Laundry. I would give her support materials and sections of the unpublished book to send to Keller and agent Lescher. Susie said we should do this soon then, because she was heading out to the French Laundry in two weeks to meet with Keller and Lescher about the book.

I supplied materials and waited.

A few days later Susie's call came, which I got on voice mail: *"You know, it's really premature for me to fly you out to California,"* she said. *"We're really not sure what we're doing here. Sorry, hope you understand."*

After I got this message, I went for a long walk in a wood, sat by a clear, gurgling stream. I considered smashing my head on a rock, punishment for my delusions. When I returned from the walk, I called Susie and to her voice mail said thanks, made a last appeal without sounding too desperate, and noted my schedule was free if she happened to change her mind.

I began plans to look for work as a line cook, put a message in to Claude Rodier at Sans Souci and a few other notable chefs in town. I made plans for some measly freelance articles. I took another walk.

The following week, Monday afternoon, Susie called again, this time from the French Laundry. I knew the minute I heard that sweet voice: There was only one reason for her to call me from California. They wanted me out there, could I still do it? A flight was leaving tomorrow afternoon, and she would ask Charlie to drop a plane ticket off that evening. In hours, with head-spinning suddenness, I would be bound for what by now had become in my mind an all but mythical place. And I would arrive in time for dinner.

Susie waited at the gate and whisked me away in a convertible, up 101 North, out of San Francisco and over the Bay Bridge, through cloudy Oakland and Berkeley and, the sky suddenly, arrestingly clear, on into the Napa Valley. She turned off Highway 29, took a left on Washington Street, and in a moment nodded at the signless brown stone building with the wooden balcony and said, "Here's the French Laundry." She turned right onto Creek Street—rustic suburbia—and into the small gravel parking lot. I would be staying at Keller's house directly behind the restaurant in a small upstairs room with a futon, a fan, and a lamp. I had time to wash my hands, splash my face (Susie told me what I had on—chinos, a jacket, and an open, button-down shirt—was fine; the place was casual), and then we left the house and walked into the garden.

It was beautiful, a grassy courtyard within walls of honeysuckle. Little lettuces and vegetables grew in raised beds. Roses, all kinds of them, were in bloom. The Chinese hackberry tree was dense and full, and a chinaberry tree stood craggy but beckoning by the front door. Lilac bushes flourished, day lilies bloomed, and in the center of a walking path, a lush herb garden encircled a young Grecian laurel tree. The sun set over the peaks of the Mayacamas beyond, turning the sky from cerulean to dark cobalt. Every sight seemed that vivid.

Susie and I sit on a wooden bench set at the back of the courtyard and are served sparkling white wine from the valley. Soon Bob and Susan Lescher arrive, and we enter the French Laundry. It is a stone and frame structure built in 1900, rustic on the outside, spare on the inside, with pale walls, low, comfortable light, white tablecloth, white china, and lots and lots of crystal glasses. We are shown to the center table in the downstairs room, a small room with seven tables. The walls are virtually bare, and the room is library quiet. Immediately I fall in love with the entire waitstaff. They are dressed in billowy collarless white shirts and floor-length white aprons, knotted in back. They are beautiful; they seem like angels.

I am aware then of being disoriented, my vision of this surreal-seeming room not completely fixed or trustworthy. It's been a long day; I'm three hours ahead of our eight o'clock reservation, already jet-lagged. Just yesterday I was in my office, trying to grind out freelance ideas for the local newspaper. We have been seated only a few moments when a waiter bows, holding a translucent triangular tray containing cones filled with pink ice cream, a blade of grass incongruously sticking out of the pinkness. The waiter says, "Salmon tartare in a savory tuile with red onion crème fraîche." Hmm, I think, and remove one of them from the tray as it moves around our table. I, corn-fed midwestern beef lover, am not a big fish eater, and I am particularly not big on oily, fishy-tasting fish such as salmon, especially *raw* oily, fishy salmon (which, I learned in culinary school, can carry parasites that do not die at room temperature). But I am in other hands now, and I bite. The salmon is fresh and clean and wonderful, and I am astonished. I cannot believe it, in fact. It's a revelation to me, this subtle balance of fresh fish and its gorgeous texture, followed by the crunchy cone with sesame seeds and that red onion–freckled cream. We are offered menus, but the concentration required for reading is so contrary to where I am that I would have to leave the room, go somewhere else before I could focus on cold words. I am delighted when I hear a waiter say, "But the chef would like to cook for you. . . ."

A plate with an anchovy is set before me. "Anchovy marinated in lemon and olive oil with baked cluster tomatoes," the waiter says, and then, "pickled salutation oysters with a cappelini of marinated cucumbers and sevruga." Two of us have gotten the oyster. I of course receive the anchovy, king of oily, fishy-tasting fish. I ignore the cute little cherry tomatoes, baked tender and still on the vine, to stare at the glistening gray anchovy fillet. Salmon is fine—a delight, really. I adore salmon compared with anchovies; salmon and I are a love affair, in fact. Again I bite, and find that I clearly have never had anchovies before. The flesh is dense and salty and lemony and wonderful.

Where am I? *This is not the world I know.*

We must be conversing, the four of us; I'm sure we are, I'm sure I'm talking and responding intelligently to questions. But the food. The food keeps coming and demands silent focus. Four different soups arrive in demitasse cups, beautiful colors, bold as paint: pale green (cold English pea soup with truffle oil), forest green (watercress), pale yellow (summer squash), and bright orange (carrot). Clearly we are being treated here as though we were royalty. They think we are the queen mother perhaps. I cannot believe we merit this attention, friend of Susie's or not. We are not the president of France and we are not Paul Bocuse and we are not *John Mariani.* But here we are, center of the main room, three or four or five waiters in their billowing loveliness attending to our glasses, which are filled with various wines throughout the meal, all of us being served different courses—four soups!—the silence of the room, the beautiful succession of plates.

Two miniature pancakes arrive on a small plate atop a pale green chive coulis and beneath sevruga caviar; they are potato blini; Susan and Bob have them instead with tomato confit and bottarga. Two different tomato salads follow, and then two fish courses: Atlantic salmon, with its crispy skin formed into a chop, served with truffles on potato gnocchi, and crispy-skinned unagi with Maine lobster, seaweed salad and ponzu sauce. These are small items on big plates, two or three bites each, and we exchange them so that we can try everything. Empty plates disappear, and new ones are set down: a littleneck clamshell containing a tiny bundle of fresh capellini, on top of which rests a single clam, the shell set into a bed of hot rock salt fragrant with peppercorns, cloves, allspice, and star anise, and the waiter says to me, "Linguini with white clam sauce"—*where am I, is that a joke?*—and "Truffle custard with ragout of summer truffles and a chive chip." I look at Susan's plate to my right; it has a little eggcup containing an eggshell with its top clipped off. Out of the eggshell a perfect potato chip rises. Susan, bigtime New York agent, takes a bit of the chip, which has a chive embedded in it, then a small spoonful of the custard, and—I'm staring hungrily at her—she makes a low-moan-ecstasy face, and I am jealous. She won't pass this one. She can't pass it because my Eye-talian *ris-*

torante special is a single clam on a perfect little bed of fine-fine pasta, one bite, which is heaven, but what ecstasy has Susan got? Four new courses arrive: braised beef cheek and veal tongue, stacked, with tomato confit, leeks, greens, and a horseradish cream; a three-bean salad with a truffle vinaigrette; haricots verts, a ball of them held lightly together with a red wine vinegar cream, on a disk of bloodred tomato tartare ringed by an emerald chive oil; and agnolotti, a kind of ravioli, with sweet white corn, summer truffles, and truffle oil. Four separate versions of ecstasy, and I cannot bear *not* to have them all, and yet I am angry and frustrated when I'm forced to pass my plate—*please, let me finish just this, just once!* Four different fish courses arrive, one for each of us (all of which must be passed), followed by two lobster dishes—variations of butter-poached lobster tail. *What is happening here?* I wonder, and as I do, a waiter arrives to show us something. He carries a small earthenware pot to each of us so that we may regard it. He says, "Moulard duck foie gras poached in truffle juice." And it is, he's not kidding: a whole foie gras floating in a clear dark liquid. I am happy but confused. The chef has especially for our table poached an entire foie gras? After all that we've had. And he's sent it out for us to look at before he cut it. The restaurant was packed; what was the chef doing back there? Soon slabs of poached foie gras arrive, with morel mushrooms, summer truffles, and root vegetables. Glory itself.

I grow dizzy from the extravagance, from the angels swirling around the table, from the sights I have seen, from the incredible new sensations on my palate, and from all the wine I've drunk. *You don't understand, this is extraordinary!* I want to say, but I don't because it's obvious, and I am a rube. I've just arrived from Cleveland; my head is unclear; I'm well past giddy. To Susan, a New Yorker entrenched in the food world there, I say, "Do you eat like this all the time?" For a moment she looks at me as if I were an idiot, then shakes her head and says, "No." I just need a check and balance here (once referred to as a "reality" check, but there is no "reality" anywhere near where I'm sitting; that is the one thing I know for certain). I keep wanting to say, *You don't understand how extraordinary this is. Do you see how the vegetables are cut? Do you see that perfect brunoise; it is a perfect and uniform sixteenth-inch dice, do you know how hard that is to do? Every single one is the same, hundreds of them, like confetti but cut by hand!* Four meat courses appear: lamb, veal, squab, and venison (Susan has the lamb I want badly, but she isn't coughing up any of that, you can see right away), and the meat is perfectly seasoned, but *perfectly,* you couldn't improve on it, it is *perfect.* Then cheese courses, perfect cuts of cheese with vegetables and dots of black dressing on pristine china, then sorbet (quinine with watermelon "carpaccio," and lychee with strawberry papaya salad), and then four *more* desserts, panna cotta, chocolate cake, chocolate-filled meringue with mint ice cream, mint oil, and chocolate shavings with salt sprinkled on top, and chocolate éclairs, three varieties of miniature tarts (blueberry, banana cream, and lemon), and hand-wrapped chocolates.

And it is done.

I float up toward consciousness and hear Susan and Susie discussing whether "Thomas" will come out to the table or if we should walk back to the kitchen. Susie notes that he rarely comes out to the dining room, and he does not much like it when he does. But soon there he is, Thomas Keller, a skinny tower in clogs, with dark boyish, wavy hair, shy smile, enormous forehead, staring at his feet throughout as though at the curtain call of a school play. Soon he looks up, smiling: narrow face with very dark eyes. He seems to me, standing at our table, natural and quiet, quick to laugh, self-effacing. I got clips on Thomas Keller and read about him on the plane that afternoon. He worked at many restaurants in New York, I knew, and one in Los Angeles. He once had a temper but got that under control. His New York experience taught him an appreciation for economy. Standard newspaper and magazine fare. But the articles also told me this: He was forty-two, and he had no formal culinary training.

I shall return to this man's house and try to take notes on the evening, but only manage to type the word *surreal* over and over again into my laptop as I attempt to compose thoughts. I keep thinking as I fall easily into sleep about those little brunoise cuts—*actual* brunoise, not small dice called brunoise—each one seemingly a perfect die, and about the seasoning: Everything was perfectly seasoned, every single bite, every one! The vegetables, cooked *perfectly*. Everything had been perfect, and perfect in a way I had learned about and talked about and written about but had never before experienced. Here it was. Providence had intervened and carried me aloft clear across the continent. This was it. I was here. I'd penetrated to the very core of the profession.

$\mathcal{T}$he two-story stone building called the French Laundry is six-teen hundred square feet, which includes the foyer-reception-wine-bar area, the main dining room, where we ate, a stone alcove off this room with four tables. The foyer and main dining room are separated by a stairway leading to two second-floor dining rooms that can seat about thirty-two people at a time, half the restaurant's seating capacity. In summer, which lasts approximately nine months in the valley, French doors open onto a wooden balcony where diners can stretch should they need a break during a three- to five-hour meal. The building was once a French steam laundry, where the gentlewomen of the valley brought their finery. But it was also a residence and, during the 1930s, a saloon with swinging doors and brothel rooms upstairs ("*Gunsmoke* style," said Al Marquez, whose parents owned and lived in the building for decades).

When a couple named Don and Sally Schmitt bought the place in 1976 for $39,000, it had been vacant for years and was unlivable, but still known to all Yountville as the French Laundry. Even dark, abandoned, and filthy with decay, it had charisma. Don Schmitt had once been Yountville's mayor and is credited by many with single-handedly transforming Yountville from a sewer into a viable and thriving community. Sally had learned to cook along the way, and they opened the French Laundry as a restaurant in February 1978 serving a single prix fixe meal each night. They opened, for instance, with a menu of pasta with clam sauce—still on the menu!—blanquette de veau, rice, salad, and rhubarb mousse for $12.50 per person. Don used a metal box for a cash register (they didn't accept credit cards); he marked up wine by only a dollar or two a bottle; family and friends did all the tablewaiting, dishwashing, cooking, and cleaning themselves. And the restaurant never once turned a table; if you had a table reserved at the French Laundry, it was yours for the whole night. After more than a decade San Francisco food editor Michael Bauer put the French Laundry on a par with Chez Panisse, the seminal prix fixe Berkeley restaurant, when he wrote that Sally Schmitt "was one of the unsung heroes of California cuisine, as much a pioneer as Alice Waters."

After a dozen years Don and Sally were ready to move on—the valley had grown too crowded for them; they needed to pioneer one more territory—and quietly put the place on the market. A few chefs took a look at it but thought it too small to turn a profit. No one made a viable offer. Then, in the spring of 1992, an unemployed chef who was living off his credit cards traveled from L.A. (where he'd been fired from his job as chef of Checkers Hotel), arrived at the French Laundry, and knew instantly that this restaurant was his destiny. His lack of employment and personal debt were of course an obstacle. Thomas Keller spent the next nineteen months gathering some forty-eight investors to buy the place for $1.2 million.

Critical acclaim for Thomas Keller began in New York City when he was head chef of Rakel. The market crash of 1987 and subsequent restaurant downscaling hurt Rakel, and Keller left the restaurant rather than turn it into an inexpensive bistro. He became a restaurant consultant, and in this capacity he had never made more money, and he had never been more miserable. An acquaintance called Keller from California to say that Checkers Hotel wanted to create a cutting-edge hotel dining room; would he be interested in taking over the kitchen there? Keller moved to L.A. In New York the economy had felled him; in L.A. it was management brought in by new owners of Checkers who didn't care about food. Keller was quickly fired for insubordination.

Now, with plenty of spare time on his hands, he created a little olive oil company called EVO. He did wine dinners in L.A., freelance. He cooked at the Beard House in Greenwich Village. He judged rib cookoffs in Cleveland. He searched for a restaurant to buy. Newspaper articles openly wondered, "Whatever happened to Thomas Keller?"

Keller had generated enough interest in New York and Los Angeles to warrant attention as soon as he opened the French Laundry in the summer of 1994. The *Chronicle*'s Michael Bauer and *John Mariani* were there almost immediately, the first of a gathering horde, and praised it lavishly. Everyone pronounced the French Laundry excellent.

Keller was now serving food his way: several small courses at a fixed price. The economy was stable and would soon gather steam. The Napa Valley was becoming a year-round tourist destination, and it was a tourism that appealed almost exclusively to people who loved to eat and drink. Keller and a St. Helena native named Laura Cunningham, who quickly became French Laundry general manager, were management, so there was no problem in this department either. He had the kitchen staff he needed. Laura aligned the front of the house and built a wine list. For the first time in Keller's career, all the pieces that make a great restaurant began to cohere.

The first year was slow, however, particularly in the winter, and the French Laundry struggled to pay debts. It hired Pat McCarty, an accountant (who had been, like her boss, recently fired, she from Stag's Leap vineyards), to organize their neglected books and juggle checks to purveyors, beg for time to pay others. Despite the stress, Keller never lost his focus on the food. As long as he cooked perfectly, he believed, solvency would come. In 1995 he was nominated for best California chef by the Beard Foundation but was not chosen. He used the good reviews and the evidence of his cooking to gather more money. Now he built a breezeway—a long, windowed corridor—off the dining room leading to a structure that would be a brand-new kitchen to give his skills their full range (no longer would he have to cook in what is now the foyer, the broken oven door crashing down on the back of his legs throughout service, sautéing in saucepans because he couldn't afford proper sauté pans). Keller won best California chef from the Beard Foundation the next year, and the year after that, in May 1997, the dark horse in a crowd including Charlie Trotter, Emeril Lagasse, Nobu Matsuhisa, and Gray Kunz, he was awarded best chef in the country.

It wasn't long after that Susie Heller said to her friend, "OK, Thomas, it's time to do your cookbook."

The celebrity cookbook is a relatively new phenomenon. In the past books were written by writers. Few chefs had the time, inclination, or capacity to write their own books. Susan Lescher and her husband, Bob, were among the first agents in the country to specialize in food writing and cookbooks. Lescher can't isolate exactly when the trend began, but she says in the last few years the celebrity chef book "is about all editors want." The celebrity chef cookbook in many ways seems to have resulted from chefs' odd trajectory out of the kitchen and into the klieg lights of media stardom.

Lescher said the first celebrity cookbook of the current wave, of the movement we're seeing now, began when Jim Finkenstaedt at Morrow published a cookbook by Michelin three-star chef Michel Guerard. Finkenstaedt, in a telephone conversation from his home in Paris, recalled that *Michel Guerard's Cuisine Minceur* was "the first really successful one, . . . a spectacular success." But two other books by three-star chefs, one by Jean and Pierre Troisgros and one by Paul Bocuse, were less successful. "Neither book did very well. And for a while nobody would touch them," Lescher recalled, suggesting that little care had been given to making these chefs' recipes accessible to the home cook. But as more people traveled to Europe and as more Americans became interested in food and cooking, the books generated some interest.

The book Lescher says turned this around was Alice Waters's *The Chez Panisse Menu Cookbook,* which she handled and which proved to be a blockbuster in 1981. The movement gathered steam through the eighties as American home cooks became more ambitious, and by the mid-1990s, with a booming economy fueling interest in restaurant dining and with the astonishing success of Emeril Lagasse leading a wave of interest in chefs' lives and work, celebrity cookbooks now towered over writers' cookbooks. Soon publishing houses coveted star chefs as though they were movie stars, lavishing big advances on them that were unlikely to be returned in royalties. The average advance today, Lescher said, was in the low six-figure range (and the chefs typically had to hire their own photographers, which can run many tens of thousands of dollars). But the price could go as high as $350,000 for a nationally renowned chef like Jean-Georges Vongerichten.

Such chefs had immediate recognition, a built-in audience, and, Lescher noted, they also had numerous restaurants where they could sell their books. But there was also the groupie factor. Editors and publishers, Lescher said, paid sums of money they knew the books were not worth "because they wanted preferential treatment at the chef's restaurant." She would not point fingers, but given the celebrity status of chefs and the prestige of having a central table at, say, the French Laundry, it's not difficult to understand how a publishing executive might rationalize a big advance.

So publishers were able to pay for it, and chefs wanted to do it. Given photographer fees, money spent on recipe testers and writers, this was not usually a moneymaking venture for the chef. The chef, Lescher said, wanted to bring attention to the restaurant and to showcase his or her food. Susie's remark to Thomas—"it's time"—was partly a rote response to what was happening in the industry; all well-known chefs now had their own cookbooks. Thomas should have his own simply as a matter of course.

But the French Laundry was different from other restaurants; his cookbook, he said, should reflect that. Also, Keller simply wasn't interested in producing yet another celebrity chef cookbook. They bored him.

The morning after I lost my virginity to the French Laundry, I was up early, still on Cleveland time. Josh, then French Laundry butcher, was breaking down racks of rabbit at 7:30 A.M. He directed me to Ranch Market for coffee. I also got a doughnut there, which seemed indecent after last night's meal. The doughnut made me a little angry, in fact, but I was hungry.

Today was a Wednesday, generally the day Keller took off (the restaurant is open seven days a week). Midmorning we walked in the opposite direction of Ranch Market to Gordon's—a restaurant, wine bar, and the kind of breakfasting spot where Margrit Mondavi might just as likely be found as, say, Thomas Keller—and here we had delicious coffee and fresh fruit at a small table outside.

Thomas explained his hopes for the book. "The French Laundry is not new," he said. "It's twenty years old. The French Laundry is bigger than me. A lot of people make the French Laundry what it is. I want this book to be about the French Laundry, not about Thomas Keller." The kinds of cookbook he admired, he said, were the ones produced in Europe, lavish with photographs not only of the food but also of the region where the food came from, with a text filled with stories about the food and about the chef, books such as *Le Livre d'Olivier Roellinger*. His favorite cookbook was *Ma Gastronomie* by Fernand Point, one of the century's greatest chefs of one of the century's greatest restaurants, La Pyramide in Vienne, a town in southeastern France. *Ma Gastronomie* is filled with wonderful stories about the restaurant and the chef. "I want it to be a good read," Keller said of his intended book.

And so I returned to Cleveland, wrote a proposal, and Susie and Thomas put together a list of about seventy-five recipes that would appear in the book and three complete sample recipes. Susan Lescher liked the package, showed the proposal to various editors; two made offers Susan considered viable, and Susie and Thomas chose Ann Bramson, now heading Artisan, a division of Workman Publishing. That is how Thomas Keller's cookbook was launched.

I was a hired gun. I'd get a flat fee, a generous one, I thought, but one that had no relation to any royalties. This was fine by me. Any money at all was gravy. Less than a year earlier I was making brown sauce in the American Bounty restaurant at the Culinary Institute of America, and now I was about to be given entrée into the kitchen of the French Laundry, to interview its cooks and purveyors, taste anything I wanted, watch the cooking, try to get inside the mind of this unusual chef, and eat several times at this place, one of the best restaurants in America.

Some said *the* best.

In September the Culinary Institute of America holds a week of food-writing courses at its Greystone Campus, which is in St. Helena, a ten-minute drive north of Yountville. Some of the most influential food writers and food critics in the country are invited to teach. Every year many of them eat at the French Laundry. During one such week in September 1997, on a Thursday night, Thomas Keller could look out the window of his kitchen and see Ruth Reichl, Phyllis Richman, restaurant critics for the *New York Times* and the *Washington Post,* respectively, and the *Atlantic Monthly's* Corby Kummer mingling in the courtyard; they had reservations together that night, along with many other food writers. The whole restaurant would be filled with food writers, in fact, but it was the presence of Reichl, the most powerful restaurant critic in the country, that would have a dramatic effect on the restaurant.

"It was really good for them," Keller recalled, noting that all the food writers were able to relax and talk with one another. "Really high energy, and everybody was drinking and having a good time. And we were really on, *really* on that night. This is the third year they've come, we *knew* everybody was coming, so we were all jazzed in the kitchen. High energy. We were doing some really good food. And we make the meal for Ruth and Phyllis and Corby and Mark [Furstenberg, a CIA baking instructor and D.C. baker and entrepreneur], and I went out afterward because I didn't look at it as a professional visit; I was looking at it as a social visit. They were there to enjoy dinner at the French Laundry; they weren't there to write about the French Laundry." Keller chatted and laughed, greeted the women with a kiss, which he would never have done, he said, if he'd thought this was a professional visit.

Six weeks later Keller received a call from a fact checker at the *New York Times.* How does it feel, the fact checker asked, to have Ruth call you the most exciting restaurant in the country?

Keller thought it was a joke.

On October 29 the *Times* ran Ruth Reichl's piece under a "Critic's

Notebook" tag. The French Laundry, she wrote, "is the most exciting restaurant in America." A meal here, she exclaimed, "is a wild ride, an exhilarating flavor carnival." She said:

> Mr. Keller loves soup, and he might begin a meal with a dazzling quartet of contrasting flavors that arrive in espresso cups. Fresh slightly bitter sorrel soup, the essence of green, is quickly followed by tomato consommé that is crystal clear but tastes bright red. Two thick soups look similar, but one is an ineffably rich lobster bisque, the other a clean smooth puree of cranberry bean.
>
> Part of the fun of the French Laundry is watching Mr. Keller negotiate the high wire, wondering if he will fail. He is not afraid to make mistakes, which increases the anticipation and keeps you on the edge of your seat.
>
> Each new dish is a challenge. The first time you order "oysters and pearls," a sabayon of pearl tapioca with poached Malpeque oysters and cavier, you feel simultaneously daring and foolish.
>
> Can he possibly pull it off? Incredibly, he does; the dish is absolutely fabulous.
>
> Before long, Mr. Keller has drawn you into his world, made you a participant in his restless search for flavor. . . . Mr. Keller's genius is in understanding that people will participate in his fantasy so long as he keeps them happy to every last bite.

That apparently is what he did the night she was there. Phyllis Richman also wrote an influential review based on that night, and Corby Kummer returned to write about the restaurant and Keller. "He got a lot of mileage out of that meal," said Kummer.

Richman noted that while Keller knew who they were, the reservations had not been made in any of their names and that all the articles written were not based solely on that single meal. "I think he's the best," Richman said. ". . . The French Laundry is as good as a restaurant gets in this country, maybe as good as a restaurant gets anywhere."

Chefs were likewise full of unusually high praise. Michael Richard, who is known to be as chauvinistic about his native France and its food as a chef can be and has been quick to claim there is no such thing as a great American chef, said of Keller, "He's one of the best French chefs anywhere." Jean-Louis Palladin said, "He has the mind of a French guy, you know? He's thinking like a French cook."

CHAPTER THREE

*L*aura Cunningham, dressed in a dark suit, her abundant brown hair pulled severely back into a ponytail accentuating high, angular cheekbones and narrow face, strides out of the French Laundry dining room, down the breezeway and into the kitchen, carrying two crème brûlées in ramekins. Thomas Keller is at the pass, *la passe* in French kitchens, a bank of stainless steel tables covered with thick white tablecloths, on top of which is a metal bar where the night's tickets are held. Thomas is in the middle of dinner service, calling orders, finishing plates, expediting. He is dressed in a crisp chef's coat, long white apron, black pants. His black clogs add two inches to what already seems too much lean height. He is motionless, holding two fingers to his lips as he stares down at tickets, determining what needs to be fired next. Laura stops in front of the pass, extends the ramekins toward Thomas.

"These are soft," she says.

Thomas looks abruptly at her, touches the browned sugar coating the custard, wanting it to be hard and smooth as glass. His finger sinks into a gluey film. Laura's lips tighten, and she sets the ramekins on the dishwasher's station, to the right of the pass.

"*Tim?*" Thomas calls to the pastry station. "Is there a problem with the crème brûlées?" He's visibly angry; he knows they've caught this error only because a gluey crème brûlée has been served, maybe several of them.

"No," Tim answers, checking a sheet tray neatly lined with brûlée-filled ramekins.

Keller leaves the pass to check them himself. He taps the sugar top; it's hard. The waitstaff brings a dozen brûlées to their station out front to save trips to the kitchen. The waiters' station happens to be where coffee is brewed and milk is steamed to a froth; the heat and humidity are evidently softening the sugar crust, a fundamental pleasure in the crème brûlée. Thomas turns to Laura and says, "No more bringing these to the wait station. When they need them, they can come back here." The front of the house expediter, a young Frenchman named Alain who wears a thick blond ponytail, listens and nods, as do several other waiters. "You've got to understand," Keller implores them. "It's a different environment in here from out there."

It is Sunday, February 22, 1998. El Niño rains have been hammering California and flooding much of Sonoma and Napa counties, saturating vineyards and wiping out roads, but the French Laundry is packed every night of the week and three lunches every weekend. The Beard awards, continual media coverage, and the Reichl article have made difficult reservations more so. A young woman named Misty handles the French Laundry's phones. At ten every morning she begins taking reservations for the date exactly two months away. In an hour the prime slots between seven and nine are filled. By the end of the day, throughout which she absorbs strangers' badgering, intimidation, threats, finagling, lying, tears, the books will be filled and a waiting list will have begun on the back of the page. Once hungry for customers during February, the French Laundry now tries to limit the people who arrive each night, always seeming to accept about ten or fifteen more reservations than it really can serve comfortably. Tonight is no different.

Waiters gossip to one another about the customers. "The guy at table eight is wearing a Super Bowl ring," says one to another. Others whisper that Michael J. Fox is expected at eight-fifteen.

Laura hustles gracefully back and forth between the kitchen and the dining room all night. This time she returns with a Tiffany bracelet, lines of diamonds leading to a huge central pearl, and stops before Thomas at the pass. Laura explains that a gentleman would like the bracelet somehow put in the food or in a dish and served.

"Does he want it in the box?" Thomas asks. He looks confused and irritated, not at the request, only generally; the night is busy, and he must contend not only with getting the food out but now with an extraordinary bracelet.

"I don't know," says Laura.

Thomas nods, his mouth closed tight. He looks at the man's ticket, a deuce at table three; he has already served them a canapé. He orders two canapé soups from D.J.'s station. He lifts a red pen and stars the ticket, saying to Laura and Alain, "Table three is now VIPed." When the soup course is done, Thomas sets an oystershell on rock salt in a bowl and lays the pearl of the bracelet in the shell, sparkling diamonds lying across mimicking rock salt crystals. He covers the bowl with a white china cloche and directs Alain to deliver it to table three.

The ticket box chatters, spitting out orders. A waiter tears tickets off and hands them to Thomas. He studies the incoming orders, then says, "Ordering four tastings. Ordering two tastings and two regular, agnolotti and crab salad, one salmon, one scallop, one veal, one lamb." Each station repeats the order it's responsible for. "Let's pick up two scallops, a salmon and a lobster. Mark, fire two veals and a sweet."

"Firing two veal, one sweet."

The French Laundry kitchen is a clean, bright rectangle, forty feet by twenty feet. One aisle runs lengthwise. Three aisles run widthwise. Two cooks man the first aisle, canapé and fish, sharing two large flattops, which deliver graduated heat, intense in the center and decreasing as you move out. Across from them are two more cooks, first-course and meat stations, also using graduated heat flattops. In the last aisle two pastry cooks work under the direction of pastry chef Stephen Durfee. They have one small conventional gas stove, a pot of oil on one burner all night long kept at 350 degrees to fry fresh doughnuts for French Laundry signature dessert "coffee and doughnuts." The cook in charge

of the composed cheese course works adjacent to the pastry cooks on
the long counter running lengthwise across the kitchen.

The pass is created at the end of the cooks' ranges, between the
canapé/fish aisle and the first-course/meat aisle, by rolling stainless steel
tables to surround a small space where Thomas can expedite and put
the finishing touches on plates, an arsenal of finishing garnishes at his
disposal kept on ice or in small plastic containers behind him and to his
left: chopped chives, chervil pluches, fennel tips, chive tips, a range of
powders, squab spice, dried horseradish, sweet pepper confetti, two
fresh sea salts (sel gris, fleur de sel), fennel oil, chive oil, thyme oil, basil
oil, balsamic glaze, chive chips, among other assorted oils, vinegars,
powders, and herbs. The cloths covering the tables are taped there with
neon green painter's tape, which does not leave a sticky residue on the
cloth. This tape is also used to label every container in the kitchen, of
which there are hundreds, none very large. Nothing in this kitchen is
very large.

That the kitchen is clean is something you sense immediately upon
entering, but you don't immediately understand why it feels so clean;
you only sense clean's effect. Slowly you realize that the room is quiet
and comfortable underfoot. Keller uses gray carpeted mats on the tile
floor. Every other kitchen I've ever been in uses big, heavy black rubber
mats with holes in them; they provide traction, and all the food and
sauce that gets slopped and spilled on them goes into those holes; at the
end of the night they can be hosed down outside while the floor is
swept and mopped. But Keller wanted carpeting because it was more
comfortable for a staff that was on its feet fourteen hours a day.

If you arrive during the day, you notice how bright the kitchen is.
Two long windows run the length of the kitchen and look out onto a
patio. Also, Keller has put in skylights, an expensive design decision requiring complicated rerouting of the exhaust systems above the stoves.
He wanted abundant natural light in his kitchen. "I knew I had to have
the kind of place that would attract people who can do this kind of
food," he explained.

My first day in the kitchen I saw a familiar face. He no longer had a
ponytail, his dark hair now cropped short. David Gilbert had been the

incoming fellow—teacher's assistant—at the CIA's American Bounty restaurant when I worked grill station. At least once he prevented me from burning the flour I was using to make a brown roux to make the damned brown sauce, a classical sauce that was then the bane of my existence. We chatted while he slid pieces of dough through an electric pasta roller. David, I learned, was from outside Detroit and had worked as a cook for Brian Polcyn at Five Lakes Grill. When I remarked on the French Laundry kitchen, David said, "That was the first thing I noticed when I came here. It didn't smell like a kitchen. It smelled like someone's home."

Details—the carpet on the floor, skylights, fresh air—piled up. Incredibly every pan looked brand-new. The pans weren't, but the dishwashers scrubbed them so hard that even their bottoms were a clean brushed silver, not that greasy carbon black that I'd seen everywhere else. Eventually the cooks have to throw out what look like brand-new sauté pans because the pot washers have scrubbed off so much metal from the pan itself that it won't rest flat; its handle becomes heavier than the pan and falls to the counter with a clink.

If you walk down the breezeway—windows on your left, and on your right a counter with shelves of glasses above it and linens below, windows and a screen door looking out onto the patio—you arrive at the pass. To your left is the dishwasher's station. If you turn right and walk the kitchen's length, you will pass through a doorway into a small butchery and prep room, a screened-in porch that overlooks the garden. I would venture to say that few butcheries or prep rooms in any American restaurant are in breezy screened porches, overlooking a garden, shaded by an enormous Chinese hackberry tree, a mountain range visible in the distance, just over a wall of honeysuckle.

Three giant kettles filled with various stocks but most often with veal stock, sit on gas flames in this room. The first veal stock (a green piece of tape on its reads "V I") in which fifty pounds of blanched and rinsed bones cook at a low, low simmer with six calf's feet, leeks, carrots, a bulb of garlic, and tomato paste. When it has simmered for about eight hours, the V I will be strained. The bones will be retained, the pot refilled with water and set to simmer again, now labeled "V II," referred to in the kitchen as the remy, short for remouillage. When this has cooked for another eight hours or so, the liquid will be strained. V I and V II, a combined total of forty or fifty gallons of it, will be combined and reduced slowly, to ten gallons, a pot labeled "F V" for finished veal.

I had spent some time in the afternoon in this room talking with Grant Achatz, currently on fish station, and Mark Hopper, currently on meat. Lunch service had just begun. Yesterday's rains had given way to a clement afternoon. A woman, seated on the wooden bench in the garden, breast-fed her baby. A gentleman went out to her, carrying today's *New York Times Magazine,* open to the crossword, and sat in an adjacent chair. Another couple joined them, evidently relaxing while they waited for their table. Grant—age twenty-three with light red hair, freckles, hopelessly wholesome and earnest—faced them. He was trimming a large black truffle that had been poached in mushroom stock. He brought a ring cutter down on the truffle to make it a perfect cylinder. Adjusting a plastic Benriner mandoline, he carefully created a dozen and a half identical silver dollar–size slices of truffle. They would fit neatly on top of one of the extraordinary scallops Keller buys from a woman in Maine.

Grant's dish had been conceived twelve hours earlier, at one in the morning. Keller and four cooks had taken positions around the cleaned stainless steel tables in the center of the kitchen, as they do every night after service, determining what orders need to be faxed to various purveyors, what new dishes they would add to the menu.

Grant had been serving the scallop with sautéed leeks and truffles, then with a scallop roe coulis, and wanted to change it again ("You get bored," he said). He had wanted to use a red wine sauce, but the braised oxtails on meat station used a red wine sauce, so that night, leaning on the stainless steel table with his colleagues D.J. (canapé), Kirk (meat), and Walter (first course), all of them beat from a Saturday night's service, Grant shrugged when Thomas asked about the scallop dish. It's hard to come up with new dishes at one in the morning. "Why don't you use asparagus," Thomas said. "What else do we have?"

"We have some truffle coulis," Grant said.

Thomas nodded and said, "Use asparagus and truffles."

Grant nodded. And that was how a new French Laundry dish was created.

At service the following night Grant sautéed the scallop, beautiful three-ounce pieces of meat, big and dense as a filet mignon. He then spooned onto the plate asparagus sauce (a puree of asparagus, thinned with stock, strained, and mounted with butter *à la minute*). In the center of this he put a spoonful of truffle coulis (made from the scraps of the truffles he'd been slicing), a brownish sauce ringed by the bright green sauce. Into the center of this sauce he spooned diced fingerling potatoes, which, besides being good to eat, elevated the scallop and kept it from sliding around in the sauce when the waiters left the kitchen, bowls in hand. He rested the scallop on the potatoes, then placed the perfect slice of truffle on top. He now spooned onto the truffle slice some sliced asparagus stalks that he'd reheated in butter with some shallot and tomato concassé, and on top of this he placed a bundle of four asparagus tips, tied with filaments of leek, and sent it to the pass.

"Pan Seared Maine Diver Harvested Scallop with Green Asparagus and Périgord Truffle 'Coulis'" was one of nine dishes he was responsible for that night. Toward that end Grant spent part of this afternoon during lunch service slicing truffle in the prep/butcher porch and tying bundles of asparagus tips with blanched leek greens.

Another new dish had also been created that night. Of Kirk Bruderer, who was off tomorrow but writing a prep list for Mark Hopper, Thomas asked what Kirk wanted to do with the veal. When Kirk said nothing, Thomas said, "How about doing a vitello tonnato? You know what that is? Classic Italian dish?" Kirk didn't seem to know, and Thomas explained that it was a basically a leftover dish, veal served with canned tuna and mayonnaise. But Thomas wanted to turn it into a chaud-froid dish, a hot component and a cold component, so he told Kirk that meat station would sauté the veal fillet as normal, but the garnish for it would be a tartare of yellowfin tuna, formed into a quenelle and rested on top of the hot fillet, itself resting on artichokes braised in wine and oil, Spanish capers, and fresh herbs, and written on the menu "Vitello Tonnato."

During lunch service, while Grant prepped the scallop dish and Mark turned artichokes, the kitchen was filled with sixteen other cooks, some working the lunch service, others prepping for dinner. The kitchen is crowded but stays clean on weekend days. When plastic wrap is needed, it is pulled from a cupboard beneath a prep station, used, then returned to that cupboard. You always know where the plastic wrap is, and the counters stay clear. Thomas works lunch service, and on this Sunday he finds the Pullman loaf of bread to make toast rounds for foie gras. Someone has torn a hole in the plastic bag instead of un-knotting it. Thomas calls out to the kitchen, "Who opened this?"

My friend David Gilbert takes a breath, leaves his workstation, and goes to Thomas for his lashings. Thomas looks at him and shakes his head, incredulous. It seems Thomas is about to say something harsh, but instead he says, "Let me show you how to open this bag." He un-knots the bag and removes the Pullman loaf. He stares at David. David nods and returns to his station.

Keller was once well known for his temper. Many of the cooks who worked under him hated him. When one of his line cooks once com-plained about a late walk-in, Keller fired the cook on the spot. You want to go home, go home, Keller said. The young cook pleaded and pleaded. But fired means fired.

Reminded about his early days, he says, "There comes a point when you've exhausted rational expression. And you've got to revert to more primitive means. But by then it's too late anyway."

So now he uses calmer means to convey his anger or disapproval. Si-lence can be more effective than a scream. And he will get angry in his kitchen, but I never heard him raise his voice. His anger is concentrated and focused.

When lunch service is over, prep for dinner begins. Thomas portions foie gras, slicing inch-thick slabs, crosshatching the surface, then resting each on parchment in a rectangular plastic container. Cutting the foie gras to the right thickness is paramount, yet he still returns from a trip to find the foie gras cut a quarter inch too thin. The proper thickness, an inch, ensures a crisp, seared surface, a warm, firm interior, with an almost molten center—the three textures of perfectly cooked foie gras.

He gives the scraps to Gregory Short, one of two sous chefs, who will roll them in cheesecloth to make the foie gras torchon, foie wrapped into a cylinder in cheesecloth and poached. Thomas then covers the container, stores it, cleans his knife, and wipes down his board so that it appears nothing at all has happened. Then he fills the pig's trotters with their sweetbread farce and wraps them in caul fat. He butchers fish, completing the task slowly, cleaning his knife, washing his board, wiping down the stainless steel table till it gleams. And then he makes the risotto farce for tomorrow's agnolotti. He has already made final menu changes and taken calls from purveyors. He occasionally feeds them, as he did Charlie Akwa, one of his fish purveyors. Charlie the Fish Lady, a former Wall Street money runner turned fishmonger, makes deliveries personally on weekends, dropping off belon oysters, and then, when pressed, agrees to a bowl of corn agnolotti.

At four forty-five Thomas has a bite to eat and sits on a stool in the breezeway speaking with front of the house staff, calling first to ask who are front waiters, who are back waiters, then moving into new menu items, such as the scallop with asparagus and truffle coulis, the vitello tonnato. He sets his station as other cooks set theirs. At around five-thirty the first guests are seated (sometimes there is a delay as last-minute changes require a reprinting of the night's menu), and the order box begins its incessant chattering; at quarter to six Thomas leaves the pass, lopes calmly across the gravel parking lot, through the opening of a tall wooden gate, and into his home to have a shower, then a quiet moment or two with an espresso. He returns to the kitchen around six, a little after, his hair still wet, and ties a fresh white apron at his waist. He is now ready for the second service of the day.

This weekend proves to be smoother than last, with Saturday's Valentine's Day going down as one of the two worst nights in French Laundry history. Customers sat too long at tables that had to turn, and there were "monster waits" at the bar, according to Laura, who must absorb the complaints and comp the champagne. As service began, Thomas demonstrated for Walter, on first course, how he wanted the cured salmon cooked (poached very gently in milk), but first-course orders kept coming and Thomas kept cooking at the first-course station while Mark Hopper, taking over for D.J. on canapé, covered that course and expedited at the pass. "I don't know why he's doing this," Laura whispered. "It's throwing everyone off." Thomas retook the pass two hours and twenty minutes into service, but everyone remained out of sync. Waiters left for an eight-top with two first courses—the poached salmon with gnocchi and a pea shoot salad, and a fricassee of belon oysters, oyster mushrooms, oyster plant, and beluga caviar—only to return to tell Thomas the table had already had that course. "I don't know where you guys are taking this food," he said to them. For a half hour he struggled. Laura came back with dishes, saying, "Twenty-five has already had their agnolotti." Thomas looked at the ticket, crossed off that course, and said, "Now I'm really lost." It was ugly.

Laura spent a lot of money comping champagne. At one point twenty-six people jammed the foyer waiting for tables; some waits lasted an hour and a half. The kitchen assembled additional canapés to keep tempers at bay, and these extra courses took a toll. This was the shit. (At the French Laundry one says, "in the shit," the direct translation of the French, not "in the weeds.")

Larry, a front of the house waiter, said, "We're doing eleven different dishes we've never seen before."

David, a thirty-five-year-old waiter and artist who looks twenty despite his height and beefy physique, approached the pass and said, "Chef, Table Twenty-seven just came in, said they don't eat meat, they called ahead."

Thomas shook his head; this was the first he'd heard of it.

Johnny, another waiter, talked at a whisper with another waiter, and Thomas said, "You want to have a conversation, have a conversation out there." He was visibly angry many times that night. When Johnny again was talking—back waiters will line up to run food as needed—he said, "Don't look that way, look this way. Pay attention to what is going on in the kitchen."

The lobster course was sent out to a four-top, but Larry returned with them. Keller looked up angrily. Larry said, "Table Two is up." No food goes to a table unless the entire table is seated. Larry set the dishes at the pass and left to check the table again. Thomas looked at Grant, who seemed to be the only cook really on top of his orders, and said, "We're gonna lose these four lobsters." Grant shook his head—that can throw his entire service off—but didn't skip a beat in his cooking. Larry rushed down the breezeway calling, "He's back, he's back." Thomas stared at the four lobster tails: two herb-roasted with a garnish of seared foie gras and "pommes Maxim" with red beet essence, two butter-poached with braised fennel, niçoise olives, and a sultana raisin emulsion. Alain looked to the chef: Could he take them? Thomas held his hand over them to feel for heat, paused, then swept his hand through the air: Send them out.

The last customers were seated at ten minutes to eleven. Their dessert course wouldn't go out until three minutes after one.

The French Laundry had accepted 120 reservations, too many for an ambitious menu; it'd offered a single menu of eleven courses, with two dishes for each course, so all the meals lasted longer than normal. The dishes themselves were cumbersome for the waitstaff; an uncomplicated course, such as pasta (risotto agnolotti with truffles and celeriac bouillon, and foie gras ravioli in a quince broth with toasted chestnuts), required three waiters to serve a six-top; the final course, "baked Alaska" with valrhona chocolate ice cream, graham crackers, and Italian meringue, required four waiters for a party of eight, tying up a quarter of the waitstaff for five or six minutes on a single table. Thomas and Laura would have to reevaluate Valentine's Day, one of the busiest days of the year at the French Laundry.

"We usually have a real critical moment in the beginning for the first hour and a half because that kind of sets the tone for the rest of the night," Keller explains. He thinks of the kitchen–dining room dynamic as an hourglass shape: the heat, hustle, tension, athleticism, and stress of the kitchen and the coolness, relaxation, luxury, refinement, and ease of the dining room, separated by the narrow squeeze of the pass, through which one thousand five-, nine-, and twenty-course meals pass each week. "When it works," Keller says, "It's beautiful."

The French Laundry serves between 100 and 120 customers a night, seven nights a week without fail, and between 70 and 100 customers each Friday, Saturday, and Sunday at lunch. Because each meal comprises numerous courses, 100 dinners is the equivalent of 250 covers at a conventional restaurant. On a slowish night 70 chef's tastings will be ordered, and 30 five-course meals, 710 courses in all, requiring thousands of plates and liners and hundreds of wineglasses. And every night there are a few VIP tables—friends of the French Laundry, investors, celebrities, regulars, and anyone dining solo—which will receive as many as ten courses *before* the nine-course tasting menu begins, with maybe a special course or two—an entire foie gras poached in truffle juice, for example—tossed in.

By eight on Sunday the kitchen is working full bore into the night's service. Husky, baby-faced David returns from the dining room with four sets of dishes in his arms, but before leaving them at the dishwasher's station, he says to Thomas, "Chef, this is Table Seven," a VIP table tonight, and Thomas looks at every VIP plate before it disappears. Usually plates come back empty, in which case David would have said only "Chef, Table Seven," but the two extra words tell Thomas to look more carefully. The kitchen is rocking now, the dining room packed. Keller looks down at the plates, then snaps his gaze back on David. "They said it was wonderful," David explains. "They're just full." Keller looks again at their plates, mostly empty but for a few pieces of meat unfinished. Then he spots something and lifts it out of the dish between thumb and index finger. He exhales. All cooks are hustling, fifth gear, no time to pause for even an instant, turning-plating-cooking, stooping at their lowboys, turning-firing-plating. But Keller appears to have all the time in the world right now, has stopped completely. "Mark," he calls to the meat station.

"Yes, Chef," Mark answers, but he does not look up. He's pulling pans from the oven, wincing at the heat, has several sauté pans working on the flattop, and he's ready to plate several dishes.

"Mark."

"Yes, Chef!" But still Mark does not stop moving. He can't, too much to do; he can't lose his momentum.

"Mark."

"Yes, *what?*" Mark says angrily, and stops to look at the chef. He had to break his sprint and come to a full stop. "Yes, *what?*"

Keller tosses a brown circle of string to Mark, and then he returns to expediting. Mark bobbles the string, then catches it. For a moment he doesn't know what it is. Then he recognizes it and seems visibly to deflate where he stands. He has sent a veal fillet to a table without removing the butcher's string that kept it tight and uniform as it cooked. He mouths the word *shit* so hard his head jerks, and he returns to his work. He's one of the best cooks in the kitchen, but his error stays with him all night.

David waits at the pass to run food. He has set a plate down on which to carry a silver soup terrine, tonight filled with pea shoot soup to be poured over a carrot custard and glazed carrots at the table. He has placed a doily on this plate and turned to say something to a waiter behind him, leaving his hand on the doily. He stops speaking abruptly, turning and saying, "Ah!" Thomas has set the scalding terrine on his hand. Cradling his hand, David looks at Thomas with alarm. Keller, leaning down an inch or two toward David, touches his own breastbone and says, "I want your attention here."

And then the kitchen hits a groove, and all elements lock into place. The chefs actually begin to move more slowly. The dance takes over, and each cook is all but fluid. The plates are beautiful. The kitchen is quiet. Thomas doesn't speak other than to order and pick up.

Visitors often arrive to say hello. During nightmare Valentine's Day Barbara Tropp, a San Francisco chef and cookbook author, appeared and thanked Thomas for a wonderful meal. More often strangers arrive: a young cook from Stars, Jeremiah Tower's restaurant, with his mother. His mother appears to be astonished, and watching the kitchen, the cooks at work, the perfect plates leaving the dining room, she whispers to her son, "It's like a watchmaker's shop." Her son just grins, clearly amazed. He senses this night, from the food and the vision of this clean, clean kitchen that he's got to work here (and in six months he will be hired).

When the night slows, after eleven, and Thomas has only a few more orders to fire, he will clean or sweep or wash dishes. This weekend Grant, returning from the walk-in to his station, spots Keller rinsing down plates and says, "That is why this is such a great kitchen to work in."

"Thomas?" Laura says, appearing with a customer, a middle-aged woman, casually dressed, nondescript. An accountant perhaps, a civil lawyer, maybe an academic. She asked to see the chef, and Laura has escorted her. Thomas sets a rinsed plate in the dish rack, places the hose into its bracket, and dries his hands. He shakes the woman's hand with a do-I-know-you? smile. The woman says, "I just wanted to tell you that in forty-seven years I can say that was the best meal I've ever had."

Thomas smiles and says, "Thank you! Thank you for telling me that. Come back again."

"I will," the woman says. She is all but breathless. Giddy. "With a smile on my face," she says, reduced to the level of a swooning teenager. She cannot contain herself—she knows better, but it's useless—and she continues to gush. He asked her to come back again, and so she says, "Thank you for saying that." The moment she hears the words leave her mouth, it's as if she can't believe she's acting this way. She and Laura head back up the breezeway, and the woman, regaining her senses, tries to explain and apologize for her behavior, pleading, "I've never done that before."

Laura places a comforting hand around the woman's shoulder. "I know," she says softly. Laura sees this all the time.

First canapé and fish stations break down. Next first course and meat break down, and they will clean and make sure their stations are set for tomorrow morning's work. They lean on the counter writing their prep lists. They gather around the stainless steel tables and discuss tomorrow's three menus, determine what orders need to be phoned or faxed tonight. And then Thomas heads home.

When I spent time at the French Laundry, I'd dress in my CIA-issued whites and Dansko kitchen clogs, pressed into a gap between shelves and a prep station facing the pass. Or I'd stand beside the pass—more comfortable, better view of the food, closer proximity to the chef—when service wasn't busy. Thomas could then occasionally lean to me and quietly say something like "Did you notice that? That's a great server," as Monica carried blini courses away. Monica was serving one of the blini to a vegetarian. The blini with tomato confit is a vegan dish until the final flourish of bottarga—dried cod roe—is grated into ruby confetti over the plate. Monica had noticed it and asked, "Chef, do you want to serve this?" Thomas looked, lifted the plate, and handed it back to D.J. on canapé, saying, "Replate this, please." He would have missed it himself. This kind of professionalism in his staff impressed him. He was the proud father of the French Laundry family.

Many of the waitstaff used family metaphors when describing Keller and their work at the French Laundry. One young woman, referring largely to the stress of the work and front of the house cohesion, said, "I shouldn't make this analogy, but you know when in families there's an abusive father? The kids stick together?" She quickly said that no one here was literally abusive, but that was the effect of Thomas, the severe, omnipotent father.

David, burned fingers cooled, said, "If you try to seek his approval, he will bury you. Like he tells his cooks, 'Don't cook for me, cook for yourself.'" Excellence, that is, not its reflection on you, was what you strove for.

On Friday that same weekend, in addition to the regular menus, he offered an offal tasting. As I stood beside the pass, I would move aside to make room for a cutting board where Thomas sliced the veal kidney (he roasted the kidneys whole and served the slices with wilted spinach and red wine vinegar sauce). I watched him slice the organ; it was cooked perfectly, and its various chambers or lobes were slightly pink and surrounded by juicy fat.

As Thomas made the first two slices, he said, "Oh, see, *look* at that." He sliced again. "See how that fat melts around it. That's beautiful. You don't see kidney like that in the United States that often." He tasted a scrap, smiled, and said, "Oh, so *sweet.*" He wiped down his board and his slicing knife and returned to the pass. "You've got to like kidney, of course."

I found his calm, in the heat of service, extraordinary: that he could take such personal pleasure in slicing the kidney, noting the color and how the fat melted around and through it and the meat's sweet succulence. More extraordinary, though, was the fact that he was serving it as part of an additional tasting menu. Most nights the French Laundry of-fered a five-course menu for sixty-five dollars; the diner chose one item from seven first-course options, one item from five fish courses, one of four meat courses, one each of five cheese and five dessert courses—twenty-six courses to choose from. Or you could order the five-course vegetarian menu.

In addition to these, he offered a chef's tasting menu, nine courses for eighty dollars, none of the dishes repeating on any of the menus. Lunch menus on the weekend consisted mainly of dishes offered for dinner, but not entirely. You could order the lobster pancake (a crepe filled with butter-poached lobster) atop a carrot butter with pea shoots and the guinea fowl for lunch, but not for dinner; you could order a scallop at lunch or dinner, but at lunch Keith served his with melted leeks and a red wine glaze, and at dinner Grant served his with juli-enned snow peas and poached scallop roe coulis, garnish that by Sun-day had changed to the classical combination of asparagus and truffles.

The three menus—five-course, vegetarian, and tasting, a total of forty different courses—were not variety and excitement enough, how-ever, for some customers. They wanted tailor-made meals and would request the chef serve them dishes that didn't appear on any of that night's menus. Thomas said, "That can be stressful. Especially when you say, 'And by the way, we're vegan,'" meaning that they ingest no an-imal products whatever, wiping out fish and meat, of course, as well as butter, cream, and most stocks. But in a way Thomas liked that pres-sure. When you pull something like that off, it's a great victory. "Stress is important," he said. "When you have to perform under pressure, you have to have stress to do it. I don't see stress as a bad thing."

But on this particular winter weekend he also decided to offer an offal tasting menu mainly because he loves to cook offal, and offal is one of his favorite things to eat. He learned to cook offal as chef of a lit-tle French place called La Rive in upstate New York where the local farmers had an abundant supply. His mentor Roland Henin taught him how to cook it. Offal was the true test of the chef. If you could take organ meats and transform them into exquisite dishes, that was cook-

ing. My Webster's dictionary defines offal as "(1) waste parts; esp. entrails, etc. of a butchered animal (2) refuse; garbage."

Keller had made a tasting menu, then, of "garbage," eight courses of
it for seventy bucks.

He began this with the truffle custard, here served with a sweetbread
ragout. Next, a crispy medallion of calf's brain with a celeriac puree and
black truffles. (I eventually had Keller's calf brain, and it was so good I
almost tipped over in my chair at Table Five in the middle of dinner,
slowly and to the side, as though I'd been turned to concrete from euphoric surprise. I later told Keller how good it tasted and remarked on
how hot the thing was when it got to the table. He smiled and said, "I
know. Brain stays hot forever. It's like tar." Now that I think of it, far
away from Keller and the French Laundry, I can't name any dish anywhere ever that has been better. That, I realize now, in contented retrospect, was the best dish I have ever eaten. It had a delicious crisp
exterior and a fatty, molten, succulent interior. It was extraordinary.
Calf's brain. "Garbage.")

For the third course he would serve the garbagiest garbage of all,
tripe. "You've got to know how to cook it," he said. He served it with
savoy cabbage, carrots, and a whole-grain mustard sauce. He finished
the main courses of his offal tasting with the whole-roasted kidney. The
cheese he served as Corsu Vecchiu, a semihard Spanish sheep's cheese,
with sweetbreads in pastry and a port wine glaze. Grapefruit sorbet refreshed the palate before the desert, "Sweetbread": French-toasted brioche
with maple sugar cream.

But the offal menu wasn't the end either. As it happened, State Senator Michael Thompson and some of his buddies had gone hunting and
killed a mess of ducks. The senator asked Thomas to prepare the ducks
for a small dinner party. Thomas said sure. But El Niño rains knocked
out some roads, and the party was canceled. Rather than waste all the
good fresh ducks, Keller printed up a fourth menu and offered it to
everyone throughout the weekend: "Degustation de Canard Sauvage de
Californie."

Again the truffle custard, on this menu served with shaved black truffles, began the meal. Then a duck confit with foie gras and Thomas's version of sauce à l'orange. He served a lobster course, butter-poached tail and one claw, with a duck hash. The showpiece of this tasting menu was the roasted mallard duck breast with braised Brussels sprouts, pancetta, and sauce au sang, a reduced duck stock thickened with duck blood ("What is considered an impurity at one time," he had said early in the day as he poured excess duck blood from his butchering into a plastic deli container, "can at another time be considered an asset"). The roasted duck was first brought to the table in a copper sautoire for the diners to view before being carved. He served a Vacherin cheese with cinnamon-poached pears and watercress after this, and dessert was poached comice pear sorbet with "cold duck gelée," then a hazelnut s'more with graham "quacker" and cocoa syrup.

I hovered over the menus that night and counted the items. A total of fifty-six finished dishes—good dishes, not cafeteria mass-produced food, but highly refined, intricately composed dishes comprising five or six separate components with no component duplicated in any other dish except for herbs—could come out of that kitchen at any given time. I needed some perspective then. How good was this?

Chris Gesualdi was working in the kitchen for a week and a half. Chris, Thomas's sous chef at La Reserve and Rakel in New York, had been head chef of Montrachet for the past four years. Montrachet is a fancy French restaurant that carries three *New York Times* stars. Chris had just left Montrachet and intended to open a new restaurant called The Tonic on West Eighteenth Street the following summer. In the meantime Chris was staging in various kitchens, postgraduate work, one might call it (he moved from the French Laundry to Restaurant Daniel to work with Daniel Boulud). I asked Chris how good were fifty-six different items on a given night? He said, "Good." He wasn't a chatty fellow, so I asked, "For instance, what did you do at Montrachet?"

Chris said, "Thirteen aps, thirteen entrées. Twenty-six. And that's *plenty.*"

Later, in an effort to explain his admiration for Keller, he said, "He's got the whole animal on the menu."

I asked Thomas did he do this a lot. Service had begun, and the pass had just been set. He walked into the breezeway where the menus were laid out on the linen counter. No, this wasn't typical, he said. He was so surprised, in fact, that he didn't take my word for it. He counted every item himself.

He turned to me. "And D.J. does—" He paused and ran through in his mind all the VIP canapés, counting on his fingers, sixteen items not seen on the menus. "That's seventy," Thomas said. "I'm shocked." Then he went to the pass to start serving dinner.

Keller had worked all six services over the weekend, and he would be back at the pass tomorrow night. He was in the kitchen between 10:00 and 10:30 A.M., and except for a twenty-minute shower before dinner service, he stayed in that kitchen, not leaving until between 1:00 and 1:30 after ensuring that the following day's menu items had been confirmed and food orders had been placed. That was a forty-five-hour workweek right there and comprised only half his days in the kitchen.

The night following these services, morning by the time Keller leaves the kitchen, is cool and dry. Thomas Keller sits on his front porch, as he often does after service, to smoke a cigarette and drink a glass of red wine. I, who have been watching service all weekend and am staying the month in an upstairs room, join him. The front of his house is peaceful, far removed from the restaurant it seems (though only a hundred or so feet away). I can hear a creek not far from the house. Silhouettes of giant pines rise against a clear night sky. Thomas evaluates the weekend, his voice quiet and composed. It has been a busy few days.

There in the dark Yountville night, stream gurgling in the background, Keller reiterates how surprised he is by the number of dishes they offered this weekend. One could argue that the variations on the truffle custard on three menus, typically a VIP canapé, didn't count, and knock that seventy down to sixty-eight, I suppose, but then, the kitchen could easily have gotten a customer asking to go off the menu and come up with eight other dishes. They were prepared to do that in an instant. So the fact remained: This kitchen put out a hell of a lot of food. And while Thomas seemed proud of it, it also worried him.

"How big can you get? How hard can you work the machine?" he asks. "It takes five guys just to make that truffle custard. One person to cut and clean the eggs, one to make the custard, someone to make the sauce, someone to chop the truffles that go into the sauce, someone to make the chive chip. And that's for an item that doesn't even make it onto the menu."

The staff is uneven. Certain cooks can handle that load, but others struggle to keep up. How can he maintain excellence and consistency and continue to grow at the same time? He asks himself this all the time. Keller drags on his cigarette, and a new image comes into his mind. Grant's scallop dish. It was two words the night before, asparagus and truffles. A dozen and a half hours later the first one arrived at the pass: seared scallop with asparagus sauce, truffle coulis, whole asparagus and truffle slices. "I knew immediately," Keller says, "this is a keeper." This is what he means by creating a dynamic, spontaneous kitchen. "It's just remarkable," he continues, "that we were able to go from a concept to a finished dish like that."

But this is not his ideal kitchen. The French Laundry, he has always maintained, is bigger than he is, was around long before he arrived in Yountville, and he hopes will continue even beyond him. He says he hopes someone like Eric Ziebold, twenty-six-year-old sous chef, will take over as chef and keep this special place rolling well into the next century. But for him he has another kitchen in mind. And as he explains it on the porch tonight, it has a utopian aspect, like Marx's ideal society in his *Communist Manifesto;* Keller's vision is equally vague and enormously appealing. In his ideal kitchen—and since he always strives to fulfill ideals, he truly hopes one day to make this happen—there is no head chef, no sous chef, no brigade. There are only five or six cooks, people like Grant, Gregory, Eric, who share similar notions of perfection. Each day they will come into the kitchen and cook, just cook. There will be no plan. They will cook as they are inclined. Each cook, equal with all others, will be utterly free to experiment, to let his or her own individual personality and creativity truly propel him or her. The key element in this scenario is this: shared standards of perfection. If this situation comes to pass, if the five or six cooks share the same notions of how to make stock, how to clean, how to keep one's station, how to finesse a sauce to silky excellence, how to cook a piece of meat perfectly, to season it perfectly, every single time, how to take a Pullman loaf out of a plastic bag, then the perpetual shackle of maintaining a great restaurant will be broken. A head chef must constantly be on people to do it better, to work cleaner, to bring this dish or that preparation to perfection. In his ideal kitchen all that effort—which depletes and enervates you, and yet that can be the main work of a day—will vanish, and with the shackle gone, he believes, a kitchen could really cook.

As he describes his ideal kitchen to me, his eyes bright at the very thought, I cannot help being impressed that after this busy weekend, six services, and the many menus—seventeen different menus when you counted them all—he is still thinking and talking about cooking, more cooking, how to do it better, how to *really* do it, what real cooking could be like.

Then he stubs out his cigarette, drains his wine. "I'm tired," he says. "I'm gonna shower and go to bed."

CHAPTER FOUR

*G*rant Achatz stands at the stainless steel counter before a white cutting board, ten-inch slicing knife, and damp towel; beside the cutting board is a plastic container on ice containing whole rouget, or red mullet. Grant can occasionally look out the window in front of him to the patio, now, in February, empty of its tables, as he reduces a dozen mullets to identical two-by-two inch fillets. They will be the main item in one of Keller's favorite dishes: Red Mullet with Italian Parsley Coulis, à Palette d'Ail Doux, and Garlic Chips (affectionately known as fish and chips).

At service, Grant will cook off two fillets so that they are juicy inside and their bright red skin is so light and crisp it will click when you tap it with a knife. They will be stacked on a disk of garlic and egg, fried crispy, creamy inside; this is set on a circle of a smooth puree of parsley; Keller will finish the dish at the pass by piling light, crisp garlic chips atop the fillets. The rich succulence of the meat, the fresh parsley, and the two garlic preparations create a luxurious but simple flavor combination, amplified by the alternating crisp-creamy layers of texture (all of which is anticipated visually by the shimmering white chips against crimson skin against the forest green coulis) to cohere into a perfect or nearly perfect dish. Because it is so clean and precise in design, the dish is exciting to make over and over again, but it can also be the most frustrating in repetition when the details are off and it does not meet its self-imposed mark of "the perfect dish."

On a clear Friday afternoon, though, this dish begins at Grant's workstation and the butchering of the fish. He butchers each separately, places the fillets in a small plastic container on ice, discards scraps, wipes the board clean of scraps and blood, and cleans his knife, before beginning the fish. Grant is one of twenty French Laundry cooks. Skill levels among the cooks vary—they are neither robotically perfect nor as uniform as Prussian soldiers in their work—but three core cooks seem to share a similar elegance in movement and image that I watched with intense fascination: Gregory Short, twenty-nine, Eric Ziebold, twenty-two and Grant, twenty-two. All were graduates of the CIA, and all were hired about the time the new kitchen opened. The French Laundry was no more or less diverse than most high-end kitchens and followed similar demographics: Mexican dishwashers, for example, women more likely to work pastry, an all-male hot line (though a former airline stewardess, an Asian-American woman named Lisa, soon moved from prep to first course, a hot line station), and most were under thirty. But Greg, Eric, and Grant seemed to me quintessential French Laundry cooks and were among those Keller usually singled out as the best.

I loved to watch Gregory cook. His movements were as fluid and sure as those of a classical dancer. He stood about five feet ten in small black leather clogs, had clipped red hair and red eyelashes. He never moved quickly when he was under pressure, but he moved continuously; whether he was slicing the duck roulade or flipping a fillet (always with a palette knive; tongs are verboten in this kitchen because they damage meat), each move had an immediate end but was also part of a bigger design that rolled out fluidly as orders were called. He would slice that roulade, then spin to his right to flip the veal fillet in the sauté pan. But that spin simply continued almost full circle to his mise en place drawer to pull two rabbits and a veal and a short rib that Keller had ordered while he had been removing the duck roulade from the poaching water. All his movements, so calm and slow, seemed nearly thoughtless. If you liked to watch cooks at work, Gregory was engrossing, a half back dancing through giant linemen in instant replay time.

That was it. His movements were so deliberate and graceful as to seem to be in slow motion. I had never seen anyone move slowly under pressure in a kitchen. And yet that was the rule here. Under Keller, cooks learned the importance of moving slowly. If you were moving fast, something was wrong—you hadn't planned well, you hadn't been efficient—and your food would suffer. To move slowly was the goal, an element of the self-discipline you learned as you became a better cook.

Gregory was from Boseman, Montana, attended a state university to study architectural and industrial design, and began cooking when that program was cut by the university. He attended the Culinary from 1991 to 1993 and, upon graduating, worked in the Pacific Northwest, learning banquets, volume cooking, under a chef named Dave Kellaway, "a certified master chef," Greg noted. "I landed here on the fish station March '96," he said.

While I spoke with Greg, he vanished every few moments. He was straining the finished squab sauce. Most stock-based sauces here are called quick sauces: bones of the animal (here, squab), browned on top of the stove, cooked with varying ratios of veal stock and a light chicken stock, with many reductions and deglazings. When Greg brought the sauce to the proper flavor and consistency, he strained it, what he was doing as he recounted his history. He poured the sauce from one steel bowl through a chinois into another steel bowl, departed, cleaned the chinois and bowl, then returned and poured the sauce through the chinois again, rapping the rim of the chinois with a spoon to hurry the sauce through (cooks never pumped sauce through with a ladle). After each straining, he examined the fine sediment caught in the chinois, then strode to the dish station to clean the chinois and bowl again and strain again. Finally he poured the sauce through the chinois, and we peered into it. It had caught nothing. Greg looked at me, grinned, and said, "That's it." He cleaned the chinois, returned it to a hook near his station, transferred the sauce to a pan, and labeled the saucepan "Squab." He had strained the sauce more than twenty times.

Eric Ziebold arrived the same month as Gregory; he can tell you the date: March 6, 1996. Eric was born in Iowa, had been cooking since age sixteen, externed at Spago in Los Angeles, and graduated from culinary school in 1994. From there he went to work for Jeffrey Buben at Vidalia in Washington, D.C. After more than a year there he confided to Buben that he missed California and hoped to return. Buben told him, "If you want to work in California, then you've got to go to the French Laundry. In two or three years it will be one of the three best restaurants in the country."

Eventually, after two short French Laundry *stages,* Keller told Eric there might be a position for him. Eric accepted.

"For me the moment you first walk in the door and see the kitchen, see how people work," he said, "it's the kind of kitchen that anyone would want to work in."

It is in these young cooks, Eric most of all, that one notices the effect of the chef's mind on the staff. As the personality of a powerful CEO of a small company, a school principal, or a theatrical director permeates the entire operation over which that person presides, so a chef's mind and personality permeate a kitchen, determine absolutely not only its standards but also its tone and tenor. The people who work there are successful in direct proportion to their willingness to embrace, to be infused with, the chef's personality. In a strong chef's kitchen those who resist the personality leave or are fired. The weaker the chef, the more nebulous this dynamic becomes. Keller was anything but nebulous. Eric, it seemed, was attempting to adopt Keller's entire thought process, to make it his own. And, as he was sous chef and second-in-command, he was apparently successful.

He had just returned from a weeks-long stage at Taillevent in Paris, arranged by Keller. (He had learned at this Michelin three-star restaurant care of ingredients by prepping asparagus that cost the restaurant eleven dollars a pound: "When you learned to be that careful with asparagus, you become that careful with asparagus that are a dollar a pound." And he learned discipline watching the cooks squeegee the insides of plastic bags to get every last drop and from the pastry station. "They scrubbed the floor four times a day, I mean *scrubbed* it, *four* times a day.") One night during service we left the kitchen for the office to talk. He was dressed for work and had helped prep but was not on tonight. On the way out he stopped to wipe crumbs off a cutting board used by the cheese station to slice bread, and in the parking lot he picked up a cigarette butt.

"Is the guest going to notice the cigarette butt in the driveway?" he asked me. "Consciously, no." Eric seemed to be in part instructing me and in part playing the role of model French Laundry employee for my benefit. He said, "It's all those unconscious things that make this a beautiful place." But he was no doubt genuine. Keller was forever picking up cigarette butts himself. And I would warrant that if Keller had seen one of his cooks spot a butt and *not* pick it up, that cook would thereby have created an insurmountable barrier to advancement in the kitchen. Most of these cooks, Keller explained to me, hoped to own their own restaurants one day; if they were good enough for that, they would treat this place as if they were the owners. If they didn't, they would never be successful, he thought, because you can't spend half a career as someone else's employee and then suddenly, one day, start thinking like an owner. If you wanted to be a great chef and restaurateur, you had to think like an owner and *act* like the owner from your very first job as prep cook, or you'd never develop the muscles for when the time actually arrived. Eric was bearing this out.

"When you see him doing it every day, you start to do it too," Eric explained, apparently refreshed and invigorated by his travels. We sat in the small two-room office—fax machine, computers, telephones, corkboard, mail slots, comfortable office chairs—an oddly sterile environment compared with the kitchen. "You watch him. He walks in the kitchen, first thing he does is clean. He'll be cleaning under that little sink by the expediting station. He cleans the oil bottles. When you see somebody do that every day, after a while you think to yourself, maybe I should be cleaning under that sink. Maybe I should be cleaning the oil bottles.

"Why?" Eric continued. "Oil bottles? So they've got oil on them, does it matter?" Meat and fish stations use white plastic liter bottles for canola oil and clarified butter. "You just pour oil into a pan, it's not going to affect the food. The bains in the sink with the spoons and whips, does the water need to be clean? No. And pretty soon you start to do it with the food, 'Oh, well, that won't be noticed.' 'Oh, that's all right.'"

Eric had eaten at Alain Ducasse's restaurant in Paris, and for one of his meat courses, the waiter sauced his plate at the table. And it was a perfect sauce, beautifully translucent, and Eric was excited but also sad because he was alone and had no one to share it with. This was the effect he strove for when he cooked.

"I made what I think was a prefect bordelaise sauce," Eric said, recalling one night when he worked fish station. Keller served the bordelaise with lobster, and Eric had brought it to that deep burgundy color, translucent with a gold sheen shimmering over its surface. "It was perfect. It was so beautiful every time I put it on the plate I thought, 'Man, that is *great*.' Grant was watching me. He thought it was too." (Later I asked Grant if he recalled this sauce from months ago. He paused, not recalling, then nodded and smiled slightly, saying, "Yeah, I remember it." He said they just stood over the sauce in the white bowl marveling.) "When you go to so much work for that sauce, when you appreciate something that much, you're not going to put something on the plate that's sloppy or bad." Eric paused. "And that goes back to cleaning the oil off the bottle."

Eric was right. And it wasn't just a matter of principle, though that was important. But more to the point, if your bottle had oil on it, that oil would get on your hands, and those hands would then leave oily finger marks on the plate when you pulled it from the warmer and again when you sent it to the pass. So it was simply logical to clean your oil bottles first.

"Thomas makes you notice so much more," Eric said.

I spoke with Grant while he butchered the mullet. He made neat stacks of the rough fillets before taking them down to portion size and then gently dragging the blade of his knife back and forth across the fish's skin, as if it were a barber's strop, to remove as much moisture from it as possible, the key step to ensuring perfectly crisp skin without overcooking the fish. Grant had taken to using for virtually all his prep a ten-inch slicing knife, the kind Keller used. Grant told me he'd learned patience and intensity here. "You have to be intense to get all the stuff done," he said. Also confidence. If you can do well here, he said, you'll do well anywhere in the world.

Grant came from a restaurant family in Michigan and attended the CIA immediately after high school. He served his externship at the Amway Grand Plaza in Grand Rapids. He landed a job at Charlie Trotter's after graduation. Charlie Trotter and Keller are often compared. They both are American, serve small portions of highly refined food in tasting menu format, and have similar expectations of standards and quality. Charlie Trotter's is likewise considered to be in the top tier of American restaurants, and some people will argue that it's the best (*Wine Spectator* readers, a discerning lot, no doubt, chose it as America's best restaurant in both 1997 and 1998). But kitchens are like people. They have distinct personalities: Some you get along with; some rub you the wrong way. And Grant had a tough time in Trotter's kitchen. He was young, barely twenty, and perhaps this was partly the reason he felt uncomfortable there. But the tension for him was enormous. He told himself he would stick with it a year, and he did. This, he knew, was how you learned. You went to the best kitchens in America, put your head down, and worked, despite the blows you had to take. You expect a great kitchen to be tough.

He left Trotter's and traveled in Europe, then returned home to decide his next move. He wrote to Masas, in San Francisco, and never heard back. He wrote to Inn at Little Washington and heard back immediately from its human resources department which, eventually, would offer Grant a *stage*. He also applied to the French Laundry, but not just once as with the other two restaurants. For the French Laundry he made a stack of envelopes each containing a letter and résumé and, as part of his routine, popped one of them in the mail every day. He had heard from a cook at Trotter's that the French Laundry was good. He had read a blurb about it in *Wine Spectator*. That was the extent of his knowledge about the French Laundry. And yet every day for several weeks he sent a letter and résumé to Thomas Keller.

"I don't know why I did it," Grant said. "I didn't know anything about the restaurant. It was kind of weird."

Keller, figuring he was going to keep getting these letters if he didn't put a stop to it, called Grant and, after talking, offered him a *stage*. Grant would give it a year exactly and no more. On the day he arrived in Yountville and appeared in the kitchen, the first thing he saw was the chef sweeping the floor, and he sensed then that this kitchen would be different.

Grant was now approaching the one-year mark but had no intention of leaving just yet.

He liked the way things were done here: the right way, and then more. "Blanching green veg, for instance," he said. He noted that the water had to be very, very salty. Keller wanted it to taste like the Atlantic. And it had to be a rapid boil. If you added vegetables (in some cases, such as fresh peas, they had to be ice cold) and the water lost its boil, Keller instructed you to throw them out and do it right. (I had met a former cook who had spent all morning not only shucking fava beans, a tedious task in itself, but also removing their skins, which is easy to do after they're cooked, but tedious and time-consuming when they're raw. Half his workday he spent preparing pounds of fava beans to be cooked. He brought the salted water to a boil and dumped in the favas. The boil vanished, Keller saw it and told him to throw the favas out and start again. The cook no longer works at the French Laundry, but he now bakes its bread.) Grant understood the reasons for this and liked this standard.

He liked the fact that all shallots here were chopped by hand and not pulsed in a Robot Coupe. When you chop shallots in a food processor (when I was a cook, I preferred this method . . . because it was faster), the cut is irregular, leaving you with some large chunks, some perfect, and the rest a shallot puree. Grant was even willing to concede that using a processor didn't hurt the food. "It wouldn't necessarily affect the food," he said. "But it affects your psyche. If you take a half hour to chop shallots, you're going to make sure they don't get wasted."

Here it was again.

I had been by this point in numerous kitchens, spoken at length with scores of chefs, cooked with and for some of them. Many, when you got them really engaged and excited about what was important, talked about exotic foods like foie gras, truffles, or clever preparations, such as sauces made from reduced vegetable juices and spices, and infused oils. At the French Laundry—which served a ton of truffles and foie gras, which reduced carrot and beet juices to use for sauces, which made a dozen or more infused oils—the best cooks in the kitchen talked about cleaning oil bottles, how to cook a green vegetable, how to strain a sauce, and the effects of chopping shallots for your station by hand.

In the chaos of your life, of the world, of the flood of sensory perception, the demands of work, family, fear of the future, the news of the world that pours into your home daily through newspaper and television—famine, war, flood—news of your life, successes and defeats, you look for patterns to make sense of it all. In the chaos of kitchen work, writing about it, watching it, working it, from the torrent of sensory perceptions, the stress of the work, the flood of food information, endless, often contradictory, I likewise looked for patterns, repetitions. So much of life in kitchens, the work of cooking, and the food that resulted paralleled the bigger picture. And here was the overriding repetition: The best cooks talked about the very basic elements of cooking.

And these good young cooks, Grant, Gregory, and Eric, I knew, were merely amplifying and extending the mind that had created and drove the French Laundry itself.

CHAPTER FIVE

Thomas Keller was born on October 14, 1955, at Camp Pendleton, in Oceanside, California, to Edward Keller, a Marine Corps officer, and his wife, Betty. He was the youngest of five boys. After Edward and Betty divorced, about four years later, Betty moved herself and the five boys east, eventually settling in Palm Beach, Florida, where she supported the family by managing restaurants in the affluent town and its considerably less affluent neighbor, West Palm. Thomas, a genial but somewhat reckless teenager, attended Lake Worth High School, was not an ambitious student, played basketball and baseball, and for a time engaged himself in less wholesome pursuits common among teenagers of the early 1970s, pursuits that ended when his mom put him to work washing dishes at the Palm Beach Yacht Club in West Palm, which she managed. This was his first restaurant job: dishwasher. Dishwasher is how many American chefs begin.

One afternoon Betty Keller nodded toward the Yacht Club's chef and said to her nineteen-year-old son, *"Watch him. Watch what he does."* Mrs. Keller sensed that her chef was about to quit; her son Thomas was out of school and ready for a real job. Thomas Keller had until then given little thought to what he would do with his life, and none at all to becoming a cook, let alone chef.

"I called up my friend Przempko [pronounced Shempko]," Keller said of the day the Yacht Club chef gave notice. "He was out of work, and I asked him if he wanted a job and he said, 'Yeah.' So we went out and partied that night. We both had a job. We were going to become *chefs*."

The Yacht Club served uncomplicated lunches and, on weekends, dinner. "We did everything," Thomas said. "We cleaned the whole restaurant. That was the first thing—bathrooms, dining room, the whole thing. Then we'd get ready for lunch. Hamburgers, french fries, sandwiches, eggs Benedict." When he didn't know how to do something, he'd call Joseph, his older brother who was then a cook at La Petit Marmite, a fashionable classical French restaurant in Palm Beach. Joseph would walk him through making a sauce, cooking a whole prime rib, broiling lobster tail. Keller smiled at the memory and said, "I remember the first time I made hollandaise. I was so excited. I ran out and told Captain John. Captain John was the dock manager. I was twenty years old. I'd never made a hollandaise before."

That year Betty gave Thomas his first cookbook, Mary and Vincent Price's *A Treasury of Great Recipes,* inscribing it, "To my wonderful son/God Bless you always."

Thomas was inspired. He would make his first fancy cookbook dish, Tagliatelle Verde con Prosciutto, one of Vincent Price's favorite recipes from Harry's Bar. "I couldn't find spinach pasta," Keller recalls. "This was 1975. No one had spinach pasta. So you know what I thought I'd do? I'd *dye* it green." The final dish, with neon green fettuccine, was not as appetizing as he'd hoped it would be. The prosciutto, which he overcooked, released all its salt, rendering the dish inedible. A kind diner, a regular and a fan of young Thomas's, tried to eat it, really did try, but had to tell Thomas he just couldn't. "That was my first venture into trying to create something for myself," he said, "being inspired by a recipe and trying to create it."

Thomas Keller remained chef of the Yacht Club for two years. "Making hamburgers," he said, "and trying to make things nice and neat and trying to keep things as they should be, making eggs Benedict every day, making the hollandaise, which was really the high point of every morning, perfecting the hollandaise."

Keller had not been born into a food family; he did not carry with him great food memories from childhood as so many great chefs do.

Food was not a primary concern in the chaotic, but spanking clean, Keller apartment on Cocoanut Row in Palm Beach. Joseph, Thomas's closest brother in age, tried to keep decent food on the table and became a cook and chef himself, while Thomas haphazardly tended toward carpentry, his taste memories were scarcely more complex than chili dogs on the beach. His mother ran restaurants, but that didn't carry with it for her or her boys a reverence for great food. Restaurants in the 1970s were a living, and Betty was to all the Keller boys a powerful and influential presence who kept the family afloat during the rootless years following the divorce. "She was the driving force of the family," Joseph said. "She showed me the strength and scope of a woman. She showed me tenacity, perfection, hard work, cleanliness." Thomas learned the same things. When asked who were the major influences on his career as a chef, he will say without hesitating: "My mom."

This story, as I gradually learned it, astonished me. The work of cooking is too hard simply to fall into it this way. You don't grow up with a disregard for food, get thrown into a cook's spot, grilling burgers and preparing old standards like eggs Benedict ("Look, Captain John! I made a hollandaise!"), and twenty years later get called the best chef in America running the country's most exciting restaurant in an era of extraordinary interest in and competition among great restaurants and great chefs. It doesn't happen that way. Yet here it had, and so what grew to obsess me about Keller was how and why it happened. What was it that drove him? Whatever *it* was, *it* was interior; he had no formal training and no extended mentoring. He learned just about everything by figuring it out himself.

I knew by this point that you could make a restaurant and sell food without striving for perfection. You could boil the shit out of your stocks, and you could cook on a filthy stove with black, beat-up sauté pans, standing on thick rubber mats slopped with sauce and food scraps, and make money in a high-end restaurant. I had done it myself, and I knew this was an option. And it was *still* hard work no matter your disregard for stocks or cleanliness. I cooked my ass off in 150-

degree heat after a long day of prep, burning my hands and arms, the skin of my hands cracking and filling with wood splinters from feeding the fire. But I really didn't care about my work—I just wanted to get the food out—and I knew it was less hard when you didn't care. But to be a great chef in America, this did not come naturally; this took hard work. And I never would have thought it would have come from chili dogs on the beach, the Palm Beach Yacht Club, and Continental cuisine served in America in 1975.

It did, but how?

Keller had given me the first clue to the answer, and it was, appropriately, in the sauce, a classical French sauce. Hollandaise. From his very first days cooking the sauce was the high point of each day. "Perfecting the hollandaise," he said. He made hollandaise day after day after day, for two years, and each day he tried to make it better than he'd ever done before.

"Roland Henin," Keller says, "he was my chef."

Henin, a sturdy, fit man, a veteran of a dozen high-end kitchens and a former instructor at several culinary schools, is currently a consultant for Yosemite Concession Services, which handles the food for the park system and Ahwahnee Hotel there, was born during World War II in Lyons, France, the gastronomic capital of the Western world. He began work as a teenage kitchen apprentice, the way virtually all European chefs learned the trade. Henin came to North America to cook at Expo 67 in Canada and stayed to travel and work, eventually winding up in Palm Beach as sous chef at the Everglades Club (less than a half mile from where Keller lived), then at the Breakers (also a walk away from the Kellers). But it was several years later that Henin met Keller on a beach in Narragansett, Rhode Island. Henin was head chef of the Dunes Club, an exclusive resort, and commanded a staff of more than three dozen cooks, one of whom was a young Thomas Keller, who remembers the kitchen as being "the size of a football field."

Palm Beach was not a place the rich chose to inhabit during the summer, and so restaurant work slowed considerably. Keller for a few years in his early twenties traveled to Rhode Island resort towns to cook and hang out on the beach. It was a good life for a young man not long out of high school. His first summer in Rhode Island Keller got a line cook's job at Clarke Cook House in Newport. He had until then cooked alone, with the help of Przempko, and under his mother's hawk eye. In Rhode Island he was on his own. Clarke Cook House served classical cuisine appropriate to mid-seventies American tastes—steak au poivre, duck à l'orange—but in the kitchen, Keller says, "it was more a fraternity thing. Five or six cooks on the line, and we'd smoke cigarettes and drink beer, pumping stuff out." He didn't learn much about food that summer, but he did learn about the dance. "I learned about being quick, how to be quick, how to begin to do the dance with four or five other guys on the line."

After Labor Day he returned to Palm Beach and cooked on his own; it was a pattern he returned to again and again throughout his career, going elsewhere to cook with others, then returning home to cook by himself. When Memorial Day rolled around the following year, Keller once again headed north.

"I basically picked him up off the beach," Henin said of the first time he saw Keller, his Lyonnaise accent still rich. "He was living on za beach in the day and doing some cooking at night. He had cutoff jeans; he was having a good time. It was summer; living was easy.

"We talk a little bit. I was kind of pressed for staff. I was having some problems feeding the staff. Staff is *always* a problem. They're there for the summer, and they're always bitching. No matter where, what, or how, they always bitch. The customer is easy, but the staff is always bitching. So I said to Thomas, 'You take care of the staff. This can be your job. Just keep them happy, whatever you want to do, just keep them happy.'

"And you know what? He turned them around. He turned their attitude around, the staff. I don't know what he did; I don't know what he cooked them. But he gave them food and made them happy.

"He was just doing good food without being extravagant," Henin continued. "Then, toward the end of the season, I lost my saucier and I offered Tom a chance, maybe, to move into this position. And he did.

He did his best. At first I just needed a body, but he gradually took over the position by making one thing more every day. And he kept feeding the staff. From that point on, I said, 'Hey, this guy's got something going on.'"

Keller says that Henin was the first person to teach him the fundamentals of cooking: how to make stocks, how to roast, how to braise. "He taught me how to peel a tomato, things that nobody took the time to show me before," says Keller. And he taught Keller that staff meal was about more than feeding the staff. Staff meal was first about how to work with by-products, utilizing leftovers to make something tasty, eye-appealing, nutritious, satisfying.

"The message underlying that," Keller continues, "was, Can you be passionate about cooking at this level? Staff meal. Only the staff sees it. If you can do that for these people, create that habit, that passion, that drive, that sincerity, and keep that with you and take it to another level, then someday you'll be a great chef. Maybe.

"Henin taught me that cooking was not just a job," Keller says. "He took me aside; he showed me the reasons *he* cooked. It was about being creative, gratification, satisfying yourself and satisfying people, that that was the raison d'être to feed people and ultimately to feed yourself. As you're feeding others, you're feeding yourself, you're getting the fuel to push yourself forward. He taught me about passion.

"Henin for me was this almost religious, divine figure," Keller concludes. "There was Zeus, and then there was Roland, the god of cooking." Keller laughs.

The first summer he learned mechanics and teamwork. The second summer he met Henin, "moving," Keller says, "from the athletic, or dance, part to the thinking part." He worked for Henin for less than one full summer, but the two remained connected permanently. Henin was Keller's chef. "I didn't learn all the fundamentals there," Keller says of scant weeks in the Dunes kitchen. "But I learned what I needed to know to learn the rest. Henin gave me direction. He directed me. You have those people who put you on track."

In the winter of 1978 twenty-two-year-old Thomas Keller was hired by two hopeful restaurateurs as executive chef of a new restaurant in West Palm Beach. The men had formerly run a carpentry shop called the Cobbley Nob, a name they thought would fit rather neatly on their fancy French restaurant. The *haut français* Cobbley Nob sat on Forty-fifth Street in an area of West Palm Beach that would be deserted were it not for the nearby jai alai courts, a situation that ensured a steady flow of potential customers to the restaurant. Thomas Keller, the gangly new chef with a mustache that did not disguise his youth, began his career as head chef here in April of that year with a repertoire of classical French cuisine. It was his first experience organizing a kitchen, purchasing food, worrying over cost control, and managing a kitchen staff. He cooked everything in clarified butter, made gallons of it every week, but it was not long before he realized that the hordes who gambled at the jai alai courts were not necessarily interested in his haute cuisine. Most of the people who came to the restaurant, he said, "wouldn't have known if I'd cooked their food in motor oil."

The Cobbley Nob died quickly and quietly. And the young chef felt lucky to unload sixty gallons of clarified butter on a local restaurant.

Keller returned to his itinerant life, cooking for classically trained French chefs in South Florida and moving north for the summer, continuing to learn. "Even though it was informal learning," Henin observes, "he always got the learning or the teaching from the old-school guys."

One of his first jobs after the Cobbley Nob happened to be chef for a French couple, René and Paulette Macary, who ran a restaurant called La Rive in Catskill, New York, on a patch of the Hudson River valley so remote it didn't have an address. The wife, Paulette, wrote the menu each day by hand. Thomas cooked alone, with René's eighty-year-old mother as his only prep cook; she minced his shallots and picked his beans. He slept in a small cabin behind the restaurant, and was in the kitchen by nine, and there he cooked by himself until closing time, when he cleaned the kitchen according to the only standard he knew.

He built a smokehouse out back to cure and flavor his own meats. He learned to use New York's bountiful livestock. He began to learn how to develop relationships with purveyors. Fantastic veal came down from Utica. He found a man in the valley who raised spectacular pigeons. He began to ask these farmers for unusual items, entrails they usually threw away since no one wanted them, things like pigs' ears, cocks' combs, and duck testicles. By good fortune, Chef Henin had landed a teaching position at the Culinary Institute of America. His credentials suited the classically minded institute, and he joined the first class taking the newly created Certified Master Chef exam. (He passed.) His young friend Thomas came down to visit an occasional class. Every now and then, on weekends when the CIA was not in session, Henin popped up to La Rive and cooked with Thomas. Unlike Americans at the time, the French loved offal—Henin did, especially, as did proprietors René and Paulette—and because it was so abundant and cheap in the Hudson River valley in the early eighties, Henin taught Keller how to cook it. Tripe and kidney, lung and brain. Henin admired cooks who could work with offal and happily indulged his protégé in the vagaries of innards. "Offal really demonstrates good cooking," Henin says, "because using offals, you need to be a good cook to do them justice. This is what cooking is all about: taking a second or third cut and elevating it to the level of excellence. Like taking some trimmings of pork and liver and making a terrine or pâté that is better than a filet mignon, that is what cooking is all about."

In winter, when La Rive closed, Keller returned to Florida and, with Henin's help, found other classically trained French chefs to work for. He learned their food, their techniques and in the spring returned to the kitchen of La Rive, where, alone with Mimi, the grandmother, he practiced and embellished upon the new methods and dishes he'd picked up. This was how he found and developed his voice, as it were, as a cook. And here he received his first attention from New York journalists, when Gael Greene and Raymond Sokolov toured the Hudson

Valley, made a chance visit to La Rive and praised Keller's food in *New York* magazine.

Keller cooked for three years at La Rive, and when it became clear that he would not be able to buy it from René and Paulette, he left. He knew by this point he needed his own restaurant in order to make a great restaurant. He wanted to create not country food but extraordinary food. But he had been enormously happy here, he said, and, as he later noted, he spent the next ten years of his life searching for his own La Rive.

Upon leaving La Rive, Keller packed what he owned and moved to New York City, embarking on what was the quintessential cook's life, not much different in style from that of the journeymen of the Middle Ages. For the next four years he cooked in numerous kitchens, never staying longer than a year in any one place. He got a job as chef at Raoul's Restaurant in SoHo, owned by restaurateur Serge Raoul, who eventually became Keller's business partner. Next he landed a job as poissonier at Polo Restaurant in the Westbury Hotel. Here he cooked with some of the best new American and French cooks working, cooks who were introducing America to genuine nouvelle cuisine under Patrice Boely and his talented but little-known sous chef, Daniel Boulud. This was Keller's first introduction to composed plates. Heretofore he had only known variations on the so-called three-plop design: meat with sauce at six o'clock, veg at ten, starch at two. But at Polo he saw asparagus served not as one of three items on a plate but as a base for something else, an integrated part of a dish; stews were not bowlfuls of meat and vegetables in liquid but structures built on top of a sauce. "Amazing cooks doing amazing things," Keller says of those days.

These cooks showed him that it was imperative to go to France—where they had come from—to stage in the great kitchens there. After writing letters and seeking connections, he landed work in a one-star kitchen, all he needed to justify leaving America indefinitely to live abroad in France. Catapulted out of Polo by these amazing cooks, he landed in a dungeon of a kitchen. The windows of his room above it were black from the coal smoke, coal he himself would have to light each morning in the ancient stoves in the cellar, illuminated dimly by bare bulbs hanging from wires. He quit after two days—"I knew if I stayed there, I would die," Keller says—and retreated to Paris, borrowing the apartment of his former boss Serge Raoul. Here he sent a flurry of letters and résumés and recommendations. Eventually, he discovered that Taillevent offered *stagiare* positions, but an American already had the spot. This American, however, had not arrived, and no one knew if he still intended to come. If he did not, the position was Keller's. Keller procured the name of this cook and telephoned him. He pretended to be from the administrative offices of Taillevent and confirmed to his satisfaction that the chef would not be coming there. He then informed Taillevent and appeared for work. Once part of a Michelin three-star kitchen, he was able to orchestrate easily a series of stages at seven two- and three-star restaurants during the course of a year.

Because Keller had mastered the basics as taught to him by chefs classically trained in France, he did not need to concern himself with them here but could focus on more refined aspects of cooking: working with foie gras, chlorophyl (the pigment in greens), and chocolate. He remembers that his year in Paris was a great confidence builder; after years of working on the assumption that he knew next to nothing, he discovered what he did know, and it was a lot, ten years worth of cooking and studying. His year in France was in effect the end of his self-styled apprenticeship.

Upon returning to New York, he was quickly hired as chef de cuisine at La Reserve, a high-end French restaurant rivaling Le Cirque and La Cote Basque.

"It was the first job I was ever fired from," Keller says, apparently forgetting that he was fired from Clarke Cook House. "Arrogance. Insubordination. Just being a jerk. I would throw the owner out of the kitchen. I yelled at him all the time. We did good food, amazing stuff, but it wasn't what the owner wanted. I wanted to do plates, I didn't want to send a rack of veal upstairs to be carved. I guess because I'd come back from France, I'd worked in all these great kitchens, I thought I was above it all. He [owner Jean-Louis Missud] put me in my place. He said, 'I don't need you in here.' It made me realize I was an asshole. I probably wouldn't have wanted me around either. It was at that point that I went to Serge and said, 'OK, let's do that restaurant.'"

"That restaurant" turned out to be Rakel, a hip, high-end boîte in SoHo serving expensive lunch and dinner to high-flying Wall Street executives. It was to be Thomas Keller's first stage for wide media attention. Thomas Keller's food—after La Rive and rural New York, after his years working with old-guard French chefs and young talented French cooks in New York, after his experience in three-star European restaurants—had become refined and distinctly his own. He'd found his voice at La Rive, he was maturing, and this maturity developed into something called finesse. The wit and sophistication that, sometimes verging on absurdity, would characterize his food forever after emerged here at Rakel.

Bryan Miller, in a two-star review of Rakel in the *New York Times,* wrote that it was "one of the handsomest and most provocative restaurants in the SoHo area, featuring an inventive menu full of surprises." Here were Keller's sweetbreads, perfectly sautéed, served on filaments of fried leeks with a sesame vinaigrette and his "cappuccino" of wild mushroom consommé served in a glass coffee cup with frothed milk on top, which Miller called "soul-stirring."

But Miller found the crab cakes underseasoned and a prosciutto, tomato, orange zest, and vodka pasta "overintellectualized." Temperatures were off—a slightly raw bit of salmon, an overcooked "ragout of crustaceans," a potato cake partly burned—and service was clunky. Imperfect notes in an otherwise exciting score, a hopeful beginning, where Keller earned many prominent fans.

The restaurant opened in January 1987. Ten months later the stock market bottomed out, and the 1980s Manhattan boom years were over. Expense accounts dried up, diners grew thrifty, and with this new mood, a more basic style of cooking became popular. Serge Raoul wanted Keller to scale back his refined and expensive tastes to produce more simple bistro fare; Keller had no interest in that. There were many factors in Rakel's failure, from its location to high food costs, but the overriding reason was simply the economy. "It was sad," Keller says now. "It was sad."

Keller was not alone. In the spring of 1990 Florence Fabricant, under the *New York Times* headline STAR CHEFS FIND THEMSELVES ON THE OUTSIDE LOOKING IN, wrote: "Recently many head chefs left well-known New York restaurants not knowing where their next kitchens would be. Geoffrey Zakarian of 44 in the Hotel Royalton, Thomas Keller of Rakel, Michel Attali of Petrossian and Ali Barker of 150 Wooster Street have spent weeks, even months, sitting on the bench."

After Keller and Raoul split, Keller drifted into the darkest period of his career. Ever in search of La Rive but finding the market in New York dead, he became a consultant. Keller says "prostitute."

"You're selling yourself to restaurants that are doing poorly," he explains. "They expect you to be a miracle worker. You go into a restaurant where people don't give a shit. It's messy, it's dirty, the food is terrible, there are no cooks to cook the food. I remember one time, I was on my knees in the kitchen saying to the cook, 'Please, please, just *cut* the chicken in *half* and put it on the *plate!*' I never made so much money in my life. I was miserable."

Then a call came from an old acquaintance asking if he was interested in becoming a chef at a hotel restaurant in L.A. Keller took over Checkers in January 1991, but six months later the hotel was sold to German businessmen.

"It was miserable, working for people who didn't care about food. I had to bring in my own purveyors. The hotel wouldn't pay them; they told me to find new purveyors. They got hung out to dry. There was nothing I could do." He occasionally ventured into the dining room— again the critical accolades picked up right where they'd left off in New York—and frequently told patrons that the hotel wasn't paying his purveyors and the operation was a sham. Once, seated at a table with some diners, he noted that the controller of the hotel ran a rotten operation and explained the reasons why. This might have been a minor incident except for the fact that the controller was one of the people at the table.

"So that was the second job I got fired from," Keller says. "Which was fine. I would have fired me long before they did.

"It's funny," he continues, noting how hard the work of a chef is. "I never gave up on the restaurant business. I felt confident I could cook. I knew I could cook. So I bummed around looking for a restaurant in L.A., which was worse than New York."

He remembered a conversation he'd had not long before with his mentor. Henin had said, "Tom, forget all this bullshit about all the people that are trying to tell you how to do things. Do something on your own. At La Rive, you were happy. You were alone and really developing and blooming. You're a young American kid. American cuisine is coming up. The wine business is coming up. I think you could put those things together. If I were you, I would look for a small place in the wine country."

"I don't have the money," he said, "I don't have the connections."

"Wa wa wa," mimicked Henin.

Keller's girlfriend at the time, a wine seller, had begun a little side business making boutique vinegars with wine left over from her tastings. It was terrible vinegar, Keller says. She also had gotten into olive oil, pumping cheap olive oil into pretty bottles. Keller, unemployed, began to study vinegar and olive oil. If they were going to make vinegar, he wanted to make it really good vinegar. If they were going to put olive oil into a pretty bottle, it was going to be the best olive oil you could buy. Thus was born EVO, Keller's small olive oil company, which he bought from the girlfriend after they split up. The company has yet to make money, but it is indeed very good olive oil.

About this time his friend, the chef-restaurateur Jonathan Waxman said these words: "There's a place up here called the French Laundry. It's for sale. You should take a look at it."

Keller made the trip. He showed up on a Monday afternoon in the spring of 1992. The restaurant was closed. But the honeysuckle surrounding the old house was in bloom, as were the ancient roses climbing an arched trellis that led into the courtyard. Keller passed under the roses and beheld the French Laundry.

Time felt out of joint. He had stepped into a different world. This was the French countryside that he loved. Here was a French country home. Here was a three-star restaurant in waiting. Here was La Rive.

Don and Sally had opened the French Laundry when Thomas Keller opened his first restaurant as a twenty-two-year-old boy chef. In retrospect, there was, when Keller passed under that creeping rose and beheld the French Laundry, a moment of inevitability, of culmination: He'd arrived. He'd never known it, but it almost seemed he'd been heading here his entire life.

There was, however, a nagging problem: Thomas Keller didn't have enough money to pay off his own credit card bill. He didn't even have a job. How on earth does a broke, unemployed cook get a million dollars from people he doesn't know?

"I woke up every day for nineteen months," says Keller, "every day thinking that someone else was going to buy the French Laundry." It was, he says, the longest nineteen months of his life.

CHAPTER SIX

"One morning, I walked into the room off the kitchen where I lived, which we were using as an office," Keller says, "and there was Laura with a reservation book on her lap sitting on a milk crate with a phone. And there was Arthur sitting at a fold-up table trying to work. I was so embarrassed and humiliated and terrified by the sight."

The French Laundry had just opened, summer of 1994. From the beginning at Cobbley Nob through Checkers, Keller had yet to make money running a restaurant. He'd never broke even. Keller could cook and always got the reviews, but also he always lost money.

And he was perfectly poised to do it again, only now there was a lot more money to lose, and he alone was responsible. One of his friends then was a man named Bob Long, a former banker and now wine-maker. Bob asked Keller to join him and some friends on a trip to Italy. Keller needed to get out of L.A., clear his head, and decide on a plan to acquire the French Laundry.

"He wanted to create a three-star restaurant; it didn't matter where," says Long. Keller had confessed to Long his ambitions of one day owning a great Michelin-caliber restaurant in the French countryside. Three-star cooking in a three-star restaurant, this was the only work Keller was interested in. It didn't matter that this was increasingly hard to do in France, let alone in America, where high-end cuisine had crashed with the market, and nouvelle cuisine, beaten into the ground by bad cooks, had been replaced by roast chicken and mashed potatoes.

Didn't matter. Bob Long chuckled and asked, "How do you start a three-star restaurant when you don't have any money?"

One of Long's friends on the trip said to Keller, forget the fact that Keller was unemployed, broke and had never made any money in restaurants. The Napa Valley itself couldn't support the kind of restaurant he described so enthusiastically because tourism, on which he'd depend for business, was seasonal; in January and February, the restaurant would be dead.

Keller nodded quietly and went to work. Rarely content outside a kitchen, he asked for jobs in restaurants during his vacation to learn how things were done in Italy, picking up details that became fundamental to his future work, such as how many yolks would fit into a kilo of pasta (thirty). They stayed with an Italian family, and each morning Keller rose early in order to make the day's pasta with the grandmother. She taught him an ingenious self-sealing pasta, the Piedmont version of ravioli, called agnolotti. It was an odd trip in a way. Keller bumped into an eclectic coterie of American foodies on holiday, people like Irene Virbila, the *L.A. Times* restaurant critic. People recognized the lanky, silent American in cook's clothes in the kitchen. He bumped into his old friend Tommy Colicchio. The trip was an auspicious one, as many had begun to echo newspaper articles that openly wondered "Whatever happened to Thomas Keller?" It was also "the beginning," Keller says, "of waking up every morning with the cold sweats." If he lost the French Laundry, he felt he would never have another chance like it in his life.

Upon his return from Italy, Keller put together a comprehensive business plan with the help of former banker Long. He needed a lawyer and went to see Bob Sutcliff, who represented a couple of prominent chefs in the area. Sutcliff was impressed with Keller's business plan; he'd never seen something so thorough from a cook. He said he'd be happy to help; it would cost forty grand. Keller said he didn't have forty grand. He reached into his little black bag and pulled out a green bottle, his EVO olive oil. Sutcliff was intrigued. They talked about the olive oil company. One thing led to another. A few hours later Sutcliff had agreed to work on spec with five grand up front. Keller and Sutcliff shook, and Keller went to his bank account to withdraw twenty-five hundred dollars in cash, his maximum weekly limit on his VISA. Seven days later he withdrew that amount again and secured Sutcliff's services.

He needed only a million plus more, and so he did what he knew best: cooked for people. Again with Bob Long's assistance, Keller found potential investors and invited them to dinner at Long's vineyard above Yountville. Here he had not only his comprehensive business plan, Long's excellent wines and spectacular mountainside views, but also a slide show of what the restaurant would look like, sample menus, and pictures of the food. While the potential investors watched these slides, they received their first bite, a tiny ice-cream cone with a scoop of salmon tartare in it. This was followed by a complete French Laundry meal, concluding with a composed cheese course—whipped Brie with tellicherry pepper and balsamic glaze—and dessert. The potential investors would get a sense of proportion and quality and the goals of the proposed business, as well as a sense of Thomas Keller himself.

Twice Keller was knocked off course by single investors who wanted absolute control of the restaurant, after which Keller had to begin the entire process over again. But he had so endeared himself to Don and Sally Schmitt that they virtually took the French Laundry off the market with a down payment from Keller of four thousand dollars. They wanted someone who they felt would care for the French Laundry and the town of Yountville that they had so diligently built. They trusted this quiet, forthright, methodical chef.

Ultimately Keller was able to convince forty-eight people that his idea would work. Bob Long never doubted it. Napa County was visited by nearly three million tourists spending $361 million at the time. There were only a few good restaurants in the valley. "And you had two hundred and fifty wineries," Long concluded, "that needed places to entertain clients. That's why you can't get a table here."

With final help from the Schmitts themselves, Keller bought the restaurant for $1.2 million.

"Everything we bought we used," Keller says of their hustling to open the French Laundry. "We had just enough money to do some cosmetics. Painted the dining room, did the ceiling over, put some carpet in. People gave me some chairs. In the kitchen we bought some refrigeration and created workstations. It had only been Sally in there before. Now there would be four of us. Stephen wasn't doing desserts then; he was first course and cheese course. And we were lucky to have a small pastry chef because there was so little room. My cooler was at the entrance into the dining room, so every time I got something from the cooler, I blocked the waitstaff from the food.

"When we ran out of money, we had to open the restaurant. We needed cash flow. The only utensils we had were the ones I had brought with me or the ones we bought used, some pots from a friend in L.A. We bought some china, some glassware, silverware, and that was it. We opened with eight pots and no sauté pans. We sautéed in pots; we cooked everything in pots.

"The first night was for investors only, forty-five people. The first two weeks were previews, the forty-nine-dollar menu reduced twenty-five percent. It allowed us not to feel so much pressure to perform at the level we wanted to perform.

"We offered a four-course menu and a five-course menu. The four-course menu fell away because everyone ordered the five-course menu. After two months we added the chef's tasting menu, which was easier on the servers, who still wrote everything in longhand on tickets, and brought in more revenue."

The small family of waitstaff and cooks that opened the French Laundry quickly found their routine. They cooked six days a week. The same staff worked every day. They had big, delicious family meals. They played softball on days off. After work they'd drink wine together. And the next day—every day, in fact—at four-thirty, when they'd begin to cook fast and hard for the night ahead, a tape was popped into the tape deck, *ka chunk,* and a deadpan voice intoned: "K. Billy Super Sounds of the Seventies Weekend just keeps on comin' with this little ditty that reached up to twenty-one in May of 1970. The George Baker selection, 'Little Green Bag.'"

And notes from a bass guitar began to pound. The sound of a tambourine arrived in a counterbeat, then the drums, the vocals, the rhythm guitar, and the kitchen began to rock. Agnolottis were filled with California chestnuts; beef cheek and veal tongue that had been braising all morning came out of the oven; foie gras was portioned; beurre monté—melted butter kept in a creamy-looking emulsified state—was whipped over a burner; lobster was cooked off; venison loin was cleaned and tied with butcher's string; puff pastry was rolled out. The night's mise en place was readied.

The second night the French Laundry was open, *John Mariani* showed up. Michael Bauer of the *San Francisco Chronicle* came not long after that; that same night the pot of oil for frying doughnuts caught fire, and someone rushed it into the backyard, where it sat like a little bonfire beneath the honeysuckle and the chinaberry tree. The oil caught fire about once a week. The butane clickers the cooks lit their burners with exploded from the heat with enormous bangs, blasting plastic shrapnel into their chef's coats. They just kept on cooking. The reviews began and never stopped. Neither did the tape of the *Reservoir Dogs* sound track and *Super Sounds of the Seventies.* In the morning Keller often found the tape in the fry oil, put there by one of the waitstaff who just couldn't bear to hear "Hooked on a Feeling" one more time.

"We bought four copies of that tape during the last five months of the old kitchen," Keller says wistfully.

Keller wasn't open half a year before he took the positive reviews and the evidence of his cooking to investors and asked for a proper kitchen. He'd convinced them out of $1.2 million with an idea and a stack of paper. *This* money came easily—you could read the reviews, you could have dinner, you could see how squeezed they were in the current kitchen—and they broke ground for the new kitchen one year to the day after they'd begun renovations on the restaurant itself.

The old two-hundred-square-foot kitchen became a bar and foyer, and a brand-new kitchen four times as big was created. There would be no music in this kitchen, no *Super Sounds of the Seventies.*

"The new kitchen changed everything," Keller says. "It turned the French Laundry into a real restaurant. The camaraderie changed. There were a lot more people. We could clean the old kitchen in twenty minutes. The new one took two hours. We were open seven days a week, lunch on the weekends, to increase revenue and justify spending half a million dollars on a new kitchen. No longer did everybody work the same days. A lot of connections between the staff were lost. They didn't spend days off together or drink wine together after work. That was the saddest part of the change."

Keller was terrified at this stage. He knew the pieces weren't all there. Just as they hadn't been there twenty years before at Cobbley Nob, or at Rakel or at Checkers. Management had been taken over completely by Laura Cunningham, who bought wines and managed the front of the house. Keller was cooking better than ever and had reached a point in his career at which he was able to work as close to his potential as never before. But this left no one watching the books, and the French Laundry was losing money. And there was no one to keep track of it. Weeks passed when Keller didn't take a paycheck so they could make payroll.

"I was remembering Rakel," Keller says, "thinking, 'This *can't* happen again. It *can't*.' I was into something bigger than I'd been in before. It was just me with people I didn't know who'd given me a lot of money. I was terrified that we were missing that one element that would ultimately bring down the restaurant.

"The first six months we were extremely lucky to lose only six hundred eighty dollars per investor. Almost thirty-five thousand dollars. I was in the shit, but I kept my focus on the food. I couldn't lose that."

And then Pat arrived. Pat McCarty, accountant. She would try to clean things up, gather the invoices lying all over the office and figure out where the money was and where debts were. Soon she found herself fending off one purveyor they weren't able to pay, then shorting a second purveyor so that she could pay the first. "They didn't know how much money they had," Pat recalls with dismay. "They didn't know how much money they owed." This information was relatively easy to figure out; what was harder for Pat was writing checks. The work was so stressful she nearly quit. "I was sending out checks when there weren't funds to cover them," she says.

But the reviews remained good, stories kept appearing, and so did customers. They made it through 1995 and then through the winter of 1996. Pat kept them organized and above water, and by the spring they were showing signs of not losing money. In May, Keller received a best California chef award from the James Beard Foundation. "After they announced the Beard award, everything changed," Pat recalls. "That day the phones started ringing and didn't stop." That spring Pat was able to find Keller and say these words: "Thomas, all accounts are payable within thirty days."

The three elements of the tripod that make a successful restaurant were for the first time in Keller's career in place: back of the house, front of the house, and financial.

By the end of 1996 the French Laundry had made a profit. Seventeen dollars. Or just over thirty-five cents per investor.

"I thought back on all that we'd done," Keller says, "everybody's hard work, my own, the stress. And I wondered, 'We did all that to make seventeen dollars?'"

And yet he was all but giddy about it. They'd turned a corner. "What it said to me," Keller remembers, "was, this is my first year—with Rakel or the Cobbly Nob or all those different places that I've been—that I've been able to make money. We were able to close the first two weeks in January for a vacation for the first time."

And when they reopened on a stormy January Monday, the restaurant was at capacity. Tourism in the Napa Valley had become year-round.

Reviews and word of mouth ensured that the French Laundry reservation book would stay full. Five months later, May 1997, Keller was
named the country's best chef by the Beard Foundation. Six months
after that the country's most powerful restaurant critic called the French
Laundry America's most exciting restaurant.

CHAPTER SEVEN

"*You* have to have enormous respect for the food," Keller said. He paused. "It's why I killed the rabbits."

Near midnight Keller extended his slender frame across an entire couch; I sat in an adjacent couch, in his living room, where we were talking generally about cooking. The rabbit story had come up at dinner at a nearby restaurant, with Laura Cunningham, French Laundry general manager, her mother and sister. We'd returned, and Thomas and I stayed up to talk, Keller apparently enjoying the end of the rare day when he did not cook.

Because I was there in the capacity of hired writer for his cookbook—had no idea I would return in my mind nearly a year later to this place, to my notes from that evening and weeks at the restaurant, for my own purposes—we talked about the book. Keller believed the French Laundry was an important restaurant and that it, like other prominent restaurants, had had an impact on the industry. Portion size, for instance. He didn't invent small portions (Trotter had been doing it for years), but the success of the restaurant and its menu, and the extraordinary media exposure he'd gotten, no doubt inspired chefs who shared ambitions similar to Trotter and Keller. Furthermore, approximately forty thousand people ate at the French Laundry each year, and that can't help opening a few people to the idea of many small portions. A subsequent rise in the popularity of the chef's tasting menu—a meal of six to nine courses designed each night by the chef—spread throughout the country, reaching even culinary backwaters such as Cleveland and Detroit and popping up in numerous low-end restaurants, ones far removed from the French tradition out of which the form sprang (such as Manhattan's Honmura An, a Japanese restaurant, and the Italian restaurant Po). Keller's whole point was that there was a perfect quantity to serve beyond which the flavors begin to dull. "I want to serve as much food as possible," he said, "without jeopardizing the intensity of the flavor."

When Keller lived in New York and didn't have a lot of money, he appreciated restaurants that offered half bottles of wine so that even penurious cooks could taste more than a single bottle; thus he and Laura, the sommelier and buyer, tried to offer a great selection of wine in half bottles. He also hoped the success of the French Laundry would encourage more people to return to classical French cuisine, the source of his methods and ideas. He seems to have been the first chef to feature a composed cheese course, and he hoped this helped diners to focus on cheese, which he thinks is important; once a rarity (other than, most notably, at Chanterelle, which offered a formal cheese service as long as two decades ago in Manhattan), the cheese course was becoming increasingly popular at many upscale restaurants.

But even here, as we spoke of such possible topics for a book that would contain scores of French Laundry recipes—Black Sea Bass with Saffron Vanilla Sauce, Sweet Parsnips and Arrowleaf Spinach and Saddle of Young Rabbit Wrapped in Applewood-Smoked Bacon with Caramelized Fennel, Potato Gnocchi and Fennel Infused Oil—Keller couldn't help returning to fundamental principles of cooking.

Beginning, as one must always begin, with stock, *le fond de cuisine,* the foundation of cooking. "The ideology of a stock needs to be understood," he said, reclined but, as always, precise, quiet, and alert. "It all goes back to respect."

For his veal stock, Keller instructed his cooks to rinse the bones, to *clean* them. Only then were they blanched, covered with water in a giant kettle and brought to a boil; mats of foam and scum (coagulated blood and protein and fat) would rise and be discarded. You would never want to eat this stuff, this foul mat. Obviously, then, you remove it. You must always be skimming, continually removing what you don't want in the finished product.

Whoever works butcher station makes the veal stock with fifty pounds of bones. These are a lot of bones to heft, to boil (it takes a long time to bring that many bones and gallons to a boil), and to strain. Keller lamented this only insofar as it prevented him from making an even better stock. "Sometimes I think we should blanch the bones twice," he said. This would result in cleaner bones and ultimately a cleaner finished sauce. "It's the base for everything," he said of veal stock.

You bring the liquid up to heat slowly, "not violently," he said. You never wanted abrupt or harsh temperature change when cooking. And as with the first stock, the second stock, the remouillage, made from the same bones, followed the same fundamentals: low temperature, long cooking time.

"What it comes down to," Keller said, "is having a high regard for food and how to think about it logically. You must have the right amount of bones and the right amount of vegetables to the right amount of tomato to the right amount of water."

Keller continued. "How do you cook green beans?" He described the key factors for perfectly cooked green vegetables: "You've got a certain amount of water, a certain amount of salt in that water, and a certain amount of beans relative to that salt and that water. All of it is important." It was simply a matter of caring, he said. Understand the method, and then execute it. There is a moment when any given item has reached perfection, he said, and you have to be ready at that moment.

Gradually—during this time silently observing the kitchen at work during prep and during service, interviewing staff, French Laundry purveyors, and through conversations like these—I was beginning to understand how his mind worked, what the qualities of that intelligence were that produced a great chef.

Keller was enormously observant, a trait in himself that he described in ways that were persuasive to me because I had failed to see myself the very things that had seemed so plain to him. In every kitchen I'd worked in or been in that had asparagus, the asparagus was either lying flat in a hotel pan, rubber bands surrounding the bunches, or still in its shipping carton. Keller's stood upright in water. In New York he used to walk past all the Korean greengrocers, and all their asparagus were in buckets of water, like gladiolas. Once you notice that and equate it to the porous cross section of their stems, the reason is obvious. "Treat asparagus like a flower," Keller said.

When a cook let milk or cream boil over on the stove, I saw a mess. Keller saw it as a question of measurement. "People are boiling two cups of milk, and it boils over," Keller said. "They never think of the fact that there's not two cups of milk in there anymore." He paused. "Most of what happens in a kitchen is logical."

The reason you don't want stocks and sauces to cook at a heavy boil was not only for clarity and cleanness but also for yield. I used to make a lamb sauce for the chops I grilled at my station, and while we followed a recipe, sometimes I ended up with a lot of sauce, sometimes as little as half what I expected. Keller said part of the reason for a gentle temperature was that at a boil, bone and vegetable disintegrate, and the resulting fragments act like sponges, soaking up all your stock or sauce only to be slammed out of the chinois into the garbage. That's where my lamb sauce had gone. I could suddenly see it in my chinois back at Sans Souci.

Some things, I thought, should have been obvious to me, but others were not. Was it obvious how delicate the flesh of fish is? If you spend enough time cutting it, it is. Keller went further with this idea. You had to cradle fish as carefully as a newborn child, he whispered. In his walk-in he wanted his fish not only packed in abundant ice, but packed in ice *in the same position it swims* to avoid stressing the flesh of the fish unnecessarily. This is logical, I suppose, but how many chefs take it this far, have a little panorama, like at the natural history museum, of fish swimming?

The extension of this was that he loved to cook and serve fish more than any other food. Fish offered a great variety of textures and flavors, worked with more garnishes, and made better presentations than any other item.

"But it's not my favorite thing to eat," he said with a smile, still stretched out, hands behind his head. "My favorite thing to eat is offal. And things that are cooked for a long time."

Offal he'd learned to cook at La Rive in the hills near the Catskill Mountains. Here he cooked alone, experimenting without fear of humiliation from older cooks and chefs. This, and the fact of La Rive's isolated and rural situation, created what was an ideal environment for self-teaching, were one so inclined. Keller was. So when his rabbit purveyor arrived with a delivery, Keller said, "Next time, bring them to me alive."

If he were going to cook rabbits, he should know how to skin, gut, and butcher them as well. The purveyor showed up but did not prove to be an elegant teacher. He knocked one rabbit out, slit its throat, pinned it to a board, skinned it, and gutted it, then left. That was it. And Keller was alone in the grass behind the restaurant with eleven cute little bunnies. Bunnies *are* cute. Soft fur, long ears, little pink noses, warm, yearning eyes. Keller didn't *want* to kill them. But he had no choice at this point and eventually cranked up his resolve and made for one of the rabbits. "Rabbits scream," Keller told us at dinner. "And this one screamed really loud." It was an awful experience, he said. He tried to kill it, but the rabbit was screaming so loud and struggling to get away the work was difficult. Then the rabbit's leg snapped as it struggled to get away. So while it was still terrified and now likely in great pain, it could no longer run away, and Keller managed to kill it. Ten more to go.

He stunned, killed, skinned, gutted, and butchered them all for service that week, and he did learn how to break down rabbits. But he learned something more. He had taught himself about respect for food and, its opposite, waste. It had been hard to kill those rabbits because life, to Keller, wasn't meaningless. If their lives hadn't meant anything, it would have been easy to kill them. He took that life, and so he wouldn't waste it. But how easy it is to forget about a piece of meat in the oven, throw it in the garbage, and fire a new one. He would not overcook this rabbit. He cared about it too much at this point. These were going to be the best rabbits ever. He was going to do everything possible, short of getting in that oven to cook with them, to make sure they were perfect. (I was later gratified to read this in Bryan Miller's *New York Times* review of Keller's food at Rakel: "Sliced loin of rabbit perfumed with rosemary is the best I have had in ages.")

But this understanding wasn't enough. A self-taught chef had to take one more step, make the critical intellectual jump: apply this new knowledge and instinct to everything you touch. This was how a chef taught himself, and this was how Keller learned respect for food.

"They taught me a great amount about care," he said, recalling the rabbits. "It's up to me not to waste them."

I don't recall how that conversation ended. We'd talked for an hour and a half. He was always tired when the restaurant ran seven days a week, ten services in all, so he went to bed, and I went upstairs to write down what we'd talked about. I typed away in the guest room of that very quiet house, and it quickly grew spooky; the conversation became haunting and benevolently haunted. The night I'd first arrived at the French Laundry, I'd thought, *I'm here.* I knew I'd arrived somewhere important. I'd felt a parallel excitement of arrival when I'd first pushed through the doors of K-8 at the Culinary Institute of America, my first day in a culinary class, knife kit in hand, tardy and out of code. *But,* I thought, *I've made it, I'm here.*

As I transcribed my notes in Keller's house that night, I realized with increasingly strong shivers that Keller had just linked that beginning and this end in a way that was powerful and convincing for me.

First, the fact that when he began to talk about cooking, the thing one began with was veal stock. How important it was to find a butcher who would saw the bones into one-inch pieces: because that size would give him the most efficient yield. Why he did not brown the bones in the oven: because he didn't always want a roasted flavor in the finished sauce; if he wanted in his final sauce flavors that resulted from roasting, he would incorporate them later. Suddenly I was back in Skills class at the Culinary, listening to Chef Pardus, *my* chef, ask if we should put garlic in the stock. Did we know how that stock was going to be used?

Would it be reduced and used for a sauce? Would that sauce want garlic? How could we know? And couldn't we introduce garlic later if we wanted it?

Keller wanted his stock clean, and so he washed the bones first, then blanched them, then rinsed them, then made the stock. You don't treat your stockpot like a garbage can, he said. You peel your vegetables. You skim everything all the time. You want everything clean, and that meant removing what you did not want in your stock. (When a student asked Pardus if it was necessary to peel carrots for stock, he had said, "Put the peels on their salad if they like peels so much." Chef Pardus held up a mound of limp, dirty carrot peels. "You want to eat this?" Obviously, then, remove it.)

Keller wished he could blanch the bones twice for the ultimate clean stock because he knew the truth of what chef-instructor Rudy Smith had told his introduction to hot foods class: "If you've got a perfect stock, you can make a perfect sauce. If you've got a mediocre stock, the best sauce you can make is a mediocre sauce."

As I typed the words that Keller had all but whispered, reclined as he was at that late hour, *"right amount of bones and the right amount of vegetables to the right amount of tomato to the right amount of water,"* I was all but transported to the classroom of chef-instructor and CMC judge Ron DeSantis. Here was Keller, a contemporary American chef with no formal training, a star chef, one far removed from the so-called fuddy-duddy world of the CIA, and yet he had virtually repeated words that had rung in my ears a year and a half earlier, in DeSantis's classroom. "You GOT that?" Chef DeSantis had boomed. "That cook MEA-SURED! Counted. We got a certain amount of bones here, we need a certain amount of water *here*. And everything is beautiful, whether it's brown or white stock. Everything works beautifully then. You have to *mea*-sure."

I had agreed in principle with DeSantis, but I also knew how real kitchens worked. You didn't measure your herbs and aromatic vegetables, your mirepoix; you eyeballed it. That was part of being a pro, not having to measure. Keller, the ultimate pro, one might say, wanted his cooks to measure.

And of course, beans. Green beans. Boy, if I'd gotten money every time one of those madmen chefs at the CIA talked about how important it was to cook your green beans properly! "Al dente vegetables don't fly here at the CIA," Chef Pardus had said in the opening class on vegetables. And from then on I heard about green beans every single week, all the way through to the last class, American Bounty, when Chef Dan Turgeon said to me, "How to properly cook a green vegetable. That's what they hammer into you here. It's really, really important. If you look at these master chefs, all they've really done is perfected, mastered those basic cooking techniques. It's what they always do, it becomes a habit. Every time they cook a green bean, it's a *perfectly* cooked green bean."

The way Keller differed from the chef-instructors I'd known was not to contradict them but rather to exceed them; he took what they taught students and brought it to crazy levels. I'd cooked fava beans for Dan Turgeon's class—pain in the neck, those little buggers, but delicious in succotash. It was the same in every kitchen. You pop them out of their enormous pods, blanch them, shock them in ice water, then peel them—cooked, the skin peels right off—and you're good to go. At the French Laundry you peeled the favas *before* cooking them and you removed that itty-bitty germ poking out the side, which can be a little bitter. Keith Willis, a new French Laundry cook on fish station, had worked at, among other kitchens, Charlie Trotter's and Lespinasse under Gray Kunz, two great kitchens. As much perhaps out of frustration as curiosity, he asked Keller, "Why do you peel the favas *before* cooking them?" Keith had never been asked to peel a fava before it was cooked, but Keller explained that the favas' color was better because acids and gases get trapped beneath its skin, dulling its beautiful pale green color as it cooks, and it stays fresher longer.

Keller wanted a ton of heavily salted water in an enormous pot. Dissolve a cup of kosher salt in a gallon of water, and that's what your blanching water should taste like; that's the salt level Keller wanted in his green veg water. He called his method big-pot blanching. Enormous pot of ocean water at a wicked boil, a teensy amount of green veg. If you cooked your vegetable this way and plunged it into a vast amount of ice water the instant it was done, you would achieve extraordinary color in your bean. You'd have a greener-than-green green bean. If he was cooking English peas or favas, he wanted them chilled in ice water before their cooking; very cold vegetables into boiling salt water produced the greenest of greens and the freshest, strongest flavor.

And of course, the importance of killing bunny rabbits. The benevolent haunting continued even here, now in the words of my gardemanger instructor, Eve Felder. "No one can tell me this," she had said. "I know how to kill a quail. I know what it's like to kill and clean a squab. I know what it's like to take down a full pig, to take down a full lamb. I'm not queasy about that. I can't be. Because that's the connection of working with food."

As with everything, though, Keller brought what he learned to its furthest logical extreme. What was true of rabbits was true even of wheat. Thus to burn a crouton was a waste of life. Not the life of the wheat but the life of the person who grew the wheat, the life of the person who baked the bread, and the life of the cook who spent time cutting that bread and burning the croutons.

This kind of observation of, and thinking about, the world around him, his engagement in it, his curiosity and intensity, and the way he used what he absorbed, all were fundamental elements in becoming not simply a chef and not a great cook but rather a great chef. Thomas Keller had been 100 percent driven toward cooking for nearly twenty-five years, a quarter century's active engagement in food and feeding people and watching how the world worked in relation to the cooking. He was smart, sensorily engaged in the world and seemed to be connected to the life core, that energy, that meaning, that order I sensed in the world and that cooking could connect you to. He tried to put all he was and all he knew into his food, always striving toward perfection, and had been doing so for a long time. To be a great chef required this much time, this much presence within the work.

CHAPTER EIGHT

"*P*ig's ears?" I asked.

"Pig's ears," Keller said. He looked up from the trotters he was stuffing at his station and said, "What are you looking at me like that for?"

Pig's ears, the idea that you could, by choice, cook and eat the hairy, flappy piece of cartilage that is a sow's ear was interesting news to me. Country folk ate all kinds of goofy stuff, that didn't surprise me, but that a pig's ear might be at home in haute cuisine did. Should I have been surprised? No. In the summer Keller's duck breast had been garnished with, the menu read "Ragout de Langue de Canard." *La langue,* I thought. *La langue.* Reaching back to my high school French, I thought I knew what that meant. And it didn't mean a ragout of duck language. It meant a ragout of the actual tongue. Could this stuff be good to eat?

Keller liked duck products. In addition to tongues, he'd learned to use duck testicles and for Sunday lunch at the French Laundry he liked to serve a poached duck egg on duck hash. Keller also loved pig. While we spoke about pigs' ears, what looked like small, thick, curved sausages braised in brown sauce in a pot on the stove. "Pig tails," Keller explained when I looked up from the pot. He shook his head and said that when he ordered them, he thought they'd be cute little curlicues that might make an interesting presentation, not tails the size of link sausage. It was an experiment about which he was not hopeful. But he'd try.

I walked to his station, what would become the pass in a couple hours, when he continued to stuff trotters, the skin from a pig's foot, with a mixture of chopped sweetbread and black truffles. He would wrap these little *paquets de porc* in caul fat, later simply to be reheated and served on a sauce of chestnuts and white truffle oil.

He also prepared pig's head dishes. This was an extraordinarily laborious but fascinating preparation in which a pig's head was boned out, leaving a big flap of head skin with plenty of fatty and succulent cheek meat. This was rolled around pig's tongue, pig's ear, and sweetbreads, tied into tight cylinder, and oven-poached all day, then cooled. It was then sliced thick, coated in panko bread crumbs, sautéed at service so that it was crisp on the outside and succulent and melting on the inside, then served on Sauce Gribiche, a mayonnaise variation using hard-cooked yolks rather than raw. Keller adored the dish. "It tastes like a hot dog," he said. "Only the very best hot dog you've ever had in your life."

His cooks used this same basic method with a similar cylinder of stuffed pig's head to make pig's head chips, but the cylinder of meat and offal would be packed in salt and hung for a couple days of curing, then frozen, sliced very thin, and cooked into chips.

This was extraordinary stuff to me. We didn't do this at the American Bounty restaurant at the CIA; I never saw such preparations in any restaurant I'd been in. Thus, when Keller first mentioned pig's ear, I gave him a funny look. "How do you prepare," I asked, "a pig's ear?"

"You cook the hell out of it," he said. "Eight or nine hours. It never really loses its crunch, that cartilage crunch. But if you dice it really fine, it almost melts in your mouth. We serve it with lobster. With honey and vinegar. It's good."

I nodded, and observed him as he wrapped small, thick rectangles of skin around the sweetbread farce and then wrapped these in pieces of caul fat. He did this almost every day. Just as he always cut and portioned the foie gras, stressing how critical the thickness was. And every day he cut the salmon, very slowly and deliberately, as if wanting to extend each task rather than finish it, then wiping down his entire station after storing what he'd just prepared. He worked very clean so that as he began each preparation, it seemed to be the first of the day.

Often the first canapé Keller sent a table, after the cornet, was a soup. He served soups in white espresso cups, sans spoon, until he noticed other restaurants serving soup this way, and he switched back to more conventional small white bowls. Canapé station chef made as many as nine fresh soups daily. They were remarkably simple; the method was this: Cook the main item—asparagus, salsify, chanterelle, celery root, fava, chestnut, what have you—till it's done, puree it, adjust the consistency, strain it. You might simplify the equation further: Cook the item, then adjust its consistency. Meaning that all carrot soup was cooked carrots liquefied. There were elements of finesse. You had to season properly. You might decide to enrich something with a fat: cream for the spinach soup, truffle oil for the pea soup. You had to choose the proper liquid to thin your puree. Chicken broth might seem like the frequent answer (and the right choice for a vegetable with a forward flavor, such as turnip), but with something as delicate as fava bean, you might only need water. Always the soups were strained. There seemed to be few things here that didn't pass through a chinois or a tamis. The result was always a powerfully flavored liquid, usually the consistency of cream, with vivid color and the texture of luxury.

During my time at the French Laundry my old Skills chef, Michael Pardus, leading a group of CIA bachelor students on their California tour, ate there. Of the thirty-six courses that he and his two companions tasted, Pardus said, he admired and enjoyed most the turnip soup. To take a lowly turnip, Pardus said, a garbage vegetable, and create a clean and beautiful soup was what he admired most. "To distill the essence of simple things into the ethereal," as he put it. "The only meal I can compare it to is the one I had at Jamin," he said, referring to Joel Robuchon's former three-star restaurant in Paris.

Keller offered the calf's brain as a first course during the winter. This had been so good when I'd eaten it I made sure to watch him cook it one evening when he was both expediting and working canapé station to give the canapé station cook a day off. He dipped to the lowboy and removed a trotter that he'd wrapped earlier and half a calf's brain, placing the items on a small pizza pan, where one kept items that were ordered but not fired. A second pizza pan was beside this, one with a clean paper towel on which cooked meat or fish drained before being plated.

Keller floured the calf's brain, looked at me, and said, "Shake and bake." He continued to call off orders and finish plates at the pass. About twelve minutes before he wanted the brain he set a small sauteuse on the graduated flattop. When the pan was hot, he poured an eighth of an inch of oil. He laid in the brain, an oval of fatty organ meat about an inch thick. When one side was golden brown, he flipped the brain, added some beurre monté—butter that had been melted but kept emulsified—and popped the pan into the oven.

He returned to expediting, cooking the pig's foot, and preparing the torchon, a cylinder of marinated foie gras quick-poached, then cut into thick slices and served cold with brioche toast and a quince marmalade. He's so tall that's he's perpetually hunched when cooking, and it's a long way down, especially with a deteriorating knee, to the oven for the lanky chef.

After ten minutes he pulled the brain from the oven and touched it to see how done it was. He set the pan back on the flattop. He finished the foie gras and the pig's foot. He put a clean sauté pan on the heat, added whole butter, then finished plating the four items. He didn't move quickly; he only moved steadily, nothing wasted. He lifted the brain out of the pan with a palette knife and set it on a paper towel to drain and rest. He spooned savoy cabbage, which had been reheated with pancetta and Spanish capers, into a hot shallow dish. By the time this was done, the butter in the sauté pan was browned. He added a spoonful of brunoise (finely diced leek, carrot, and turnip), chives, salt, and a squirt of sherry vinegar. He spooned this over the golden brown brain. Simple as that. The brain was so hot that the vinegar-butter sauce bubbled and frothed as it spread across the surface.

Fish courses followed canapé and first courses, and one of Keller's favorite items to work with here was lobster. He sometimes roasted it, but he preferred to poach it in butter. The key to working with lobster was gentle temperature, he said; in violent heat the meat seized up, preventing the absorption of flavors and creating a rubbery texture. And you could neither flavor nor control the meat as well if you cooked it in its shell. Keller did not boil his lobsters. Instead he poured boiling water over them live and let them sit for two minutes. The outer layer of flesh cooked enough so that it pulled away from the shell while the interior remained raw. Removing the tail, claw, and knuckle meat while the lobster was still hot was critical; if they were cold, the fat in the meat would congeal, he said, and stick to the shell, making it harder to remove. At service Grant or Keith on fish station would submerge the lobster tail into creamy butter that was poaching hot, not boiling hot, for five minutes or so. The lobster that resulted was so tender some people sent it back thinking it was undercooked; they weren't used to tender lobster. This was an easy but extraordinary way to cook lobster.

Keller used the poaching butter all over the place. He loved butter. "Butter, butter, butter, give me more butter" was one of his favorite quotations from the chef he most admired in history, Fernand Point. And every day the fish station cook would create fifteen or twenty pounds of what they called beurre monté. If you melt butter, its components separate; by starting with a little water, just a tablespoon or so, and whisking the butter into it one chunk at a time, you could keep those components together in an opaque yellow fluid that was pure whole butter. You could cook things in this stuff, use it as a base for sauces, add it to other sauces as an enricher. When the meat station cook popped a fillet of veal that he'd just seared into the oven to finish cooking, he'd first coat it with a ladle of beurre monté; this helped keep the fillet juicy and flavorful, and the coating of oil ensured even heating. When the fillet was done, it rested submerged in a pot of beurre monté. The butter added flavor to the meat, but more important, because of the density of the butter, its ambient weight, juices didn't pour out of the meat, but remained within it. Beurre monté stayed about 180 degrees near the stove and was thus the perfect resting temperature; part of the reason it stayed hot through service was that each piece of meat coming out of a four- or five-hundred-degree oven tended to heat the butter up, and the butter conversely helped lower the temperature of the meat, slowing the cooking but maintaining it at the perfect serving temperature.

"We use an enormous amount of butter at the restaurant," Keller said, "but a lot of it is just used as environmental control and flavor and not added fat or added butter."

He liked old-fashioned butter sauces. I was surprised and delighted to see Gregory one afternoon whipping up a béarnaise sauce, a classical French butter and yolk emulsion, a variant of the hollandaise Thomas had made once a day for two years as a young man, then a mystery to him. I had a special fondness of béarnaise, in effect a hollandaise flavored with tarragon and shallot, because it was the first classical sauce I learned to make at home. I hadn't been to a restaurant that served a béarnaise sauce since I was a kid in the seventies. After the reduction sauces of nouvelle arrived on the scene, and the country grew concerned about the amount of fat it ate, béarnaise and its associates all but vanished. Keller served it with reverence. "It's one of the great sauces," he said. Gregory veered from the classical preparation by using red wine vinegar instead of tarragon vinegar; he cooked the yolks in this and a little water; he'd finish it at service with fresh-chopped tarragon, and serve it for Valentine's Day dinner with rabbit sirloin wrapped in a sheet of crisp russet potato. Gregory's version was lighter than one would have seen in the seventies, but it was still the old-fashioned butter and yolk emulsion classified at the turn of the century by Escoffier.

Keller was relentlessly drawn to such things, not only out of sentimental nostalgia but also because, apparently, such dishes provided a great foundation for new ideas. And so he proudly served dishes like a duck à l'orange (which he'd cooked as a young man at Clarke Cook House in Rhode Island) and lobster thermidor, classical French preparations that crossed the ocean because they were so good but that were overdone and eventually badly done and became clichés. Keller took advantage of both the cliché and its retro pleasures, but he could do so because of their fundamental truth and integrity. These dishes would never have been adopted in America and turned into clichés had they not been so good in the first place.

Lobster thermidor, according to *Larousse,* as well as the *Dictionaire de l'Académie des Gastronomes* and Craig Claiborne, was created at a famous restaurant in Paris in January 1894 on the occasion of the opening of a play by that name. Its premise is lobster with a mustard-flavored cream

sauce, glazed under a broiler, and served in its shell. Keller's was virtually no different. He simply used his raw lobster tails, put them in a
small gratin dish, added some lobster glaçage (actually the creamy lobster broth, also served as a canapé) and popped it under the salamander.

Keller served sole Véronique, a famous preparation, classified by Escoffier. A flat piece of sole is folded into a little package, then poached
in a quick fish stock made from the trimmings, lemon juice, white
wine, and water; the stock, here called a cuisson, is reduced to a syrup,
mounted with butter, poured over the fish, and the sole is garnished
with, according to Escoffier, "a nice bouquet of very cold, skinned and
depipped Muscatel grapes."

"When you're trying to be inspired, where do you turn?" Keller
asked. "My favorite dishes are very traditional dishes, sole Véronique,
quiche Lorraine, daube of beef, the short ribs that we do. I love sole,
but I wanted to do sole that had a little more structure to it than the flat
piece of sole sautéed. So sole Véronique came to mind because of the
way it was folded; it becomes a thicker piece of fish, almost like a little
package. That's how I learned it anyway. So what we'll do is make a
stuffing of sultana raisins and brioche croutons so that we actually stuff
the sole. Raisins are ripened grapes. The sauce is a classic glaçage. Sole
Véronique reduced to its essence is fish and grapes. Ours still has the integrity of sole Véronique, but we've given it a modern interpretation."

This surprise—that the French Laundry, not only one of the best
restaurants in the country but also one of the hippest, the hardest reservation to get, the one with the most cache, served béarnaise sauce, lobster thermidor, and duck à l'orange—was twofold: a revelation about
Keller and his food and a confirmation of what I'd been taught in my
very first days as a culinary student. The confirmation was this: that all
the finest cuisine in the Western world originates in the technique of *la
grande cuisine,* classical French technique. The revelation was how that
fact had become manifest in a such a thoroughly American chef, a boy
who came of age in mainstream America in the 1970s and who returned to that culture as a self-taught chef, the culture of his youth, for
guidance in interpreting *la grande cuisine,* and the results, while remaining within the confines of classical French cuisine, were sentimental,

nostalgic, intellectual, occasionally funny, often ironic. Yes, irony added an extra, sometimes dominant dimension to eating his food. His mushroom purveyor, Connie Green, had pointed me in this direction.

I interviewed a lot of Keller's purveyors, a peculiarly intense crowd, often feeling as I did like the journalistic camera in *Citizen Kane* searching for the Rosebud link to all things, the buried fact that would explain, absolutely, Thomas Keller. Connie lived in a house on the side of a mountain, more or less wild like the fungus that was her trade. Shallow plastic crates filled with chanterelles lay all over the floor around a tin fireplace, drying. We sat at a table near the kitchen, where she'd set out a pound of truffles for me to take back to the restaurant. Her dog, Casey, threw up a green slimy tube near the couch, and Connie, annoyed, said, "He's older than dirt and still insists on eating socks once a month." She poured glasses of red wine and told me about her trade but also about Keller.

When Connie first had dinner at the French Laundry, not long after it opened, she knew something unusual was afoot in the kitchen. She had come with two friends, and when one course appeared endowed with a nautical theme, complete with a flagpole skewer onto which was hoisted a flaglike sautéed duck kidney, she wanted to laugh. "There seemed to be some kind of irony that was going on," Connie recalled, "some kind of inside joke. It was as if the beauty of the food weren't enough." And then it struck her like a gong; she knew the truth. "*Thomas Keller,*" she said, "*is Dr. Seuss's illegitimate child.*"

Those two observations—Dr. Seuss (what post–World War II American childhood was not filled with Dr. Seuss?) and inside irony—were new to me, but I sensed immediately she was right. They provided the key.

Reichl's review had made special note of a dish Keller called oysters and pearls, a sabayon—a savory custard, really—with pearl tapioca, an oyster, and caviar. I'd eaten this dish, and it made me laugh, not just a chuckle but extended, quiet laughing, as if someone was telling me a hilarious story. I had been dining solo, so I probably looked no different from a person you see on a park bench carrying on an animated conversation with himself.

When I hung out in the kitchen, there was time for brief exchanges with Keller before he walked off to put something away, to get something, take a phone call, or answer any number of questions from his cooks. I asked him why he thought to put an oyster in tapioca pudding. He said, "Certain things you just know." When I pressed, he said, "It's just logical."

I said, "Putting an oyster in tapioca is not a logical thing to do."

"For me it was," he said.

"How?"

"Tapioca, pearls," he said. "Where do pearls come from? Pearls come from oysters, right? So to me it's completely logical. How does it taste to you?"

I asked, "What do *you* think?"

"I've never tasted it," he said.

"Excuse me?"

"I know that's not a good thing for me to say," he confessed. "But I know it tastes good. You don't have to stick your hand in fire to know it's hot." And he headed out of the kitchen toward the walk-in.

Oysters and pearls is a very sensual, perhaps sexual dish, what with the aphrodisiacal oyster, the creamy-slippery mouth feel, the rich sabayon, the pearls, the salty-fishy-ocean perfume of the caviar. But it can seem plain silly as well.

One is inclined to arrive at the French Laundry in a mood of grave purpose. You are seated at a table with a crisp white cloth, wineglasses sparkling, the ivory walls of the room bare. The restaurant is library quiet. Yours has likely been a hard reservation to get, and you expect to spend a lot of money, especially given that you've heard the wine list is good (you're in the Napa Valley after all). Some people have said it's the best restaurant in the country. Others have claimed it's the best in the world. Expectations are titanically high; therefore they demand a certain sobriety. This is no time for joking. You expect to have one serious meal here. And then you get tapioca pudding with an oyster in it.

I was just beginning to understand that there was, as Connie had noticed her first time there, something more than the food going on. You could accurately describe this food with words like *humor* and *irony,* terms that fly well in English lit seminars but that smack of pretension when referring to food. Indeed, ever since I'd learned the basics of cooking in Skills, I'd felt fairly secure—even a little bit above it all (a sure sign of ignorance in any foodie)—in my position that food and cooking were not "art," as so many people simply assume. The chefs, critics, and foodies who flung the term *art* around as if it were a given, I had learned, were sure to carry on with a lot more self-important hooey if you stuck around. No, despite the fact that "Cooking is art" was widely considered a given, I knew that cooking was craft only, a humble one that could achieve greatness with refinement and skill, but always craft. Keller himself thought this way. "I don't like to use the word *art*," he said when a friend suggested his cookbook would reflect his art, "because we're dealing with food. To me food is not art." Bravo, I thought when he said that, and thank God.

And here I was, using the word *irony* to describe his food. But there *was* irony in oysters and pearls. To serve caviar, one of the most expensive foods on earth, an item that connotes luxury, taste, refinement, elegance, class, on tapioca pudding, given that item's literal and sensory associations with infantile childhood, was ironic. The oyster, this odd bulb of wiggly, slippery muscle, was the Seuss element negotiating these different worlds—adulthood and infancy—that made it funny. The caviar eggs, little black spheres popped against your palate (alongside the larger copycat tapioca spheres), perfuming, with worldly elegance and luxurious seduction, remembered comforts of childhood, enhancing the bland pudding with its ocean salt.

You can go too far with this kind of dissection, of course, and risk losing your shoe in the swamp of self-important hooey you so deplore, but such pleasures were available to people who cared to think about food this way. For those who didn't, the obvious would suffice: It tasted really good. How could it not? A savory pudding, gently flavored with oyster juice and vermouth and seasoned properly, was pleasant to eat; an oyster, if it's a fresh, plump oyster, tastes delicious; good caviar is what it is. You don't have to stick your hand in fire to know it's hot.

But I had to change my mind about food and art right here; looked at from numerous vantage points, oysters and pearls was artful. Some dishes, like the calf's brain, weren't artful in that humorous, ironic way; they were just delicious classical preparations. Every now and then a dish failed, and in the midst of such perfection the failure was glaring and depressing. I had always wanted to try the French Laundry signature dish tongue in cheek, small pieces of beef cheek and calf's tongue that had been braised, then stacked and served with frisée, horseradish cream, and tomato, a small elegant tower, but when I did, I found it to be, well, insipid. The sauce had been overcooked, and so its flavors were muddy, its texture gluey. But worse, the meat was tepid. Braised meats have to be served hot, or their flavor is flat and their texture grainy. This dish, arriving, as all dishes here do, with almost magisterial promise to delight and entertain, made one sad instead. This was simply bad execution by the first-course cook during a busy night, and I knew how easily this could happen, but errors are magnified when they occur against such a beautiful backdrop.

With the cheese course Keller could turn goofy on you. He'd serve things like a "Caesar salad," which was not the traditional Caesar but used the same elements to feature Parmesan cheese. He made a Roquefort trifle and served it in a little glass parfait dish, taking private pleasure in the subversive act of using a French cheese in what was a traditional English dessert. To serve cheddar cheese, he created a dish called soup and sandwich, a miniature grilled cheese sandwich set beside a little demitasse of clear tomato soup, potato chips, and coleslaw.

"Grilled cheese sandwich to me was always Wonder bread and Kraft Singles," Keller explained. He had liked grilled cheese as a kid; the elements (bread and cheese) were obvious cheese course items, so the intellectual task was to transform them into the proportions and taste expectations of haute cuisine. Use slices of good brioche and an excellent farmhouse cheddar, and cook it just like a grilled cheese sandwich. Serve it with perfectly clear tomato water. Fry paper-thin potato chips in clarified butter, and sprinkle them with fresh caraway powder. "And there you have it," Keller said, "a composed plate that resembles something you grew up with, but still, it's creative haute cuisine."

The tomato water (water that drips out of pureed tomatoes and is then passed through a coffee filter is perfectly clear and powerfully flavored) allowed him to be playful in many ways. Years ago he offered a shrimp on the rim of a martini glass as the server poured clear tomato water from a silver martini shaker; he called it shrimp cocktail. He once froze this water, shaved it like Italian ice, then served it as a gazpacho snow cone in a conical paper cup, garnishing it with diced cucumber, onion, peppers, and a grilled shrimp. Unfortunately he called it grilled shrimp snow cone, and people thought he was serving frozen shrimp. "People didn't get it," Keller recalled. "I had one chance, and I blew it."

So he achieved irony and humor, not only with contrasting textures and products, but also with wordplay and associations from mainstream, middle-class America, transforming the ideas of America's oft-maligned lowbrow food into bona fide, often extraordinary haute cuisine.

Desserts too were playful in similar ways. Classically based, but in the context of a French Laundry meal, they added the further dimension of thematic variation, resulting in a pleasant recollection of earlier parts of the meal (which may have occurred two or three hours previously) in the same way that themes recur in plays or orchestral scores. Stephen Durfee, the pastry chef, might send out a canapé dessert soup if a table's meal began with a canapé soup. So a cream of walnut soup or a blueberry soup at the end of the meal might recall the creamy lobster broth or pea soup that began it. Keller served a variety of blini, two tiny potato pancakes, each little bigger than an elongated fifty-cent piece, often topped with caviar. Durfee can send out banana blini for dessert and top them with sweet pearls of chocolate tapioca. And to finish the meal, elegant small jellies might be sent out; unable to help himself, Keller would send out with those jellies peanut butter truffles and call the course PB & J, recollecting again a common and favorable pairing in American *basse cuisine*.

I don't know if I'd have recognized this had I been a one-time customer at the French Laundry, but as I experienced the restaurant, my total immersion in it, I realized that there was a lot more going on here than food. It ultimately felt as if the chef were engaging in a dialogue with you through food but not necessarily about food. Eating was not a consumption of food but rather an exchange of ideas, an interaction of personalities. It could be emotional, and thus the impact on some people was extraordinary, as it had been for that woman who'd come back to thank Keller and was reduced to blubbering gratitude for which she had to apologize.

My final night in Yountville that winter I had my third French Laundry meal. It lasted more than four and a half hours. I did not order. I was VIPed—as is every solo diner, friend, or stranger—and Keller would thus cook for me ("if you would like," the server said), sending me an array of canapés before the chef's tasting began and including myriad dessert courses as well. Nineteen courses in all, with five desserts, four half bottles of wine, and a double espresso. Midway through the meal I needed the bathroom and a minute to stretch my legs. When I returned, Laura Cunningham noted that "Thomas was mad" when informed I was up. *Why?* he wanted to know.

At first I thought, *What does he expect?* I'd been there two hours and had numerous glasses of wine. There was no formal intermission in this situation. But then I wondered about it from his point of view. He was working to serve me an extraordinary meal. It was *not* unlike my walking out of a theater during a performance put on for my benefit, and he thought it terrifically rude (though the restaurant was full and I wasn't the only VIP). The knowledge of his irritation made me realize that he was actually performing. Indeed this meal entertained me like a play or orchestral performance. Better than most, I'd venture. The work of a single distinctive mind and voice performing at its peak for an eager and receptive audience.*

---

*1. Cornet of salmon tartare with red onion crème fraîche is a savory tuile. (St. Urbain Pinot Gris 1995.) 2. Parsnip soup. 3. Potato blini with tomato butter and bottarga. 4. Salmon belly, a thin sheet of it virtually painted onto a plate in a circle, served very cold, with a Meyer lemon vinaigrette, chives, parsley, and dill. 5. Malpeque oyster nestled into a bed of julienned pickled cucumber and topped with a quenelle of sevruga caviar. 6. A chunk of Dungeness crab atop a fine julienne of vegetables, and beneath broiled eel, served with a soy-based sauce, chopsticks at the side of the bowl. 7. Broiled sardine in a raisin emulsion sauce, with balsamic glaze. 8. Truffle custard with chive chip. (Corton Charlemagne Grand Cru Bonneau du Martray, a 1994 white Burgundy.) 9. A potato degustation: potato ravioli on sliced new potatoes with truffles, in a truffle butter sauce. 10. Pan-roasted monkfish tail, with onion ring, onion glaze, and monkfish liver. 11. Lobster thermidor with salsify. (1987 Oak Ridge Cabernet Sauvignon.) 12. Pan-roasted quail with

To eat this way, to eat even a five-course meal here, was to experience not only a range of luxury food items (truffles, foie gras, fresh hearts of palm) and extraordinary technique (calf's brain, pig's head, beautiful soup, superlative mashed potatoes), as one would expect from any restaurant with Michelin three-star expectations of itself, but also an entire meal that arrived out of a unique intelligence—quirky, eccentric, distinct. Keller was not unlike a stage actor who brought his own intellectual and spiritual voice to a role, not unlike a novelist who could not help exploring his own concerns on the page with a voice and syntax as distinct as a fingerprint.

Keller's social mind had formed, or solidified, in middle-class America during the 1970s, so this was the culture he tapped for ideas—PB & J, soup and sandwich, Caesar salad. From the French Laundry's beginning a dish called mac and cheese has remained, in various forms, on the menu. It is not Kraft's macaroni and cheese, of course; it's butter-poached lobster tail that he serves with some sort of pasta and some form of cheese. Originally it was an actual gratin of macaroni, but as business increased, he didn't have enough gratin dishes and so altered the preparation, serving the butter-poached lobster tail on creamy orzo and beneath a Parmesan crisp (crisp cheese that stayed true to the notion of a gratin). But regardless of the form, it was called mac and cheese, connoting simplicity and comfort, and it tasted that way too.

Keller often served surf and turf at the restaurant. When he began cooking, surf and turf—lobster tail and filet mignon—was served at the best Continental restaurants, the apotheosis of class back then (save room for a Galliano after-dinner drink!). *Surf and turf,* then, can only

---

ris de veau and quail sauce. 13. Veal with polenta, brilliant green Brussels sprout leaves on top. 14. A cheese tasting: Vacherin on vol-au-vent, goat cheese on beet sauce, a blue St. Agur with grenadine-poached quince. (1996 Vin de Paille, from Alban Vineyards, in the Edna Valley, California.) 15. Grapefruit sorbet with brunoise of citrus fruits. 16. Cream of walnut soup. 17. Banana blini with créme fraîche and chocolate tapioca. 18. Pineapple, cut like a pork chop, the rough brown skin imitating bone, on top of deep-fried pastry cream and crème fraîche. 19. Ile flotant, meringue filled with chocolate mousse, on sauce anglaise, garnished with a chocolate "salad," chocolate shavings dressed with mint oil and fresh sea salt. (Double espresso.)

be used ironically in light of what we now consider sophisticated food. Keller's surf and turf dishes combined numerous seafoods and land foods: lobster tail with sautéed foie gras, for instance, braised oxtail with roasted monkfish, scallops with cocks' combs. Calling it surf and turf was important. A dish or a combination, lobster tail with a medallion of veal, say, wasn't enough; Keller needed one more dimension to make the dish interesting to himself, and in this case it was a literal device to connect the dish with a 1970s American classic. Keller was not alone in this. Many American menus used this term and others like *mac and cheese,* as one would expect (Michael Symon's Lola menu, for one; he used the terms *mac and cheese* and *surf and turf* as well, and had even put his own neo-béarnaise with goat cheese on the menu). But the relentlessness of the associations with the 1970s and the strength and originality with which Keller evoked them bordered on the extreme.

Another excellent lobster preparation regularly featured at lunch was one Keller called peas and carrots. In composing a dish that would use the inelegant but tasty knuckle meat from the lobster wrapped in a pancake, and served with a carrot and butter emulsion sauce, Keller and his brigade needed one more element to finish the dish. What, they asked themselves, goes with carrots? If you're an American who came of age in an era of the TV dinner and frozen vegetables, peas go with carrots. "I'm not sure why peas and carrots were ever put together," Keller said, "but they were, and I think in most Americans' minds, it's pretty common." Say the words *peas and carrots,* and you're immediately transported to the frozen foods section of the grocery store. And so he finished the dish with pea shoots, a perfect flavorful bundle of greens, seasoned with lemon-infused oil, vivid against the bright orange sauce.

A danger in this kind of time-specific wordplay was alienation of a large segment of his audience, the parents of baby boomers, who came of age in the 1930s, 1940s, and 1950s and did not share the emotional connection, those older, wealthier folks very likely to dine at the French Laundry but who would not necessarily flock to see *The Brady Bunch Movie* or collect, in addition to wines and cigars, Mattel Hot Wheels cars. Waitstaff was continually explaining items that relied on unfamiliar cultural references in the menu.

Calling something surf and turf or peas and carrots of course doesn't change the flavor. It only alters the idea of a dish, enhances or skews one's perception. This was one way a chef brought his mind to bear on the food. Sometimes the creation of a dish had nothing to do with the diner; it had to do only with the chef's pleasure. When Keller found fresh hearts of palm in Hawaii, he couldn't wait to start using the product. (Hearts of palm, the tender, velvety core of the peach palm, in fact the "unborn" leaves or shoots of the tree, had not been grown in the United States until 1992, when an American experimented with the Central and South American staple, sometimes called pejibaye, in Hawaii and found the soil and climate perfect for the crop.) Sections of the ivory hearts of palm are hollow; you could fill them, but with what? Keller thought they looked just like marrow bones, the four-inch sections of beef bones he bought for marrow (to be floured and panfried for a meat garnish). So it was only natural for him to want to fill those hearts of palms with a puree of marrow beans, a large, starchy white bean. He then breaded and panfried the stuffed hearts of palm. Marrow bean was a perfect filling, and the finished item, perhaps coincidentally, looked just like a gigantic version of the fried marrow.

Other instances of creating a simple and common dish—a lemon tart with whipped cream, for example—were likewise illustrative of his methods. The pleasure of creating this dessert for Keller was in determining how to sweeten and flavor the cream that would garnish the tart. What would go well with lemon? He had to look no further than tea for the answer: *honey* and lemon. He would garnish the lemon tart with a honey whipped cream. This was only logical.

So here was the mind at work and the food that resulted, from the common lemon tart to the luxurious and seemingly infinite variety of foie gras preparations, to the Seuss-like creation of oysters and pearls, to solid classic technique (calf's brain), to an appreciation of genuine hands-on cooking (braises, offal), to modern interpretations of French classics, to K. Billy's *Super Sounds of the Seventies* (surf and turf, béarnaise sauce, peas and carrots), to soup and sandwiches and gazpacho snow cones.

When mushroom lady Connie Green said to me, "It's as if the beauty of the food isn't enough," she was right. And this after all was the only way that food might achieve the condition of art. Keller could move from the absurd to the sublime in the span of two courses; indeed he could even make that fantastic leap in the very same dish. The sublime and the absurd, in your mouth at the same time, and the tension between the two could make you laugh aloud in that library-quiet dining room.

Keller had proved to me, despite himself, that he was an artist. The justification for his dishes could be found in every element that came together in the final presentation. The rinsing of the veal bones—even before you blanched them, to make stock with which to make the final sauce for the saddle of lamb with a lamb sweetbread and lamb cheek ravioli—seemed fundamental to the excellence of the finished dish. He didn't use a dozen different elements; he used as much lamb as possible. He intensified the lamb. His soups were so concentrated and strained so well that they became more than the thing itself: carrot soup that was brighter and more flavorful than an actual carrot, soup that was the very essence of carrot, a distillation and purification of the carrot. Or as Keller put it, "You'd have to have several carrots in your mouth and chew them up to get the flavor of one spoonful of carrot soup." This was what was so exciting about eating at the French Laundry: how you could taste one of Keller's dishes and something inside you would say, "I see." And it might be about carrots, which you have been eating your entire life, but suddenly you really *understand* carrots. And then you hear yourself thinking that ridiculous thought, and you laugh. And you have another sip, truly enjoying your soup, and you have a third sip, and it is gone, and you are sad because you want just one more sip. Or you will taste foie gras and say, "Now I understand what all the fuss is about. *This* is foie gras. Now I see." Or, "Ah! So *this* is a truffle." You understand, if you eat at the French Laundry and you are receptive to such experiences, that Keller has indeed reduced the extraordinary range of food at his disposal and distilled it or brought it through careful cooking to a state in which its fundamental and enduring essences are available where they were not before—whether with a carrot, a truffle, duck tongue, or beef short rib. And the reason why this was ultimately so satisfying was its underlying morality: Keller's notions of waste and the life-affirming act of cooking, his ultimate respect for the food and the life bound up in it. As his mentor recalled of the boy Thomas, hired to feed the staff, "I don't know what he did, but he turned them around and gave them food and made them happy."

That he brought to this food, always based in classical French technique, cultural associations of middle-class America solidified him as a uniquely American chef. There were many American-born chefs working within the French-based but distinctly American confines, and the ones like Keller and others of his generation—Charlie Trotter and Charlie Palmer, Larry Forgione, Jasper White, David Burke, the list was long, but the most influential were likely the TV chefs, such as Emeril, Mario, Susan, and Mary Sue—were the ones who might one day establish something that could meaningfully be called American cuisine, could *write* it, as Keller's mentor, Roland Henin, had said to me.

"The grandfather and grandmother of American cuisine, one of them is still alive," Henin said, referring, of course, to James Beard and Julia Child. "And the first generation of cook, Larry Forgione and company, I had them as students twenty years ago. Give them a chance to mature in order to make the anchor for this American cuisine that's emerging. What it is going to be I don't know, but people like Thomas are going to write it." Keller, he said, had reached a point in his career where he could work, Henin said, "without interference. And I think he could be one of the first second-generation American cooks that has really established some of the components of what American cuisine can be or should be or is."

And by "writing" this cuisine, Henin meant codify, establish a base for it, a common language and standard. For instance, there is a standard for blanquette de veau, a refined veal stew. There may be infinite variations, but say "blanquette de veau," and there is a shared understanding of what that is. Or daube of beef, or sole à la meunière, or peach Melba.

American restaurants are reluctant to use a similar language. In America the menu would read "Ragout of Downhome Farm's Milk-fed Veal with Glazed Heirloom Onions and a Fricassee of Wild Mushrooms," because American cuisine doesn't yet have its version of blanquette de veau in its culinary repertoire. American cuisine can be broken down into regions, all of which have their regional specialties (hoppin' john in the South, chowder in New England, et cetera), but it has no broad collective repertoire beyond fast food. The seeds of a beginning, however, might be in surf and turf and mac and cheese and soup and sandwich. In a decision that embodies the current respect for and sheer dynamism of American cuisine, Alain Ducasse—the first chef ever to earn six Michelin stars for his two restaurants, the superstar of contemporary French haute cuisine—was soon to open a restaurant in Paris called Spoon, which featured such dishes as macaroni and cheese, chicken wings, BLTs, barbecued ribs, and Caesar salad.

That there is no standard, or classical, American cuisine is not surprising. French cuisine developed for centuries before it began to be codified and written. America was still a babe compared with Europe. In America the first great American "chefs," Beard and Child, were not even chefs but rather TV personalities and cookbook writers, entertainers. Most people can't even name an actual American chef predating 1970, beyond perhaps Chef Boyardee. What few chefs were known were French. Alice Waters became perhaps the first famous American chef, but not until she published *The Chez Panisse Menu Cookbook* in the early eighties. Today Americans' food knowledge is booming, and American chefs have taken center stage, both in the kitchen and in front of the camera. They are all of a similar generation, and they are truly a "generation" of American chefs who, for the first time in this country's history, equal, if not surpass, their French colleagues cooking in America, a claim that could not have been uttered before in this century.

CHAPTER NINE

One afternoon in the French Laundry kitchen, speaking with Keller about his cookbook while he portioned foie gras, he said he did not want to be portrayed in the book as a so-called master chef. He wanted to be portrayed as, he said, "a Buddhist monk in search of perfection." This drive toward perfection was the ultimate component of his personality. I think a lot of chefs are creative with food, are passionate about it, are smart, have good staffs, find good products, manage their businesses well, bring unique and original voices to their food, raise it to an artful level, but the pursuit of perfection, the relentless pursuit, had made Keller who he was and was, more than anything, responsible for his acclaim, his success, and the fantastic food he served at the French Laundry.

Indeed I had realized this shortly before leaving the Culinary Institute of America. There was no "secret" to great cooking, and the ultimate knowledge and skill didn't come from outside oneself. Your own values and your own standards; they in the end were all. At the Culinary, though, the standard was an implied perfection, not actual perfection, because we were students and screwing up all the time under ideal-world conditions no less, conditions that some chef-instructors likened to Disney World, conditions we'd be unlikely to know in the industry. Keller was actually achieving something close to actual perfection in his kitchen, and this to me was astonishing.

He had never relinquished his standards. When it became clear that

Rakel could not survive the sluggish economy that followed the 1987 market crash, his partner, Serge Raoul, told Keller he'd have to scale back, turn Rakel into a bistro, serve the bistro food that had become so popular. Keller wasn't interested. He hadn't spent his life cooking in order to make money, and so he always felt comfortable cooking, both in lean years and in fat years. He liked to cook. Of the cooking life, he told one interviewer, "I always knew it would take care of me—or, if nothing else, I knew I'd be able to eat every day." And so when he was given an ultimatum—change your cooking style (and therefore your standards) or leave—the decision was clear.

"I wasn't changing," he told the interviewer. " . . . If I would compromise my standards, it would be the end of, it would be the end of me."

To renounce his standards, would be to renounce his very being.

The ultimate mystery, then, concerning Keller was where did his standards, his drive for perfection, originate, and what had made it so strong that it could withstand the excruciating rigors of professional cooking, two decades of not making money, finally to succeed on the level of the French Laundry.

The summer following my immersion in the French Laundry, Keller flew to Cleveland to work on the cookbook. He couldn't concentrate on anything but the French Laundry when he was in Yountville; the cookbook would never get done if he didn't get out of town.

I have to say that regardless of standards of perfection, the future of American cuisine, cooking-as-art sophistry, having a chef of Keller's caliber hanging out at your house, talking about food for an entire weekend, is a blast; there were even those hanging-out-with-talented-chef moments that verge on cliché but that one hopes for nonetheless, like the rue surprise. Needing a break one afternoon, we went for a walk in my middle-class suburban neighborhood, which is composed entirely of houses, trees, and lawns. Strolling along the sidewalk, Keller suddenly stopped and said, "Look at that. Rue." A neighbor was growing the plant, an herb rarely used in America anymore, in his front lawn.

"What do you do with rue?" I asked.

"I like to glaze onions with it."

I recalled that my wife had been to the farmers' market that morning and had bought, among other things, a fresh bunch of white onions ("Beautiful onions!" Keller exclaimed when he saw them). Keller leaned over a small stone ledge and picked a few fine branches of the bluish gray–green plant, and later that evening, there was the chef of the French Laundry at my stove glazing beautiful onions in my filthy pan.

Another moment. We sat out on the front porch talking about food technique for the book, spending an hour alone on foie gras, and there, before my eyes, Keller came up with a new preparation of foie gras and I was able to watch it happen in a way one almost never got to see, to be present at the moment of creation of a new dish, when Keller discussed poaching technique.

Part of the reason he seemed to like foie gras was more than that duck liver was an extraordinary substance to put in your mouth; it was also that his foie timing had been perfect. When he'd left for France, fresh foie gras did not exist in the United States; it was not produced, and it was illegal to import. Shortly after he returned, what would become Hudson Valley Foie Gras was just beginning to raise ducks for foie gras, and it soon became widely available. Most American chefs had to teach themselves how to work with foie gras; Keller had learned the proper way to clean and marinate foie gras (marinating ratio: nine grams of salt, one gram of sugar, one gram of pepper for every five hundred grams of foie gras) and the many ways of preparing it. His favorite cold preparation was the torchon, which means "dish towel" in French, a method of turning scraps left over from sauté butchering into the ultimate preparation: Foie scraps or whole lobes were marinated, then rolled up tightly in cheesecloth—so tightly it oozed through the pores of the cloth—to form a cylinder, poached quickly, just long enough to melt the pieces together, cooled, rewrapped, hung for a few days, sliced and served with brioche toast and some pickled cherries or a quince marmalade. He liked to poach whole foie gras. When he worked at Taillevent in Paris, an Englishman would fly in once a month to dine at the restaurant and would order and eat an entire foie gras that had been poached in truffle juice. It was critical, Keller said, that he'd learned

these techniques in France because not only did he now know how to
serve it, but he knew the pitfalls to avoid (slicing it too thin for sauté,
for example, or serving oxidized, or gray, foie gras).

"The foie is such a versatile thing," he said, a lawn mower buzzing in
the distance, his image framed against full maple leaves, macadam street
with fire hydrants, telephone poles. "I'm finding more and more ways
to use it. I'm getting to the point where I may even do a foie menu. We
confit it, we poach it, we do the torchon, we freezer cure it, we serve it
raw, we sauté it, we do the puree of foie, whole roast it. We've done just
about everything we can with it." He chuckled. "Like Bubba Gump.

He continued. "The idea of poaching a foie gras is very simple. You
take the foie out of the package, score the whole foie gras as you would
a slice, put it in an earthenware dish or a crock, or put it in a pot, whatever you have; the only thing you have to be careful of is to make sure
you have it in a big enough vessel so that you can get it out when it's
cooked. It turns molten. When it's cooked, it's soft and fragile, so you're
gonna need to be able to get into the vessel to get it out.

"What we do at the restaurant, we heat up the truffle juice, and
when that comes to a boil, we pour it over the foie gras and put a top
on the crock that we use and put it in the oven for twelve or fifteen
minutes at three hundred and fifty degrees, let it sit for two or three
minutes, then remove it, slice it, serve it with some of the broth. That's
really how simple it is. We put some brunoise in there, some shallots,
some chives, some parsley, chopped truffle. We may do a mushroom
stock poach instead of truffle juice, but it's that simple. We could poach
it in a bottle of Gewürztraminer, which would be a great thing to do."
He stopped and smiled at the new idea. His thoughts had run this way
because earlier in the foie discussion he'd noted that he doesn't like to
drink Sauternes with foie gras, or other rich sweet wines traditionally
served with it, but prefers a wine that offers more contrast, something
like a Gewürztraminer. "We could poach it in a bottle of Gewürztraminer, which would be a great thing to do," he said. "I've never done
that before, but I think I will when I get home!" His smiled broadened;
then he thought a little more. "Serve it with grapes. Gewürztraminer-

poached foie gras." He nodded. "This is the season when we can get some really nice grapes."

By the end of the summer it was on the menu and in the cookbook. At first he poached it in the wine, then clarified that wine, gelled it, and served it with slices of the cooled foie gras. But he didn't like the brownish hue the wine picked up. So now he discards the poaching liquid and gels fresh Gewürztraminer, which, when stirred up, looks clean and white as crushed ice. So a waiter brings sliced foie gras to the table on a bed of crushed ice and then spoons from a silver bowl onto your plate what looks to be more crushed ice but is actually the gelled wine; it works almost like a sight gag, but it's also a proper foie gras service.

Granted, these moments—the rue, the sight of Keller cooking in my kitchen, the Gewürztraminer preparation—were personally, selfishly gratifying, but I was getting somewhere in my ultimate aim: By the end of the second and last full day of talking, Keller revealed the origins of his perfectionism, the source of all that he was as a chef, the Rosebud I'd been searching for.

We sat out on the back deck beneath a towering black locust tree on what was a perfect July evening. Keller seemed tired, and he spoke very softly as though to conserve energy. We'd been talking all day, and we'd be barbecuing chicken later and having a couple of people over for dinner and we had planned on a final hour or so to finish our two-day dialogue on food and cooking, his cooking, and I directed us toward perfectionism. When he tried to define perfection, he could only circle its meaning. "It doesn't exist," he said, "because once you reach it, it's not perfect anymore. It means something else. The bar rises to some other plateau."

Perfection, he said, "is an ideal. I would never want to think that there was perfection in cuisine because it would end the drive."

He spoke of a dish he thinks of as perfect, his sautéed red mullet with a parsley coulis, perfect in conception, taste, appearance, and in repetition, a dish in which the smallest errors glare.

This led to the notion of compromises. A chef was *always* compromising. ("Show me a chef who isn't compromising," he'd once said, "and I'll show you a chef who's not working.") When the mullet was almost but not quite perfect, only then could you intuit what perfect might be. "It's the compromise that creates perfection," he said. "You can only understand perfection by the compromise.

"What makes a person strive to do his very best?" he went on. "Some innate motivating gene? I don't know. . . . I guess when I started, I grasped on to the emotion of it, to who these people were who were doing these things. I feel now that I could have done many things in life other than cooking, and done them well, had I been in a different situation. In hindsight, I was very lucky to have been raised by my mother in such an ideal way as to allow me to understand the details of things. A lot of it is based on having to do certain chores around the house. You clean the bathroom, which was my job. There was only one way to do it. Everything had to shine. Everything had to be just perfect. Her definition of perfect. Which became my definition of perfect. To this day, no matter what I do, it's kind of based on cleaning the bathroom."

He smiled, then laughed and said, "That's kinda funny," and laughed some more.

To this day, no matter what I do, it's based on cleaning the bathroom.

"So I've taken one deal that she taught me and compounded it into who and what I am. Paying attention to detail and making sure that it was done and done right. You put a piece of tape on a box in the refrigerator, it should be straight, because why would you put it on crooked? You cut a piece of foie gras, it should be perfect because if it's not, it's a waste. If you're cooking something in the oven you should make sure you take it out at the right time. At one point in the oven it is perfect, and that's when you should be aware of it and take it out."

This attitude was difficult to live with, but even more difficult was trying to have a staff of twenty cooks maintain a similar attitude. "It's not in most people's capacity of comprehension to think like that," he said, to strive for perfection like that, to do things like store your fish in the same position it swims. "To a lot of people, it's just a job. 'How can I get in there and do a good job and get out so that I can reap the benefits?'

"For me, you buy into the whole thing for your whole career or you don't do it. You don't create good habits all of a sudden. They were created somewhere in the beginning. You can't say, 'Yeah, I'm going to have a bad habit here, but when I leave here, I'm going to have a better habit.' That doesn't happen.

"You can tell those people who are naturally in tune with what's going on, with what they're doing. How they treat equipment, how they treat products, how dirty they get during the course of an evening. All those elements. Do you really care about everything that's going on around you, do you really care about everything? Or just the finished plate? Because it doesn't begin with the plate. It begins when you wake up. It's got to be a philosophy. You have to be determined, determined to do it every day. If you're going to have a clean plate, you've got to have a clean oil bottle.

"It's very hard to explain to somebody," he said, creating an imaginary dialogue between himself and a cook: "'Yeah, I want you to be perfect.'

"'What does that mean, Chef?'

"'Well, try to make sure that counter is clean every night.'

"'*Yeah* . . . ?'

"'And translate that into everything that you do.'"

That was what Keller himself had done. It had begun in the bathroom as a boy to please his mom. And he had translated that into everything that he would do for the rest of his life.

Shortly thereafter I closed my notebook. It was time to cook dinner.

EPILOGUE:

IT BEGINS WHEN YOU WAKE UP

And there the journey ended. I could stop cooking and write and move on. I was somehow free. I'd come to know three outstanding American chefs, each one of whom had been cooking his entire adult life and had made people happy doing it. In fact all three of these chefs had stated that a main reason, if not *the* reason, they cooked was that simple: to make people happy. If they failed in this, the work was for nothing. Didn't matter how good the technique was, how artful the food, or the personal standards they'd brought to bear on it.

Keller made people swoon with happiness when they tasted his food. Michael Symon made people happy just being at his restaurant. And then he cooked really good food for them. Brian Polcyn loved to cook, and he made people happy too. He didn't make Ron DeSantis happy, however, or the other CMC judges, but those judges weren't there to be pleased. That was an exam, and they were working. I remembered writing in my notes that if Brian didn't earn the CMC title, it was maybe because of his independence. That, I think now, was wrong. I'll guess now that the reason he ultimately failed was that in that situation happiness was anathema to the CMC exam. It wasn't the point and had no place there. Skill, technique, knowledge, those things did have a place, absolutely; they were the *craft* elements of cooking that the test aimed to measure. But you did not cook to make people happy at the CMC exam, and while Brian couldn't have understood this then, and perhaps I'm reading more than I should into the notion of cooking, my guess, my hope, is that deep down he knew this, that the core of his being, his soul, knew that gladness had nothing to do with what was going on here, and thus he was incapable of cooking to his full potential.

The Culinary Institute of America was an extraordinary place; I never failed to feel the rush of the air there, the pursuit of excellence, the professionalism, the intelligence that its president, Ferdinand Metz, and his team had woven into a building and an idea. The school taught the basics. It didn't teach soul. That was an individual concern regardless of place. Great cooking either was in your soul or wasn't; maybe you were born with it, maybe it was hard-wired into your mind during its formation, while you were cleaning the bathroom, perhaps. Maybe *that*—soul—was the "it" that the CMCs kept trying to define that a chef has or does not have. The "it," the soul, was therefore, I had learned, a standard.

But by the CMC standards—those set primarily by the CIA, an institution that did not attempt to teach soul or happiness, but rather technique and knowledge and theory and practice—many CMC candidates did succeed. Perhaps the ones who succeeded, then, not only were technically gifted but also had never cooked to make people happy in the first place and therefore did not have that particular cord bound up in their standards. Maybe they'd cooked for money, as a job only, and happened to be really good at it. Good reason to cook: a job, a paycheck. Maybe they cooked because a kitchen was the only place in the world they felt comfortable, and so the world of the kitchen became a kind of family for them; I had known and worked with this kind of cook. Maybe they cooked because it pleased them personally and they were content to ride this one out. Maybe they cooked for the sport, the adrenaline rush of working a line, the way some people lifted weights or became compulsive joggers. If they had begun cooking for these reasons, cooked their whole lives this way, had never needed to make people happy to justify their work, their existence—and how many professions did?—then this absence built into the CMC test would never bother those chefs; that kind of chef would not feel its absence and would just cook as he or she always did.

If, on the other hand, cooking for *people* was how you had always connected to the work of cooking, if pleasing people in a visceral way had always been your ultimate aim, then you were going to have trouble with the CMC exam because your main connection to the work didn't exist in this environment and you were therefore a different cook here.

I'd learned a lot at the CMC exam. Not least of all the Escoffier poulet sauté, a great way of prepping and cooking chicken. The test bolstered my enthusiasm for and admiration of forcemeat. It confirmed what I'd suspected even before arriving: that there were, as the test claimed, objective criteria for judging how well food had been prepared, that there were clear and definable criteria for calling one plate good and calling another great.

Brian Polcyn now taught forcemeat at his alma mater, continued to consult for Northwest Airlines, was wooed by real estate developers to open new restaurants in the suburbs of Detroit, cooked at Five Lakes, and remained the devoted dad of five and a husband who left work for home to cook for the family, then returned to work to cook for his customers, and he was loving it. Was he going to take the CMC exam? He still didn't know, but he sensed that he would. He was feeling pressure from his superiors at Schoolcraft College, who wanted the entire staff to be certified at the master chef level. They offered him a semester off, with pay, to study and would cover all his expenses. But money wasn't the issue for Brian. It was still too personal.

Whatever he decided, Brian Polcyn would continue to cook and to teach because this was what he loved and who he was. And he would cook and teach prosperously. Both the restaurant and the teaching provided healthy salaries by themselves; together, and combined with his consulting work, they made life comfortable for him doing what he loved best. This was something that no certification could provide.

The certification process had nevertheless changed him and had an impact on his restaurant. The week after he returned from the CMC exam, he put a new item on the menu. Poulet Sauté Stanley, with cayenne and curry. It didn't sell; most of Brian's customers thought he was just being cute because the Detroit Red Wings were at the time engaged in the Stanley Cup play-offs.

For me, the actual end of the CMC test was not when Brian shook Dieter's hand and relinquished his paper toque. It ended two days later outside Detroit at the home of one of his restaurant's investors. The investor had asked Brian to prepare a meal for him and his associates in celebration of the closing of a multimillion-dollar business deal. The investor wanted a meal commensurate with the occasion. Brian decided to begin the meal with a smoked chicken consommé with brunoise vegetables and rich chicken quenelles. But a consommé foremost, he said, smiling, his teeth gritted, "because last time I made consommé, they didn't *like* it."

Brian watched as the soup was ladled over the garnish and served to the businessmen. The investor lowered his head before the bowl and, with both hands, swept steam into his face. The investor smiled. So did Brian. *Now* he was cooking.

Michael Symon remained to me the antithesis of the certified master chef. He had standards, but they had less to do with forcemeat that felt smooth against your palate than with fun. His standard in large part was this: If you weren't having fun, you were doing it wrong. Bad method, faulty technique. That was why nearly his entire staff had been with him for years at two different restaurants, a situation that is virtually unheard of in this itinerant industry.

He'd learned the fundamentals at the CIA and adapted those to his own needs. It's significant that Symon's favorite instructor there was Corky Clark, the madman who ran fish kitchen. What Corky taught didn't have a lot to do with technique or precision—he was a bang-it-out kind of chef—but he had personality and intensity, and they were what Symon connected to. You could learn the technique anywhere, but personality was what distinguished a chef like Symon and the chefs Symon admired. He also happened to bring away from fish kitchen an extraordinary respect for fish. He loved to butcher it; he set up his fish butchering cutting board inside the walk-in cooler to keep the fish as cold and as fresh as possible until the moment it was cooked. This was important too.

Symon's food was all fun and personality, something that didn't really count in a CMC test that tried to measure objective excellence in food preparation. What Symon had was something that would gall a CMC who had to struggle to make his restaurant work even though the food might have blinding technical polish. Symon had the intangible stuff that was ultimately more important than the food itself, at least in the restaurant business. He had imagination and a sense of humor, and this was in the air and on the plates at Lola. He personified American bounty and affirmed in his menu that the main quality by which American cuisine could be classified was the difficulty of classifying it. It was big and bold and metamorphic; there was nothing objective about it. But most of all, it was *fun*.

Like Keller, Symon fell into cooking almost by accident. He wanted to wrestle and be a wrestling coach. He lived for wrestling. A perpetual concern of any wrestler is making weight; Symon spent much of his adolescence denying himself food so that he could wrestle at 105 pounds. His mom was a dynamite cook, and so the house was perpetually filled with the smells of great food cooking, fresh vegetables, herbs, garlic. When he was fifteen, during a wrestle-off in practice, he broke both bones in his forearm, the radius and the ulna, and dislocated his elbow. He would never compete on the mat again. To fill his time outside school, before his cast was off, he became a cook. He found he not only liked cooking, but, more, he led the kitchen. Even as a sixteen-year-old in his first job as a cook at a pizza and ribs chain, he set the pace at service, became the leader.

"It was real natural for me when I was cooking," he recalled. "People's minds work in different ways, and I've always had the ability to look at fifteen tickets and know what I have to do and what everybody around me has to do to get it done. . . . You're the pacemaker, and there's one in every kitchen, he's controlling the tempo. I have the ability to slow everything down or make it happen."

Food, for years forbidden, became the driving force of his career after those two bones snapped. Now Michael Symon, a decade Polcyn's junior, a decade and a half Keller's, was ahead of the game, still in his twenties, newly married, and with a new house. He was *beginning*. And yet at that age he was a leader in the culinary scene in his hometown, a prosperous restaurateur, and just offered his own local TV show. He had his eye on a space on the city's East Side that would soon become available; he hoped to buy it and open a genuine French bistro, provided he would find a young French chef. He wanted a young, classically trained French chef; this was critical. One day he also hoped to have a truly fine restaurant, a four-star establishment that would rank with the likes of a French Laundry. The future was bright and had been even at the pizza and ribs joint. It had never been otherwise. You could hear it in his laugh.

Thomas Keller was the synthesis of CMC perfection and Symon's American bounty and shrewd sense of fun. To me the French Laundry, that spot of earth, that stone building, was the very heart of cooking in America; Keller was it, the answer to what I'd needed to find once I set foot in the first Skills class in search of the perfect veal stock. Keller combined extraordinary technique and knowledge with humor, imagination, and intelligence, and he did so in a setting straight out of a Monet painting. It was the perfect combination, and Keller never underestimated the importance of the place he had found. There was a reason he had achieved such stature and success where he did, and not in New York or L.A. He believed that the French Laundry was alive and that it would always have its own life according to its own dictates and fate, regardless of him. "I think of it as a living thing; it has its own cell structure," he said.

This was how he saw the world, and this was how he understood cooking, with a Zenlike spirituality but with his feet firmly grounded. Cooking had never been a means to an end for Keller. That was why he never got sidetracked by money or the lack of it. The first thing was care for food.

"It goes back to the rabbit story," he said. "At some point you either have to learn or be taught the importance of the food that we eat. It's not about thanking God or anybody, that's an individual thing, but it is about understanding the relationship between you and the food. And how that relationship has to be nurtured. It has to go from point A to point B with the same feeling of affection.

"Every step of cooking is manipulation," he continued. "Somehow manipulation has become a bad word, a negative thing. In my definition manipulation is what I do every day, and I do it in a wonderful way."

Cooking was a series of manipulations, and if you manipulated a foie gras or a scallop or an asparagus stalk perfectly at every step—and also appreciated, if not relished, each step—you could have perfect food. Because the best cooking was done slowly and the best chef was the one who moved with the greatest deliberation and the finest attention to the physical world.

At the bottom of Thomas Keller was a capacity to absorb himself absolutely in the mundane tasks he performed daily. It began, apparently, at the Palm Beach Yacht Club, under the watch of his mom, Betty, as he made hollandaise sauce daily. Every day he separated yolks and whipped them hard over heat, then added clarified butter. Every day he was mystified by the thick, creamy result but terrified that it would break at any instant. Every working day for two years. He never tired of it. On the contrary, he reveled in it. It was "the high point of each day." He never took the hollandaise sauce for granted; it remained, till he left, a great mystery. It was never perfect. He never mastered it. If he ever had, the task would have become monotonous, if not unbearable. But instead he *pursued* the perfect hollandaise sauce with relentless intensity. And to this day, he will tell you that he still derives great pleasure from classical emulsion sauces because of his young experience with hollandaise and that he likewise derives great pleasure from *all* the tasks he repeats daily: butchering salmon, portioning foie gras, turning artichokes, or peeling asparagus.

He loved this. He loved to wipe a counter clean. Because this was where perfection began. At this clean counter was where we learned not to waste anything and not to err, because when you made a mistake or when you didn't care, or you didn't appreciate that carrot that you were peeling, it was a waste of life itself.

We are becoming, Keller lamented, a nation of noncooks. In restaurants, he said, "cooking has become short order, sauté. What can I get that I can throw in a sauté pan or on a grill? How much really do I have to process this thing once I get it in the back door? . . . Shortcuts in cooking have resulted in noncooks." While the French Laundry received pigs' heads and entire baby lambs to break down, most restaurants received their meat in preportioned, Cryovac packages. This had been my experience. I cooked a thousand strip steaks as the grill cook at Sans Souci, but I would never have known where on the cow those strips had come from; the only butchering required was slitting open the plastic. Shortcuts in cooking in fact was a form of not caring, therefore a form of waste.

I was happily surprised to hear Thomas Keller say that his favorite aroma, perhaps his favorite thing to do as a cook, was to brown floured meat in hot oil. As he went on, that idea of the aroma became so vivid in his memory that it excited him into a description of the braising process, and his voice seemed almost disembodied. The short ribs: *That* was cooking.

"It's not just cut, sauté, and serve," the voice said. "It requires a cook to cook in many different ways. Those are the things I like to do, cooking that has some process behind it, some thought, some technique that results in deep flavors and a lot of character, something that's more than what you started with. A filet mignon is a filet mignon, which is raw and then becomes grilled or sautéed. It's no more now than when it began; it's just cooked. Short ribs are a whole different animal from where they began. They transcend into such a full, satisfying taste and aroma, and the process of doing it is so satisfying.

"Again the process of cooking it is such a nice thing to do. Meat marinated in red wine, which has been cooked off with aromats. Marinate it overnight; then take the three components apart: liquid, aromats, and meat. Then we clarify the marinating liquid. Again always searching for the cleanest, brightest flavors; you need to clean up everything as you go. Clarify the red wine. It's very simple to do because there is albumen from the blood in the marinade. You bring it up to a boil, it all coagulates, you skim it off, and it's clarified. It comes back more clear than it was when you put it in. So you've got your clarified red wine, your meat, your vegetables. You coat the meat with flour, and in a large rondeau you brown it off, and that caramelization of the flour and the meat—that aroma? Of that meat? Whether it's oxtail or short ribs, it has a depth to it that's like no other meat. You really say, 'Wow, this is what it's all about.' It really gets you excited. There are very few things left that give me that kind of pleasure. . . . It's a classical braising technique."

Classical. That was the piece I first began with, entering the CMC exam, and now it had become the final piece of the equation, but connected as it was with the notion of perfection—perfection as an aim, as a direction, not an end—it had broadened considerably. Classical didn't mean old, and it didn't mean fuddy-duddy, and it didn't mean dull. Here is what it meant: always, ever. Combine this kind of definition of classical with the striving that we call perfection (pleasure and pursuit of it in mundane tasks, avoidance of waste as a reverence for life), and you have in conception something that approaches divinity.

Classical braising was not something invented in Europe. Classical braising had been going on for five thousand years, probably a lot longer, given that *Homo sapiens*'s ancestors were eating meat millions of years ago. It was going on at the French Laundry, Lola, Five Lakes Grill, and home kitchens across the country and the world today. The real reason we love braising goes deeper than the fact that it takes a long time and involves many steps and therefore many opportunities to be perfect. When we braise meat, we can if we choose, connect ourself with everyone who has ever braised meat and everyone who will ever braise meat. To smell that floured beef as it hits the oil sizzling, to pull the braising pan from the hot oven and marvel at the clear layer of fat, gold in hue, but crystal clear on the surface of the deep earth brown sauce below, as countless men and women have done throughout history, and will continue to do, to share that with them, to connect to that same pleasure, that amazement, to connect to that same gratitude.

This is the kind of satisfaction that people who truly love to cook are after. We seek, in our collective struggle, to learn more and to cook better, but we are in fact reaching for that connection to humanity that we've lost or maybe never had or simply want more of.

This connection will forever elude us until we learn to move deliberately, to take a long time, to make sure our counter is clean every night. And it will elude us if we ever lose sight of cooking's fundamental importance to others.

Keller, in his twenty-five years as a chef, I guessed, had fed one million people. Probably more. This was a good thing. He was a good, thoughtful cook. The work had provided him a livelihood. It had made him famous in food circles in his country and beyond. But more important than that, and this was everything, it was the good use of one life, and he knew it. No less so for Brian Polcyn and for Michael Symon. By the time they reached Keller's age, they would likely have served a million people or more. Maybe they already had. They all were great chefs; they never forgot for a moment what the work was all about: to cook for people and to make them happy.

APPENDIX

Selected Recipes from Brian Polcyn's
Certified Master Chef Exam and Five Lakes Grill

DUCK TERRINE
WITH SHIITAKE MUSHROOMS
AND ORANGE-GINGER SAUCE

SPICY SMOKE-ROASTED PORK LOIN WITH
GREEN APPLE—HORSERADISH SAUCE

GRILLED VEGETABLE TERRINE

GREEN BEAN SALAD WITH BACON VINAIGRETTE

POULET SAUTÉ STANLEY

FIVE LAKES GRILL FIRECRACKER SHRIMP
WITH PINEAPPLE RELISH

Duck Terrine with Shiitake Mushrooms and Orange-Ginger Sauce

This is a classical terrine using what's called a straight forcemeat method—a fine classical preparation. The better your knife skills, the better it tastes. This recipe fills a one-quart terrine mold. (You might want to render and save the fat for duck confit or cooking potatoes.)

1 5-pound duck	1½ cups Madeira
Pork butt as needed	9 ounces pork fatback
12 silver dollar–size shiitake mushrooms, stems removed	2½ ounces duck liver
	1 egg white
2 tablespoons garlic, chopped	Salt, pepper, pâté spice to taste
2 tablespoons shallots, chopped	½ cup heavy cream

Bone the duck, reserving breasts, leg, and thigh meat. Save all fat, skin, and sinew for other uses. Reserve one half of the duck breast, split lengthwise, for interior garnish. The remaining duck meat should total twelve ounces. If you are short, add more duck or pork butt.

Sear the reserved breasts in a hot sauté pan; remove and cool. In the same pan, sauté the mushrooms until soft, set aside to cool. In the same pan, sauté garlic and shallots, and deglaze with Madeira; reduce to a paste; set aside to cool.

Grind leg and thigh meat with the pork fat and duck liver on smallest die. (Keep this meat mixture as cold as possible at all times; it's helpful to store your food processor and grinder in your freezer before using; and also grind meat into a bowl set in ice.) Place ground meat in a food processor along with garlic-shallot mixture, egg whites, and seasoning; then puree until smooth. Fold in the cream. Poach a small piece in water and taste to adjust forcemeat seasoning.

Line a one- or one-and-half-quart terrine mold with Saran wrap. Fill the mold one-quarter of the way with the forcemeat. Next, line shiitakes upside down the length of the terrine, being careful not to go all the way across width wise. Fill another quarter of the way, and line the duck breast in the same manner. Fill mold another quarter of the way, and line the remaining shiitakes right side up. Fill the mold with remaining forcemeat, fold Saran to cover, then place a lid on the mold or cover with foil.

Bake in a water bath in a 325-degree oven until the internal temperature reaches 150 degrees.

Remove from oven, uncover, and cut a piece of cardboard to fit interior dimension of terrine mold. Place on top with up to four pounds of weight, to compact the forcemeat as it cools. Refrigerate overnight, until ready to serve.

Orange-Ginger Sauce

Zest from ¼ orange and lemon each
1½ teaspoons grated ginger
1 cup marmalade
1 cup chutney
2 tablespoons lemon juice

2 tablespoons dry sherry
½ teaspoon powdered ginger
1½ teaspoons honey
1 teaspoon dry mustard
¼ teaspoon cayenne

Combine ingredients in a food processor and blend until smooth.

Serves 10

Spicy Smoke-Roasted Pork Loin with
Green Apple–Horseradish Sauce

This pork loin and following salad and tart were all part of Brian Polcyn's buffet platter. This is an excellent way to cook and serve pork, especially during summer when the weather's hot—an inexpensive cut of
meat elevated by the flavors of smoke, spices, dried herbs, and a simple,
brightly flavored sauce.

1 pork loin (about 2 pounds)

Spice Rub:
 ½ tablespoon Dijon mustard 2 teaspoons dried thyme
 1 garlic clove, minced   2 teaspoons dried savory
 2 teaspoons dried sage   Salt and pepper

Combine ingredients for spice rub, and smear the mixture onto all surfaces of the loin. Sear the loin on all sides in a hot pan with a coating of
oil. Smoke loin in smoker for 20 minutes, then place in a 300-degree
oven until the internal temperature of the loin reaches 140 degrees, or
place in a barbecue grill with desired wood chips and cook until to
same internal temperature. Allow to cool slightly, then wrap the loin
tightly in plastic wrap, then refrigerate beneath a weight or weighted
pan to achieve an oval shape.

Green Apple–Horseradish Sauce

1 Granny Smith apple
¼ cup white wine
¼ cup lemon juice
1 cup mayonnaise

¼ cup fresh horseradish root,
    grated
Salt and pepper to taste

Peel, core, and slice apple. Poach the apple in the wine and lemon juice until it's soft. Puree apple in a blender. Push through a sieve. Allow to cool. Combine with the remaining ingredients, and season to taste.

Serves 10

Grilled Vegetable Terrine

The colors of the layered vegetables make this a visually dramatic dish. It's flavorful and healthy—another great buffet item and one that should be prepared a day ahead of serving. It's an interesting dish from a technical standpoint in that the dressing is built into the dish, and as the dressing is gelled, it also serves to hold the terrine together.

1 eggplant	Salt and pepper to taste
2 large carrots, peeled	2 tablespoons olive oil
2 red peppers, roasted, seeded, and peeled	1 tablespoon gelatin
2 yellow squash	4 tablespoons water
2 zucchini	½ cup balsamic vinaigrette (recipe below)
4 ounces shiitake mushrooms, stems removed	

Slice all vegetables one-eighth-inch to one-quarter-inch thick, season with salt and pepper, and toss in olive oil. Grill until tender but not black.

In a small pan, bloom gelatin in the water, then dissolve over low heat and add to balsamic vinaigrette.

Line a terrine mold with plastic wrap. Lay strips of eggplant perpendicular to the mold, positioning each slice so that half of it hangs over one edge (the hanging part will be flipped back over to cover the mold after it is filled). Brush the eggplant with the vinaigrette. Layer zucchini; brush again with the vinaigrette. Continue layering the carrots, red pepper, yellow squash, and mushrooms until the terrine is full. Fold the eggplant back over top. Wrap tightly with plastic wrap, and chill overnight.

Turn out terrine onto a cutting board. Unwrap, and slice with a warm knife.

Balsamic Vinaigrette

2 tablespoons olive oil	1 teaspoon garlic, minced
2 tablespoons canola oil	1 teaspoon shallots, minced
2 tablespoons balsamic vinegar	Salt and pepper

Combine all the ingredients and mix well in blender or with whisk or submersion blender.

Serves 10

Green Bean Salad with Bacon Vinaigrette

Green beans are at their peak in summer, just when the heat makes cold dishes so appealing. This is a great simple salad, enriched with a bacon vinaigrette, but it is paramount that you cook your beans perfectly. But *perfectly*.

4 plum tomatoes, peeled
10 pieces of bacon, cut into ⅛-inch strips
5 shallots, thinly sliced
½ cup veal or chicken stock
¼ cup cider vinegar
¼ cup olive oil

¼ cup chopped herbs (parsley, chives)
50 haricots verts, trimmed, blanched in heavily salted, vigorously boiling water, and shocked
Salt and pepper to taste

Cut tomatoes into petals, remove seeds, and julienne. Render bacon, and reserve two tablespoons of fat. Braise shallots in white veal stock or chicken stock. Combine vinegar, olive oil, and bacon fat. Toss all ingredients together. Top with bacon.

Serves 10

Poulet Sauté Stanley
(Adapted from *Escoffier: The Complete Guide to the Art of Modern Cookery*)

The poulet sauté method is the very best way I know to cook chicken because each piece of the chicken cooks separately, and therefore the breasts can be kept juicy. It provides an elegant way to serve a half chicken on a single plate. And once you've got the idea of the preparation, you can vary it in infinite ways. This is a white sauté, but the method works beautifully for brown (caramelized) preparations as well (while the meat is resting, make the sauce with the browned bits in the pan: Pour off excess fat, add shallots and fresh tarragon, deglaze with vermouth and a little stock or water, season, and strain—that's it. Do the same thing, but add slices of Kalamata olives, chopped tomato, and a chiffonade of basil for another variation, et cetera).

5 3-pound chickens
Salt and pepper to taste
2 tablespoons clarified butter
9 ounces thinly sliced onion
Cayenne and curry powder to taste*

1 cup heavy cream
1 ounce butter
10 fluted mushrooms, cooked
10 slices black truffle

Disjoint chickens as described on page 86, and remove all skin. You should have ten each of a boneless breast with wingette attached and frenched, a boneless thigh, and a frenched drumstick.

Season the meat with salt and pepper; then stiffen the pieces in clarified butter without coloring chicken. Remove breasts. Add onion, cover pan, and cook about 30 minutes in a 375-degree oven. Return breasts to pan, and cook for another 15 minutes, or until all pieces are done. Remove meat to a warm dish, and cover. Add cayenne and curry to

*Not optional.

onion. Cook for 30 seconds; then add cream. Simmer for 10 minutes. Puree, then pass through a chinois, return to stove, and reduce by one-quarter. Finish with butter.

Return chicken to pan, and coat with sauce. Arrange on serving platter with a bouquet of mushrooms on side. Top with ten slices of black truffle.

Serves 10

Five Lakes Grill Firecracker Shrimp
with Pineapple Relish

This is a crowd pleaser at Polcyn's restaurant in Milford, Michigan: spicy deep-fried shrimp, artfully presented. It's the kind of thing he can't take off the menu because too many people would complain.

12 large Gulf shrimp, peeled
   and deveined
¼ cup Thai chili-garlic sauce
12 wonton wrappers
1 cup pineapple, small dice
½ red pepper, small dice

½ bunch cilantro, chopped
¼ cup olive oil
1 lime, juiced
2 scallions, chopped
Oil for deep-frying
2 strands dried angel hair pasta

Make four slits widthwise across each shrimp belly to prevent shrimp from curling as it cooks. Toss shrimp in Thai chili-garlic sauce. Wet about a quarter of each wonton wrapper; roll each shrimp in a wrapper, so that the wrapper forms a cylinder. Combine the pineapple, pepper, cilantro, olive oil, lime, and scallions, and warm in a pan. Fry shrimp in 350-degree oil until golden brown. Drain on paper towels. Deep-fry angel hair pasta quickly. Place shrimp on spoonful of relish; garnish with fried pasta.

Serves 6

Selected Recipes from Michael Symon
Lola Bistro and Wine Bar

GINGER CALAMARI WITH
GREEN ONION SAUCE

SHRIMP COCKTAIL (SHRIMP WITH ANCHO CHILE SAUCE)

CORN CREPES WITH BBQ SAUCE AND SOUR CREAM

ROASTED BEET SALAD WITH
HORSERADISH VINAIGRETTE

SLASH AND BURN GROUPER WITH
CRAB TATER TOTS, AVOCADO, AND RED PEPPER COULIS

CRÈME BRÛLÉE NAPOLEON

Ginger Calamari with Green Onion Sauce

This is the best calamari I've had anywhere. It hadn't been too long since I'd been to Spain and eaten calamari served in many ways when I first had these; fried crispy, they're absolutely the best. Symon makes them sparkle with the flavors of ginger and pepper; don't short either or the marinating time. Deep-fry properly—in plenty of hot oil—or they'll be soggy and unpalatable.

8 ounces calamari, cut into ¼-inch rings (check tentacles to remove any beaks, and check bodies to remove any cartilage)

3 ounces (about a 2-inch piece) fresh ginger, peeled and grated

Ginger ale to cover

Toss calamari with ginger and let set for 1 to 4 hours in a small container. Add ginger ale just to cover, and marinate overnight.

1 cup flour
3 tablespoons peppercorns, ground to powder in spice or coffee grinder
Oil for frying

Combine flour and pepper. Heat an inch of oil in a high-sided pan. When oil is hot but not smoking, toss calamari with flour to coat, and deep-fry till golden brown (careful, calamari are easily overcooked).

Serve on top of green onion sauce.

Green Onion Sauce

3 scallions, roasted till tender

4 cloves garlic, roasted till
     tender

1 teaspoon water

Salt and pepper

1 egg yolk

6 ounces olive oil

Puree scallions and garlic with water and salt and pepper. Add yolk. With blade running, drizzle in oil slowly till mixture is smooth and creamy but light, not as heavy as a mayonnaise.

Serves 4

Shrimp Cocktail
(Shrimp with Ancho Chile Sauce)

You'll never poach shrimp in plain water again after you've tried it this way. Here what seems to be a contemporary method is in fact old. By adding aromatics and spices to the water, you're making what's called a court bouillon (or quick stock), and the flavor infuses the meat of the shrimp. Ancho chiles, dried poblano peppers, are a great flavor for any number of salsas.

Poaching Liquid:

2 quarts white wine
2 quarts shellfish stock or
   water
2 teaspoons salt
1 pound onions, thinly sliced

2 bay leaves
1 ounce cracked peppercorns
Parsley stems
2 ancho chiles, crushed
1 tablespoon coriander seeds

18 U-12 shrimp (12 to a pound, or 1½ pounds of shrimp)

Combine poaching liquid ingredients and simmer 30 minutes. Poach shrimp gently until done, about 5 minutes. Don't overcook. Shock shrimp in ice water. Peel, devein, and refrigerate until ready to serve.

Ancho Chile Sauce

12 ounces ketchup
2 cups whole peeled tomatoes
2 ounces rice vinegar
2 tablespoons chopped garlic
2 tablespoons chopped
   horseradish

3 tablespoons chopped onions
4 ancho chilis, stems and seeds
   removed
2 tablespoons brown sugar

Combine all ingredients, then cook until reduced to about two cups. Puree in a blender and cool.

Corn Crepes with BBQ Sauce and Sour Cream

As firecracker shrimp is to Five Lakes, these corn crepes are to Lola: can't take them off the menu. Frank Rogers, Symon's sous chef, has likely made his fifteen thousandth crepe by the time you read this. The crepe is a vehicle: Symon began by filling it with chorizo and asiago cheese, and you would do well to do the same, or use your imagination and fill it with something even better. This recipe calls for duck confit, and you can't go wrong with duck confit ever, but it's the crepes that make this dish Michael Symon's. (And the BBQ sauce is an excellent all-purpose sauce.)

Crepe Batter:

½ cup corn kernels
½ cup flour
2 eggs
4 ounces milk
1 teaspoon corn oil
¼ teaspoon salt

Pepper to taste
½ cup red bell pepper, chopped
½ cup green bell pepper, chopped
¼ cup scallion, chopped

Puree all ingredients in food processor till combined.

Pour a teaspoon of oil into a small hot sauté or crepe pan. Ladle in two ounces of batter. Cook till lightly browned, about 2 minutes. Flip crepe, continue cooking for about another minute; remove to a rack to cool. Repeat with rest of batter.

8 ounces duck confit

Michael Symon marinates duck legs and thighs overnight with coriander, cumin, black peppercorns, juniper berries, crushed bay leaf, salt and pepper, and a pinch of cinnamon. He then submerges them in duck fat and brings the oil to a simmer on top of the stove; when the skin begins to render, he places the duck in a 275-degree oven till the meat is fork tender, about three or four hours. He transfers legs to a container, pours the cooking fat over legs, and stores them submerged in the fat. (The confit should sit at least a day and is best if left to "ripen" at least a week.) When it is ready to use, he wipes fat off legs and thighs and pulls meat from the bone to add to the crepe.

BBQ Sauce

1 tablespoon butter
1 cup chopped red onion
2 tablespoons minced garlic
2 tablespoons minced jalepeño
½ cup espresso beans, mashed with the flat side of a knife
4 ounces Worcestershire
4 ounces tomato paste
1 ounce apple cider vinegar

1 ounce balsamic vinegar
½ cup packed brown sugar
2 ounces apple cider
4 ounces veal stock
1 tablespoon chile powder
1 teaspoon cumin
1 teaspoon coriander
Sour cream as needed

Melt butter and sweat onion, garlic, and jalepeño. Add the remaining ingredients and cook on very low heat for 1 hour. Strain through a chinois.

TO FINISH:
Wrap two ounces of duck (or chorizo and asiago cheese) in corn crepe with a tablespoon of sauce; heat 10 minutes in a 400-degree oven, or until hot all through. Garnish with more BBQ sauce and sour cream.

Serves 4

Roasted Beet Salad with Horseradish Vinaigrette

This dish features two underused, but common plants. Here they are combined in a perfect summer salad. Grill a piece of salmon, place it on top of this salad, and you have an extraordinary entrée.

1 large golden beet
1 large red beet
Olive oil for brushing
3 tablespoons grated horseradish
2 ounces rice vinegar

2 tablespoons orange juice
Salt and pepper to taste
1 ounce truffle oil
3 ounces extra virgin olive oil
2 bunches watercress

Brush beets with oil and roast in a 325-degree oven until tender through the center. Cool, peel, and cut into quarter-inch slices.

Grate horseradish into the vinegar and orange juice, add salt and pepper, and slowly whisk in the oils. To serve, layer beets in alternating colors on a plate. Drizzle with half the dressing. Toss the watercress with remaining dressing, and divide evenly on top of the beets.

Serves 4

Slash and Burn Grouper with Crab Tater Tots, Avocado, and Red Pepper Coulis

Symon says *Food & Wine* begged him to use this recipe for its ten-best issue, but he insisted on the midwestern regional favorite pierogies and Great Lakes fish, so herewith the most popular Symon composition: spiced grouper with awesome tots and a simple avocado salsa. Here, as always, his excellence is in his simplicity.

6–8 fillets of grouper
2 tablespoons Busha Browne's jerk paste (available in specialty markets)

Slit a pocket in each piece of grouper. Smear each pocket with a teaspoon of jerk paste.

Red Pepper Coulis

1 shallot	1 ounce white wine
Olive oil	2 ounces chicken stock
½ pound red peppers, roasted, peeled, and seeded	Salt and pepper to taste
	1 teaspoon cilantro, chopped

Sweat shallots in olive oil; then add peppers, wine, and stock; bring to a simmer, then remove from heat. Season with salt and pepper. Let cool, then add cilantro, and puree in a blender.

Avocado Puree
  2 avocados
  Juice of 2 limes
  Salt and pepper

Combine ingredients and mash with a fork or potato masher. Cover and refrigerate till ready to use. If not using immediately, return the avocado seeds, which will keep the avocado from oxidizing (turning brown).

Crab Tater Tots

2 pounds potatoes, peeled	4 ounces bread crumbs
2 ounces butter	2 tablespoons chives
3 yolks	8 ounces lump crab meat
3 ounces flour	Oil for deep frying

Boil potatoes till tender through the center; drain, let moisture steam off; then rice, mash, or pass through a food mill. Work in the rest of the ingredients while potatoes are still hot. When the mixture has cooled, incorporate the crab. Form into spheres the size of golf balls.

TO FINISH:
Preheat oven to 450 degrees. Deep-fry eighteen crab tater tots and keep warm. Sauté the grouper in a hot sauté pan in a small amount of oil, about 2 minutes. Flip grouper, and put pan in the oven to finish cooking, about 5 minutes.

To assemble, spoon a circle of red pepper coulis in the center of a warm plate. Place three tater tots on the sauce. Place a grouper fillet on the tots. Spoon a dollop of avocado puree on top of grouper.

Serves 6

Crème Brûlée Napoleon

Vintage Michael Symon: delicious, simple. It's a by-the-book brûlée (that is, vanilla custard), but it's something that can be done ahead of time and then quickly and easily put together on a plate, without losing the two essential satisfactions of the crème brûlée: custard and crunch.

4 tablespoons chopped almonds
3 tablespoons sugar
6 sheets phyllo dough
6 ounces butter, melted
Powdered sugar for garnish

Combine almonds and sugar. Brush one sheet of phyllo with butter. Sprinkle with sugar-almond mixture. Lay a second sheet on top; butter and sprinkle with sugar mixture. Repeat with third sheet. Cut into nine equal squares. In a second pan, repeat process.

Bake phyllo in a 350-degree oven until golden brown, 2 to 5 minutes. Cool and store in an airtight container until ready to use.

Crème Brûlée

1¼ quarts cream
1 vanilla bean, split lengthwise
2 tablespoons peeled grated
    ginger

8 ounces sugar
10 ounces yolks (about 10
    yolks)
Zest of 2 oranges

Combine cream, vanilla bean, ginger, and half the sugar in a pan, and heat till sugar is melted. Allow bean to steep, then remove, scrape seeds into cream, and discard pod. Combine remaining sugar with yolks and orange zest in a bowl, and whisk till combined. Add one-quarter cup of the hot cream mixture to the yolk mixture, and whisk. Pour in remaining cream mixture while whisking. Pour mixture into a container that will give a depth of about two inches. Place in a water bath, and bake in a 325-degree oven for 50 minutes, or until it is barely set at the middle.

TO ASSEMBLE:

Spoon about two ounces of brûlée onto a plate, place a phyllo square on top, and continue to alternate brûlée and phyllo with two more squares of phyllo. Garnish with powdered sugar.

Serves 6 to 10

Selected Recipes from Thomas Keller
The French Laundry

OYSTERS AND PEARLS

SAUTÉED CALF'S BRAIN WITH SAVOY CABBAGE, PANCETTA,
AND BROWN BUTTER SAUCE

PAN-SEARED SEA SCALLOP WITH ASPARAGUS
AND PÉRIGORD BLACK TRUFFLES

"CAESAR SALAD" — PARMIGIANO-REGGIANO CUSTARDS
WITH ROMAINE LETTUCE AND PARMESAN CRISP

CREAM OF WALNUT SOUP

Oysters and Pearls
(Adapted from *The French Laundry Cookbook*)

Ruth Reichl's story about the French in the *New York Times* helped make this dish a French Laundry signature dish. It's a seemingly bizarre, but extraordinary pairing: tapioca pudding, oysters, caviar. Keller has never tasted it. "I know it tastes good. You don't have to stick your hand in fire to know it's hot," he told me.

16 meaty oysters, such as Malpeque or other variety, scrubbed

Tapioca:
  ⅓ cup small pearl tapioca
  1¾ cups milk
  1¼ cups heavy cream
  ¼ cup crème fraîche
  Salt to taste

Sabayon:
  4 egg yolks
  ¼ cup reserved oyster juice (from above)

Sauce:

Black pepper
3 tablespoons dry vermouth
Remaining reserved oyster juice
1½ tablespoons minced shallot
1½ tablespoons white wine
  vinegar

½ cup butter, cut into 8 pieces
1 tablespoon minced chives
1 to 2 ounces osetra caviar

This recipe uses the oysters as well as their juices. When selecting oysters, choose those with the thickest shells; they will have the most juice. Timing is important in the completion of the dish. The cooking should be one continuous process, so have the cream whipped, the double boiler hot, and the remaining ingredients ready.

Soak the tapioca in one cup of the milk for 1 hour, setting it in a warm place to speed up the rehydration of the pearls.

Shucking the oysters: Reserve the oysters and all their juices in a bowl. Trim away the muscle and the outer ruffled edge of the oysters, and place the trimmings in a saucepan. Reserve the whole trimmed oysters, and strain the oyster juice into a separate bowl. You should have about one-half cup of juice.

Cooking the tapioca: Strain the softened tapioca into a strainer, and discard the milk. Rinse the tapioca under running water; then place it in a heavy pot.

In a bowl whip one-half cup of the cream just until it holds its shape; reserve in the refrigerator.

Pour the remaining three-quarters cup of milk and three-quarters cup of cream over the oyster trimmings. Bring to a simmer; then strain the infused liquid over the tapioca. Discard the trimmings.

Cook the tapioca over medium heat, stirring constantly with a wooden spoon until it has thickened and leaves a trail when a spoon is pulled through it. Continue to cook for another 5 to 7 minutes, or until the tapioca is fully cooked, has no resistance in the center, and is translucent. The mixture will be sticky, and if you lift some on the spoon and let it fall, some should still cling to the spoon. Remove the pot from the heat, but keep it in a warm place.

For the sabayon: Whisk the egg yolks and one-quarter of the oyster juice in a metal bowl set over a pan of hot water or a bowl-shaped double boiler. Whisk vigorously over medium heat for 2 to 3 minutes to incorporate as much air as possible.

The finished sabayon will have thickened and lightened, the foam will have subsided, and the sabayon will hold a ribbon when it falls from the whisk. If the mixture begins to break, remove it from the heat and whisk quickly off the heat for a moment to recombine.

Stir the hot sabayon into the tapioca along with a generous amount of black pepper. Mix in the crème fraîche and the whipped cream. Season lightly with salt, remembering that both the oyster and caviar garnish will be salty.

Immediately spoon one-quarter cup of tapioca into eight four-inch-by-five-inch gratin dishes (each with a three- to four-ounce capacity). If this is done correctly, the tapioca should be a creamy pale yellow and the tapioca pearls should be suspended and not sinking in the mixture.

Refrigerate for up to a few hours before serving.

To complete: Combine the vermouth, remaining oyster juice, shallot, and vinegar in a small saucepan. Bring to a simmer, and reduce until most of the liquid is gone but the onions are still glazed and not dry. Whisk in the butter piece by piece, adding a new piece when the previous one is almost melted.

Add the reserved oysters to the sauce to warm. Place the tapiocas on a sheet tray and into a 350-degree oven for 4 to 5 minutes, or until they just begin to soufflé. Arrange two oysters and some of the sauce over each gratin, sprinkle with chives, and garnish the top with a quenelle of caviar; serve immediately.

Serves 8

Sautéed Calf's Brain with Savoy Cabbage, Pancetta, and Brown Butter Sauce

Keller's preparation of calf's brain, a classic French dish, crisp exterior, the hot, molten interior, the brown butter—is simple and exquisite. Brain tastes mild, not unlike sweetbreads, but its texture is much finer; the mild flavor requires aggressive seasoning with salt and pepper. It's delicate, so handle it very carefully. This dish is a snap to prepare (see page 297 for a more elaborate description).

½ onion, chopped
1 carrot, chopped
1 leek, chopped
1 parsley stem
2 cups white veal stock or
    chicken stock
2 sprigs thyme
1 bay leaf
1 calf's brain (two separate
    lobes), cleaned
Salt and pepper to taste
Flour for dredging

Canola oil as needed
¼ cup beurre monté (optional)
1 cup savoy cabbage, julienned
1 ounce pancetta, julienned
3 ounces butter
1 teaspoon Spanish capers
½ teaspoon sherry vinegar
¼ teaspoon chives, finely
    minced
½ teaspoon root vegetable
    brunoise (optional)
Kosher salt to taste

The day before cooking the brain, combine the onion, carrot, leek, parsley, stock, thyme, and bay leaf, and bring slowly to a boil. Pour over the calf's brain, and let cool. The liquid should completely cover the brain. Refrigerate.

Preheat oven to 375 degrees. Remove brain from liquid, and trim as much excess skin as possible. Pat dry. Season brain liberally with salt and pepper. Dredge in flour, then pat to remove excess flour. Heat oil in a pan over medium high heat. Sear brain. When it is crisp on one side, flip, coat with beurre monté, and place in oven for 10 minutes, or until done; then remove to a paper towel to drain. Sauté pancetta and savoy cabbage until the cabbage is tender. Keep warm. In a small saucepan, melt butter, add the capers, and continue cooking until it is nicely browned. Add vinegar, chives, and brunoise, and season with salt. To plate, spoon equal portions of the cabbage mixture into the center of two warm plates or bowls. Place brain on each; spoon butter sauce over brain. Discard the bay leaf before serving.

Serves 2

Pan-Seared Sea Scallop with Asparagus and Périgord Black Truffles

"I wanted something that would be almost impossible to do, something that would really blow Chef away," Grant Achatz recalled when re-creating this recipe of a dish he served during the winter of 1998 (see page 239). "The concept was on circles. The 'bull's-eye' of sauces, the scallop, a perfect truffle disk, the twirl of asparagus ribbons, all on a round plate with a circle pattern on the rim. As far as 'tight dishes' went, it was at the top. To me everything about the dish said Thomas Keller: The repetition of ingredients in different forms, the lavish use of truffles, a very 'tight' presentation, and a perfect balance of flavors on the palate."

Scallops:
    4 each large fresh sea scallops
    Kosher salt and white pepper to taste
    Canola oil as needed
    Unsalted butter as needed

Season scallops with salt and pepper. Thoroughly heat a sauté pan at medium-high heat. Add oil to pan. When oil is hot, sauté scallops until well caramelized. Flip and sear, add butter, and occasionally baste to finish cooking.

Asparagus Garnish:
    1 bunch small asparagus
    Salted water (see page 292)
    1 leek

2 tablespoons root vegetable
    brunoise (carrot, turnip,
    leek)

Peel stems of asparagus (reserve all trimmings for coulis). Cut tips from stalks. Cut the top third of remaining stalks on a bias into thin slices. Thinly slice bottom two-thirds of the stalks lengthwise to form ribbons. Blanch tips and bias cuts and ribbons separately in the boiling salted water. Thinly julienne leek, and blanch until tender. Tie tips in bundles of three with leek julienne.

Asparagus Coulis

Stem trimmings from 1 bundle of asparagus

Salted water for cooking asparagus (see page 292)

Ice bath

2 tablespoons chlorophyll (optional)

4 tablespoons chicken stock

2 tablespoons unsalted butter

Kosher salt to taste

Blanch asparagus in a large quantity of the salted water (water should not lose its boil when vegetables are added). Shock trimmings in ice bath, and strain. Puree with a few ice cubes in a cold Robot Coupe. Pass the mixture through a tamis. Combine puree, chlorophyll, and stock in a saucepan, and heat. Whisk in butter. Season to taste.

Périgord Truffle Coulis

2 large Périgord truffles

1 pint mushroom stock

2 tablespoons butter

1 teaspoon sherry vinegar

Kosher salt to taste

Freshly ground black pepper to taste

Poach truffles in mushroom stock until tender. Using a mandoline, cut four thin slices of truffle from the truffle with the largest diameter. Punch out four circles from each disk with a circle cutter (circles should be one and one-half to two inches in diameter). Add all truffle scraps and remaining truffle to a blender. Add enough of the mushroom stock to blend truffles. Slowly add butter in small pieces. Add vinegar. Season to taste.

TO PLATE FINISHED DISH:
Spoon a tablespoon of asparagus coulis in the center of a warm plate. Spoon a tablespoon of truffle coulis inside asparagus coulis. Add a small pile of bias asparagus, finished with butter, root vegetable brunoise, and tomato diamonds inside the "bull's-eye" of sauces. Set seared scallop on top of asparagus. Heat slices of truffle in butter, and set on top of scallop. Twirl ribbons of asparagus to form a circle, and place on truffle disk. Top each with an asparagus tip bundle.

Serves 4

"Caesar Salad"—Parmigiano-Reggiano Custards with Romaine Lettuce and Parmesan Crisp
(Adapted from *The French Laundry Cookbook*)

This is a French Laundry cheese course, and it's vintage Keller, an interpretation of a classic American dish: The cheese becomes a custard; all the other classical components of the Caesar salad remain the same, but you'd never know you were eating Caesar salad.

Dressing:

1½ tablespoons chopped garlic
1½ tablespoons chopped shallots
¼ cup balsamic vinegar
2 tablespoons Dijon mustard
1 teaspoon lemon juice
2 salt-packed anchovy filets, deboned, soaked in milk to cover for 30 minutes, and patted dry
1 egg yolk
1 cup extra virgin olive oil
1 cup canola oil
Freshly ground white pepper

Puree the garlic, shallots, vinegar, mustard, lemon juice, and anchovy in a blender until smooth. Remove to a mixer with the paddle attachment, and beat in the egg yolk. With the machine still running, slowly drizzle in the oils. Season with the pepper. The completed dressing can be stored in the refrigerator for a day; after that it may lose some of its flavor.

Makes 2 cups

Custard:

⅔ cup heavy cream	2 eggs
⅔ cup milk	1 egg yolk
3½ ounces Parmesan cheese, cut into ½-inch pieces	Kosher salt and freshly ground white pepper

Place the cream, milk, and Parmesan in a saucepan, and warm to a simmer. Turn off the heat, cover the pan, and let the flavors infuse for 45 minutes.

Whisk the eggs and yolk together. Reheat the cream mixture until it is hot; then, while whisking, strain the cream and milk over the eggs to temper them. Season the custard with salt and pepper.

Ladle one ounce of the custard into twelve one- to two-ounce aluminum baking tins, timbale molds, or other molds, cover with a lid or aluminum foil, and bake in a water bath at 250 degrees for 30 minutes, or until cooked. The edges will look set although the very center may not be. Remove the molds from the water bath, and refrigerate the custards for at least 2 hours or up to 2 days.

3 cups chiffonade of romaine lettuce, cut from the "hearts" or small inner leaves	12 1-inch (or the diameter of the molds) Parmesan crisps
2 tablespoons Parmesan cheese	Parmesan shavings for garnish, made with a vegetable peeler
Freshly ground black pepper	Balsamic glaze
12 croutons (from a baguette), cut ¼-inch thick	

Toss the romaine with about two tablespoons of Parmesan cheese and just enough dressing to coat the lettuce lightly. Add pepper to taste.

Place a spoonful of dressing on each plate. Run a small paring knife around the edge of each custard, and dip the molds briefly into hot water; unmold the custards on the croutons, and center one in each pool of dressing. Lay each Parmesan crisp over a custard, followed by a stack of the salad. Place shavings of Parmesan over the romaine, and garnish the plate with the balsamic glaze.

Note: For Parmesan crisps, sprinkle a tablespoon of grated Parmigiano-Reggiano onto a silpat or other nonstick baking surface, spreading it into a circle, and bake for 8 to 10 minutes at 325 degrees. For balsamic glaze, reduce two cups balsamic vinegar to one-half cup; this should be done over very low heat, with no simmering, and should take about 2 hours.

Serves 12

Cream of Walnut Soup
(Adapted from *The French Laundry Cookbook*)

This works as a dessert by itself, as a "canapé" dessert, or as a sauce (for, say, bread pudding). Whatever way, the soup itself is ethereal; it's like drinking walnut marshmallows.

Walnut Cream:
 1¼ cups (5 ounces) toasted ¼ cup milk
  walnuts, rubbed of excess ¼ vanilla bean, scraped (seeds
  skin and chopped   and pod reserved)
 2 cups heavy cream

Place the walnuts, cream, milk, vanilla seeds and pod into a saucepan. Bring to a simmer; then reduce the heat to keep the liquid just below a simmer. Let the flavors infuse for 30 to 45 minutes. Strain the infused liquid into a saucepan, and discard the walnuts and vanilla bean. You should have about one and one-half cups of walnut cream.

Pear Puree:
 1 large pear
 1½ cups poaching liquid
 Walnut oil

Peel and core the pear; cut into eight wedges. Put the wedges in a saucepan with the poaching liquid and bring the liquid to a simmer. Cook for about 15 minutes, or until the pears are completely softened and have no resistance when tested with the tip of a sharp knife.

 Heat the walnut oil. Remove the pears and one-third of the poaching liquid to a blender. Puree the pears; then, with the motor running, pour the hot walnut cream into the blender to combine (the cream must be hot when it is added to the puree or the soup may break).

Strain the soup into a saucepan through a fine mesh strainer. Serve warm in a demitasse cup sprinkled with a few drops of walnut oil.

Note: For poaching liquid, bring a bottle of dry white wine (such as a Sauvignon Blanc) to a boil and skim off any foam that rises to the top. Add 3 cups of water and 1 cup of sugar. Return liquid to a boil to dissolve sugar, remove from heat, and stir in the juice of 1 lemon. This can be refrigerated for up to several weeks.

Serves 8 (2 cups)

ACKNOWLEDGMENTS

The author would like to thank these people who either helped to make this book possible or who greatly influenced it:

Ray Roberts, Elizabeth Kaplan, and Michael Naumann. Brian Polcyn, Michael and Liz Symon, Thomas Keller and Laura Cunningham; also, Tim Ryan, Ferdinand Metz, Susie Heller, Richard Ruhlman. And most important: Donna, Addison, and James.

FOR THE BEST IN PAPERBACKS, LOOK FOR THE

In every corner of the world, on every subject under the sun, Penguin represents quality and variety—the very best in publishing today.

For complete information about books available from Penguin—including Penguin Classics, Penguin Compass, and Puffins—and how to order them, write to us at the appropriate address below. Please note that for copyright reasons the selection of books varies from country to country.

In the United States: Please write to *Penguin Group (USA), P.O. Box 12289 Dept. B, Newark, New Jersey 07101-5289* or call 1-800-788-6262.

In the United Kingdom: Please write to *Dept. EP, Penguin Books Ltd, Bath Road, Harmondsworth, West Drayton, Middlesex UB7 0DA.*

In Canada: Please write to *Penguin Books Canada Ltd, 90 Eglinton Avenue East, Suite 700, Toronto, Ontario M4P 2Y3.*

In Australia: Please write to *Penguin Books Australia Ltd, P.O. Box 257, Ringwood, Victoria 3134.*

In New Zealand: Please write to *Penguin Books (NZ) Ltd, Private Bag 102902, North Shore Mail Centre, Auckland 10.*

In India: Please write to *Penguin Books India Pvt Ltd, 11 Panchsheel Shopping Centre, Panchsheel Park, New Delhi 110 017.*

In the Netherlands: Please write to *Penguin Books Netherlands bv, Postbus 3507, NL-1001 AH Amsterdam.*

In Germany: Please write to *Penguin Books Deutschland GmbH, Metzlerstrasse 26, 60594 Frankfurt am Main.*

In Spain: Please write to *Penguin Books S. A., Bravo Murillo 19, 1° B, 28015 Madrid.*

In Italy: Please write to *Penguin Italia s.r.l., Via Benedetto Croce 2, 20094 Corsico, Milano.*

In France: Please write to *Penguin France, Le Carré Wilson, 62 rue Benjamin Baillaud, 31500 Toulouse.*

In Japan: Please write to *Penguin Books Japan Ltd, Kaneko Building, 2-3-25 Koraku, Bunkyo-Ku, Tokyo 112.*

In South Africa: Please write to *Penguin Books South Africa (Pty) Ltd, Private Bag X14, Parkview, 2122 Johannesburg.*